D0336533

02. MAR 88.

11. MAR 88.

12.

KENT COUNTY LIBRARY

C080383129

354. 42065/RO2

CHATHAM LIBRARY

Books should be returned or renewed by the last date stamped above.

13

C 08 0383129

THE CASE
FOR THE
CROWN
The Inside Story of the DPP

THE CASE
FOR THE
CROWN

The Inside Story of the Director
of Public Prosecutions

Joshua Rozenberg

Foreword by
The Rt Hon Sir Michael Havers, QC

Wellingborough, Northamptonshire

First published October 1987

© Joshua Rozenberg 1987

C08038 3129
354. 42065/ROZ
KENT COUNTY LIBRARY

All rights reserved. No part of this publication may be reproduced, stored
in a retrieval system or transmitted, in any form or by any means,
electronic, mechanical, photocopying, recording or otherwise, without
prior permission in writing from Thorsons Publishing Group Ltd.

British Library Cataloguing in Publication Data

Rozenberg, Joshua
The case for the crown.
1. Great Britain, Department of the Director of Public Prosecutions
I. Title
354.41065   KD8348

ISBN 1-85336-011-2

Equation is part of the Thorsons Publishing Group

Printed and bound in Great Britain

1 3 5 7 9 10 8 6 4 2

Contents

Foreword

by The Rt Hon Sir Michael Havers, QC
Lord Chancellor, Attorney General 1979-87

It has always been a surprise to me that the BBC has not until recently had its own legal correspondent in the sense of a 'feature' lawyer who could deal with topical legal events on the radio news in the same way that Dominick Harrod covers economic events.

The comparatively recent appointment of Joshua Rozenberg has been a great success. He is a good lawyer who speaks concisely and with authority. He interviews lawyers sympathetically but in a determined manner so as to get the real facts. I know many people who have been interviewed by him who share my respect for his ability and his integrity.

I viewed the prospects of writing this foreword with some dismay; I wondered how a book on the subject of the Director of Public Prosecutions could fill out over 200 pages and I feared that the chapter that covered a number of cases since the beginning of the century might be no more than padding.

I was completely wrong. What the author has so cleverly done is to take a number of famous cases and relate them to the responsibility of the DPP of the day and show how he dealt with each one.

This has shown to me an entirely new aspect about these cases, most of which I knew quite well and some of which occurred during my time as Attorney General.

If the establishment of the Crown Prosecution Service marks a fundamental change in our approach towards the administration of criminal justice, for the Director it marks a complete transformation. Over the past 100 years the role of the Director had grown from that of one man, working in his chambers in the Temple, to that of a senior and powerful servant of the Crown, heading a Department of more than 200 people. But although the role had grown in size, its essential nature remained the same: to provide specialist advice on criminal law and to take decisions and conduct proceedings in respect of the most complex, important or sensitive cases. With the advent of the Crown Prosecution Service that 'specialist' or 'exclusive' role has gone. Save for certain very minor offences, the Director, as head of the Crown Prosecution Service, now becomes responsible for all prosecutions started by the police and relies on a nation-wide staff of thousands.

The next hundred years are going to be very different from the first, as the new Department seeks to apply the high standards of consistency and fairness in decisions across the whole spectrum of criminal offences that historically the DPP sought to apply to a few. The timing of this book's publication is, therefore, of peculiar significance: it is more than a commentary on the operation of an existing Department; it is an important analysis of one which has yet to prove itself. It is as important to look back at the one as it is to look forward to the other and in both exercises the author has succeeded in an entertaining and stimulating way.

I have much enjoyed reading this book which I believe will have the wide, interested attention which it deserves.

Introduction

To find out what this book is all about, I suggest you turn immediately to Chapter 1. It's not very long, but it should introduce you gently to the rest of the book and persuade you it's worth reading. This Introduction is just meant for people who like Introductions.

Sir Thomas Hetherington, who announced that he would be retiring from his post as Director of Public Prosecutions in September 1987, inspired this book and gave me all the help he possibly could when the time came for me to write it — even though he knew it would be a 'warts and all' book rather than what the civil service calls an 'official history'. You can read the fruits of Tony Hetherington's own researches and extracts from the interviews he gave me in the pages that follow. He even persuaded some of his senior staff to talk to me — not something I imagine they found very easy.

This book has no footnotes. I suppose I have been influenced by my training in radio, where footnotes, captions, references and subtitles are rather hard to put across. They also seem to be rather difficult for book publishers to manage these days. In times gone by — when footnotes really were printed at the foot of the page — they were just about acceptable. Nowadays, when you have to turn to the end of the chapter or the back of the book to read the footnotes (I'm not sure which is worse), you either scurry around trying to find them and completely lose the author's train of thought, or else you ignore them and worry that you've missed a crucial addition or a late amendment along the lines of 'this provision has now been abolished under the 1987 Act, and the last forty pages may be ignored'. So my view is that if a thing is worth saying, it is worth saying in the text. If it was only worth a footnote, it can probably be left out.

Purists who want to check my quotations need not worry, though. If no reference is given then the quotation is generally from an interview I recorded myself with the speaker, and on that you will have to trust me. References are normally given for other quotations, though the keen researcher may have to look up the page numbers himself in the index of a book to which I might refer. There is a list of the books I have used at the back of this book, and some of them, in turn, have excellent bibliographies.

Another reason for doing away with footnotes is that this book is not intended exclusively for lawyers. I hope it will be of value to everyone who takes an interest in the criminal justice system of England and Wales (I have not tried to deal with Scotland and Northern Ireland, both of which have different arrangements). Academics and lawyers who expect serious books to be written in a dense, impenetrable style, full of passive verbs and subjunctive moods, will have to forgive my attempts to use simple English. And I'm sorry if the style is too colloquial for you. There is no list of abbreviations because the only one I use is *DPP*, and if you don't know what that stands for you'll find out on page 1.

In the hope of appeasing those feminists who think I should always write *he or she* instead of *he*, or perhaps even the unpronounceable *s/he*, I hereby declare that, throughout this book, the masculine shall be taken to embrace the feminine.

This book was completed in June 1987, shortly after the Conservative government was returned to power at the General Election. At the time the election was called, the Criminal Justice Bill was still going through parliament; it was a wide-ranging measure, affecting the DPP's work in a number of different ways. Most of the Bill was lost when parliament was dissolved but the Opposition agreed to support the section of the Bill which created a Serious Fraud Office, and this, as you will see in Chapter 5, was duly enacted as the Criminal Justice Act 1987. The government announced that it would be reintroducing the remainder of the Bill — with some modifications — early in the new parliamentary session, and this will no doubt become the Criminal Justice Act 1988. Some of its expected provisions, particularly those affecting extradition law, are also described in Chapter 5.

Just as this book was going to press, Allan Green, QC was named as Sir Thomas Hetherington's successor. He will become the tenth Director of Public Prosecutions on 1 October 1987. Until a few months earlier, Allan Green had been senior prosecuting counsel at the Old Bailey; he therefore had considerable experience of advising on prosecutions, but none at all of running a large government department. A major training programme was thus planned for him.

Mr Green's appointment should have been announced much earlier. By accepting the job he gave up the promotion he could reasonably have expected to the High Court Bench, which carries with it a very attractive pension. But as DPP, although he would receive the same salary as a judge, his pension would be nothing like as good: it would be based on his years in the government service, starting — rather late in life — with his appointment as DPP. Not unreasonably, Allan Green held out for something like the sort of pension Sir Thomas Hetherington would be receiving after a lifetime in the civil service — and not surprisingly, the Treasury refused to pay up. Sir Michael Havers spent his last days in office fighting to get Allan Green his pension: the Attorney had warned the Treasury he was prepared to take the issue to the Prime Minister if necessary. Eventually the Treasury made some concessions, and Mr Green took the job. Like his predecessors, he can expect a knighthood to go with it.

Allan Green was the first Director in history to be appointed by the Attorney General rather than the Home Secretary. The Attorney who made the appointment was Sir Patrick Mayhew — on his first day in office — as Sir Michael Havers had by then gone on to become Lord Chancellor. I will be calling Lord Havers by his former title throughout this book to make it clear that I am referring to his period in office as Attorney General.

Law books usually say that the author has attempted to state the law on a particular date. This one does not, as I have tried to anticipate the Criminal Justice Act 1987, which is not likely to take effect before 1988.

As I say, parliament had been dissolved, and most of the government's Criminal Justice Bill had been washed away with it. The one part that remained created a Serious Fraud Office, and in Chapter 5 I will be explaining how the new body will work. So it would be misleading to say, as lawyers usually do, that in this book the author has attempted to state the law on a particular date: I have tried to anticipate the Criminal Justice Act 1987, which is not likely to take effect before 1988.

The other area where I have had to anticipate events is in the staffing of the Crown Prosecution Service. A major reorganization is going on at senior level, and I have had to predict where everyone is expected to be when the music stops. There will be further changes, and no doubt this book already contains some mistakes. If you spot them, you are welcome to write to me at Broadcasting House.

This is not a highly opinionated book. My aim, as a working journalist, has been to present enough facts for readers to form their own conclusions. Occasionally you may find areas of interpretation which spill over into comment, and so I must stress that any opinions in this book are mine alone, and must not be taken to represent the view of my employers. After all, the BBC doesn't have any views, does it?

I must also stress that none of the people I have interviewed or quoted in this book can be assumed to agree with my interpretation of their actions or remarks; nevertheless, I hope I have not betrayed the officials and others who trusted me enough to let me record and reproduce their views. My gratitude goes to all who have helped me.

Some, however, must be singled out for special thanks. The Attorney General at the time I wrote this book, the Rt Hon Michael Havers, QC, MP, gave the project his blessing and kindly agreed to write the Foreword. Kenneth Winfield MBE, who has a lifetime's experience of work for the Director of Public Prosecutions, did much of the initial historical research and generously allowed me to draw on his unpublished work. At Crown Prosecution Service headquarters, the Records Officer, Stuart Orr, and the Press Officer, Geoff Kenton, greatly lessened the burden of further research. Their colleague Howard Lloyd, the Director's Private Secretary, was not only responsible for taking many of the fine photographs in the pages that follow, but also for tracking down and selecting the items to photograph.

But, above all, my thanks must go to Sir Thomas Hetherington, KCB, CBE, TD, QC, for his initial encouragement and unfailing support.

It is at this point in an Introduction that the author usually thanks his wife and children for putting up with his absences (consider yourselves thanked). He then names a team of secretaries who have deciphered an undecipherable handwritten manuscript. In that context I have nobody to name but Mr Alan Sugar, who produced the cheap, slow but totally reliable Amstrad PCW 8256 word processor on which I typed the entire book. Actually, 'typed' is a bit of an exaggeration. It's about time I tried using more than one finger.

JOSHUA ROZENBERG
London, June 1987

ONE

The 'D'

'The papers have been sent to the Director of Public Prosecutions' is a phrase which never fails to send a shiver down the spine. It conjures up an image of an all-important, all-knowing being, who has within his hands the power to decide the fate of his fellow men and women. Seeing that well-worn cliché in the newspaper, you were sure the case was important (otherwise why call in the Director?), difficult (otherwise why wouldn't the police have prosecuted?) and bound to be fascinating. Knowing, too, that it would be months before the Director of Public Prosecutions would be announcing whether some poor unfortunate was to end up in the dock at the Old Bailey only added to the sense of tension. The reality, of course, is now very different. And that reality is what this book is all about.

To the public, he is known as the DPP. In his department, he is always addressed formally in the same way as a government minister: 'Yes, Minister' becomes 'Yes, Director'. In reply, he adopts the normal civil service practice of calling all his staff by their first names. When they talk about him to outsiders they call him 'the Director'. When they think he is not listening, they call him 'the D'.

We know surprisingly little about the Director of Public Prosecutions. Despite the fact that his office has existed for more than a century, despite the great popular interest there has been in the prosecutions that Directors have handled over the years, despite the academic interest in the way past Directors have exercised their heavy burdens of responsibility and discretion, no book quite like this has ever been written before.

In it I shall tell you about the nine men who have completed their service in this most sensitive and delicate of roles. Then I shall be looking critically at some of their most celebrated cases. We shall visit the Director's inner sanctum, a surprisingly plain and modest room for a man who wields such power. And I shall be exploring the close and subtle relationship the Director of Public Prosecutions has with the Attorney General, a relationship so flexible and practical that it can be seen as one of the most impressive achievements of our unwritten constitution.

But at the heart of this book is the quiet revolution of 1986, a revolution which has radically changed the criminal justice system of England and Wales and transformed the role of the Director of Public Prosecutions into the key public prosecutor that he has never been before. For more than a hundred years, the DPP only dealt with a small number of cases rather vaguely defined as being of 'importance or difficulty' — or which required the Director's intervention 'for any other reason'. So until 1986 the DPP ran a small, self-contained London office of some 80 lawyers. Now, he is responsible for up to 1,700 lawyers working throughout England and Wales. Add in the non-lawyers and you get a huge new government department of some 4,000 people, prosecuting a million cases a year and costing £150 million a year to run. It is called the Crown Prosecution Service.

The police in England and Wales do not prosecute people any more. (Neither do the Scottish police, but there is nothing new in that.) Whenever a defendant has been charged by a police officer with a criminal offence, the police must send the papers to the Crown Prosecution Service. It is then up to the lawyers working for the service to decide whether or not the accused person should go before a court, and what charges he or she should face. If the Crown Prosecutor decides to drop the case, there is nothing the police can do about it any more.

So, for the first time, the prosecutors are independent of the police. Of course, it is still the job of police officers to investigate crimes and catch criminals. But the Crown Prosecution Service in England and Wales now has the job of conducting the case in court — or dropping it altogether if it chooses to. Almost everyone thinks this is a good idea in principle. Before the Crown Prosecution Service was introduced, virtually one acquittal in two in the Crown Court was because the case had been thrown out by the judge — at staggering cost in terms of time, money and human feelings. Even the police accepted the principle of an independent prosecution service. But where there are doubts is in the way it has been put into effect.

Launching the Crown Prosecution Service on 1 October 1986 the Director of Public Prosecutions, Sir Thomas Hetherington, summarized its main objectives:

- to be, and to be seen to be, independent of the police;
- to ensure that the general quality of decision-making and case preparation is of a high level, and that decisions are not susceptible to improper influence;
- to provide flexibility to take account of local circumstances;
- to continue prosecutions while, and only while, they are in the public interest;
- to conduct cases vigorously and without delay;
- to undertake prosecution work effectively, efficiently and economically;
- to seek to improve the performance of the criminal justice system as a whole.

Those are fine ideals. But how well are they working? Are the Crown Prosecutors right when they say it is not in the public interest for certain people to be prosecuted? Are there enough Crown Prosecutors to do the work? And are they really up to the job? These are some of the issues I will be facing in the pages ahead.

And then there is the safety net. Strangely, it is still possible for a private citizen to prosecute anyone he wants to. The full weight of the criminal law, and the rigours of a public trial leading perhaps to a fine or imprisonment, can be initiated by anybody who thinks an unsuspecting member of the public should be tried on a criminal charge. I am not going to encourage you to start your own private prosecution: indeed I think there is a strong case now for abolishing them altogether. What I will do is to tell you how you can thwart a private prosecution if somebody brings one against you.

The Director of Public Prosecutions has no power to investigate crimes himself. That is a job for the police, not the prosecutors. And in theory the Director cannot even order a police enquiry. But he can ask the police to investigate possible criminal offences he may have heard about, and of course in practice the police will never refuse. Indeed, they will sometimes work quite closely with the prosecutors, particularly in fraud cases. And the police sometimes ask the Crown Prosecution Service for advice on a pretty fundamental question: whether a person they are questioning should be treated as a potential witness or a likely defendant.

One thing, though, must be made very clear. Not everyone who commits a crime in this country is prosecuted. Many people are never caught, of course. Of those who are, some merely receive a caution from the police. This can be formal (there are Home Office guidelines) or informal (I was once stopped for speeding on an empty motorway by a police officer who told me: 'at twenty to five in the morning, sir, take a bollocking').

But some people do not escape with a caution, however expressed: they find themselves charged by the police with a criminal offence (or summonsed some weeks later). That is when the prosecutor's discretion comes into play. First he has to decide if there's a 'case' — enough evidence to satisfy the court. Then he has to decide if the prosecution is in the public interest. The case will only come to court if the answer to both those questions is 'yes'.

TWO

Nine Lives

The first Director of Public Prosecutions took office in the year 1880. Thirty-five years earlier the Criminal Law Commissioners had concluded that

> the existing law . . . is by no means as effectual as it ought to be; the duty of prosecution is usually irksome, inconvenient, and burthensome; the injured party would often rather forgo the prosecution than incur expense of time, labour and money. When, therefore, the party injured is compelled by the magistrate to act as prosecutor, the duty is frequently performed unwillingly and carelessly. . . The direct and obvious course for remedying such defects would consist in the appointment of public prosecutors.

I shall be saying a little more about the history of these early days in my chapter on the Crown Prosecution Service (Chapter 4). A great wealth of detail can be found in John Edwards' first book, *The Law Officers of the Crown*: anyone who now writes about the Attorney General or the Director of Public Prosecutions owes Professor Edwards an enormous debt of gratitude. But all you need to know for now is that the passage I have just quoted was not an isolated flash of inspiration: during the half century leading up to the Director's creation in 1879, attempts had been made time and again to create a system of public prosecutors. All had failed.

The Prosecution of Offences Act 1879 was different. While proposing a new officer to prosecute in cases of 'importance or difficulty', it recognized that the existing prosecution arrangements worked pretty well in most cases. There had been an Act in 1856 which required each county to maintain an efficient police force; and cases of great public importance were already being reported by the police to the Home Office which advised the local force what to do, or instructed the Treasury Solicitor to take on the case. So the supporters of the bill which was to become the Prosecution of Offences Act 1879 did not propose a wholesale abolition of existing prosecution arrangements: that was still a hundred years away. All they wanted was somebody to look after the cases which were falling through the·net.

The role of the Director of Public Prosecutions was first defined in Section 2 of the 1879 Act:

It shall be the duty of the Director of Public Prosecutions, under the superintendence of the Attorney General, to institute, undertake, or carry on such criminal proceedings . . . and to give such advice and assistance to chief officers of police, clerks to justices, and other persons, whether officers or not, concerned in any criminal proceeding respecting the conduct of that proceeding, as may be for the time being prescribed by regulations under this Act, or may be directed in a special case by the Attorney General. The regulations under this Act shall provide for the Director of Public Prosecutions taking action in cases which appear to be of importance or difficulty, or in which special circumstances, or the refusal or failure of a person to proceed with a prosecution, appear to render the action of such Director necessary to secure the due prosecution of an offender . . .

When we come (in Chapter 4) to an Act of the same name passed more than a hundred years later, you will see that the two statutes have remarkable similarities. They both speak of the Director's duty to act in cases of 'importance and difficulty'; they both impose a duty on him to give advice to the police. Commas are sprinkled around with a little less abandon nowadays, but both statutes say the Director shall act 'under the superintendence of the Attorney General': neither Act explains what this means (although I shall attempt to in Chapter 10). Both statutes say the Director of Public Prosecutions must be a barrister or solicitor of not less than ten years' standing. Both Acts say, in almost identical language, that where the Director tells a magistrates' court he has started proceedings the court must send the papers to the Director for him to send on to the trial court. Both Acts preserve the right of private prosecution (see Chapter 9). Both Acts impose a duty on magistrates' clerks to let the Director of Public Prosecutions know if a case, once started, is dropped or proceeded with too slowly: once he knows about the case, he can step in and take it over. Professor Edwards describes this as the 'kernel' of the original Act, 'providing as it did the effective machinery for enabling the Department of Public Prosecutions to exercise surveillance over what was going on in the criminal courts throughout the country. The sanction of knowing that, in the event of any such delay, failure, or refusal, the Director was empowered to step in and see the prosecution through to its conclusion was properly thought to provide the remedy for many of the evils previously diagnosed but lacking an effective cure'.

The 1879 Act provided for the Director of Public Prosecutions to be appointed by a Secretary of State — in practice, the Home Secretary. Arguments in parliament that the right man to appoint the Director was the man who was to 'superintend' his work eventually found favour a hundred years on, when the law was changed: Sir Thomas Hetherington's successor is the first Director to be appointed by the Attorney General. Another change is in the Director's salary. Before the age of inflation the Victorians were confident enough to state in the Act itself that the Director of Public Prosecutions would get a salary 'not exceeding two thousand pounds'; nowadays the Director is paid the same salary as a Permanent Secretary or a High Court judge, £65,000 a year in 1987/88.

The Prosecution of Offences Act 1879 came into operation on 'the first day of January one thousand eight hundred and eighty'. Since that day nine men have completed their terms of office as Director of Public Prosecutions. I propose to tell you a little bit about each of them.

Sir John Maule (1880–1884)

John Blossett Maule, QC had been Recorder of Leeds for nearly twenty years when he became the first Director of Public Prosecutions. As a barrister and part-time judge, he was not an impressive choice for the job. Perhaps those appointing him deliberately chose someone who was unlikely to rock the boat. His naturally quiet and cautious approach was no doubt refined as the result of the time he had spent sitting in court. He was given no staff apart from an Assistant Director and three clerks, and no department of his own — officially, he was part of the Home Office.

Even so, it is clear that Sir John Maule (as he became in 1882) chose to interpret his powers in an unnecessarily restrictive way: he felt he could do little more than send the papers to the Treasury Solicitor whenever he thought a prosecution was justified. Maule's responsibility for the case was then effectively at an end and the Treasury Solicitor would handle the prosecution. In Maule's view it wasn't the job of the Director of Public Prosecutions to prosecute: 'as long as people elect to carry on their own prosecutions,' he said, 'I have no legal right to interfere or interpose, and it is only when they apply to me and I learn in that way what they wish for my interposition, that the interposition is well-founded or warrantable'.

Like all his successors, Sir John Maule came in for plenty of uninformed criticism. But unlike the most recent Director, Sir Thomas Hetherington, Maule felt he could not answer back. Naturally, this made things even worse. The inevitable crisis came in 1883 when Maule refused to authorize the prosecution of two alleged blackmailers. A private prosecutor went ahead instead: the two men were convicted and given heavy sentences. There was such a row about it that the Home Secretary Sir William Harcourt set up a committee of inquiry into 'the present action and position of the Director of Public Prosecutions'.

Evidence was given by the Director and his Assistant, and also by the Treasury Solicitor, Augustus Stephenson. In a naked bid for power which must have stood comparison with the television soap opera *Dallas*, Stephenson persuaded the committee that he could make a much better go of the job. He was, after all, doing most of the work already.

The committee reported a year after it had been set up:

> We are of the opinion that the existing system — which in its inception was necessarily of a tentative character — requires modification and development. At present the Director of Public Prosecutions is consulted and determines upon prosecutions, but takes no practical part in their conduct, a duty which is remitted by him to the Solicitor to the Treasury . . . It appears to us that it would conduce both to efficiency and

economy, if the duty of deciding in which cases the State should undertake the prosecution were united in the same Department with that upon which is devolved the duty of practically conducting the prosecution when determined on.

The committee then had to decide who should get the combined jobs of Director of Public Prosecutions and Treasury Solicitor. But if the DPP were to take on the additional work, he would need to recruit more staff.

We have, therefore, come to the conclusion that it will be the better plan to unite the two branches of the work under the control of the Treasury Solicitor, who has already at his disposal a numerous staff accustomed to the conduct of criminal prosecutions, and who, under the arrangement proposed, would only require such moderate addition to his establishment as would enable him to advise on questions of law and practice, or as to any step or steps to be taken in the conduct of the prosecution, or to decide as to the necessity of special costs in any particular case not conducted under his instructions. This work now performed in the office of the Director of Public Prosecutions, as explained to us in evidence, is not of an extensive or onerous character, and does not require much time or labour. If this recommendation is adopted, there will no longer remain any duties for the Director of Public Prosecutions or his Assistant to discharge; and the two offices could forthwith be merged and consolidated by appointing the Solicitor of the Treasury to the office of Director of Public Prosecutions.

Stephenson had won. The Director of Public Prosecutions had vanished in all but name.

Sir Augustus Stephenson (1884–1894)

As I have just explained, Augustus Frederick William Keppel Stephenson was Treasury Solicitor at the time when John Maule was appointed the first Director of Public Prosecutions. Since the seventeenth century the Solicitor to the Treasury has been the government's senior legal official: though his responsibilities have waxed and waned over the years, at the time Stephenson held the post the Treasury Solicitor was responsible for a major slice of government legal business.

Immediately after the committee of inquiry recommended in May 1884 that the jobs of Treasury Solicitor and Director of Public Prosecutions should be merged, the Prosecution of Offences Act 1884 was passed to put the recommendation into effect. All appointments made under the 1879 Act were automatically revoked, and 'the person for the time being holding the office of Solicitor for the affairs of Her Majesty's Treasury' became Director of Public Prosecutions.

So on 19 August 1884 Stephenson duly received a letter written on behalf of the Lords Commissioners of HM Treasury enclosing a copy of the new Act and asking him to 'undertake and perform the duties of the office of Director of Public Prosecutions' with effect from four days earlier. 'As regards the Assistant Director and Mr Young, the Senior Clerk,' the letter continued, 'my Lords regret that the Department as now reorganised will not contain

appointments in which the services of these gentlemen can be made available
. . .' — one of the most charming ways of sacking people I've come across.
Stephenson, on the other hand, got a rise of £500, which was added to his
existing salary of £2,500.

Sir Augustus Stephenson (as he became in 1885) was robust and strong
willed. As befits a Treasury man, he was also careful with the pennies: he
felt it right to resist the temptation to prosecute at public expense in cases
which a private prosecutor could handle perfectly well without his help.
It seems that even a hundred years ago some people saw the Director as
'the Public Prosecutor', a man for all prosecutions — which Stephenson was
at pains to stress was not his role.

Although Sir John Maule had submitted a report to Parliament covering
his first three years, it was Sir Augustus Stephenson who introduced the
principle of making an annual report on his activities. (This practice was
suspended from 1915 to 1987, when Sir Thomas Hetherington published
the first report on the work of the Crown Prosecution Service.) Stephenson
used his annual reports to reply to his critics: John Edwards notes in his
book on *The Law Officers of the Crown* that Stephenson referred in his first
report to three cases in which his action had been variously described as
'reckless and deplorable' by a trial judge, as a 'neglect of duty' by a local
political association, and as 'scandalous and iniquitous' by a defence solicitor.
Stephenson then went on to point out that the Attorney General and the
Home Secretary had been satisfied with the way he had exercised his
discretion in these cases; his report also reveals that the judge's comments
had been rebutted in the House of Commons at the Director's request.

In the summer of 1889 the Treasury published its response to proposals
for reorganizing the Treasury Solicitor's department. Most of the
recommendations related to pay, pensions, hours of work and so on, but
among them is the following gem:

> The Committee recommend the employment of shorthand writers and of
> the telephone. As regards the former, the experiment can best be tried
> by the Solicitor [Stephenson] making shorthand a requirement in one or
> more of the first assistants whom he engages. How far the telephone can
> be used with advantage is a question on which my Lords will await a report
> from the Solicitor after he has had an opportunity of considering it; and
> he should, at the same time, inquire whether the application of speaking
> tubes between his own room and those of the officers with whom he is
> in most constant communication will effect any economy of time.

It is perhaps worth noting that there are no 'speaking tubes' — or even their
modern equivalent, the voice-activated intercom — between the various
rooms which make up the Director's head office, perhaps to avoid the risk
of internal eavesdropping. But at some time between 1889 and today the
decision was made to introduce the telephone, including a secure but now
rather ancient system which enables ministers and senior officials to speak
to one another on direct lines without their calls going through the public
exchange or even the internal Whitehall switchboards.

Professor Edwards says that Sir Augustus Stephenson's annual reports covering the period from 1884 to 1894 leave little doubt that he was subjected to much uninformed criticism. Among his most persistent critics was the Lord Chief Justice, Lord Coleridge, who even went so far as to table a motion in the House of Lords criticizing Stephenson for his delay in getting hold of some crucial documents. Stephenson was able to prove that this delay, which had allowed a defendant to escape abroad, had not been his fault — but it was clear that the public bickering between the Lord Chief Justice and the Director of Public Prosecutions could not be allowed to continue. Stephenson was quietly sacked without any reason being given: 'compulsorily retired' was the phrase used.

Hamilton Cuffe (Lord Desart) (1894–1908)

Sir Augustus Stephenson was succeeded as Treasury Solicitor and Director of Public Prosecutions by one of his Assistant Solicitors, Hamilton Cuffe. Again there was an abrupt shift in emphasis, as Cuffe chose to lower the temperature of public debate by not responding to criticism of his office. Presumably this was what the government had wanted from the holder of a job whose only previous occupants had both been removed from office.

Hamilton John Agmondesham Cuffe — who was sent to sea as a midshipman at the age of 12 — was the second son of an Irish peer: he became the fifth Earl of Desart on his brother's death in 1899. The former sailor steered the ship of state safely round the rocks of controversy which had sunk Stephenson, but as the years went by it became clear that the increasing workload was more than one individual could manage. The government's solution was to re-establish a separate Director of Public Prosecutions under the new Prosecution of Offences Act 1908; Desart gave up the job but remained Treasury Solicitor until his retirement a year later in 1909. He was to live until 1934.

Sir Charles Mathews (1908–1920)

Sir Charles Willie Mathews was the first Director of Public Prosecutions to head his own department — in effect, the first real DPP. The Prosecution of Offences Act 1908 repealed the section of the 1884 Act uniting the posts of Director and Treasury Solicitor, and again gave the Home Secretary power to appoint the Director of Public Prosecutions. The man he appointed was born Charles West but later became stepson of the comedian Charles Mathews, whose surname the young Charles took by deed poll; after a successful career at the Bar including a period as Senior Treasury Counsel at the Old Bailey, Charles Mathews became Recorder of Salisbury before his appointment as the first independent Director in 1908.

Despite the creation of a new department, the policy seems to have been very much 'business as usual'. The new Director of Public Prosecutions continued to operate under the Prosecution of Offences Regulations made as long ago as 1886 (regulations which were to survive for a total of sixty years until they were finally replaced in 1946). Mathews took over most of the staff who dealt with prosecution work in the Treasury Solicitor's department, including the men who were to become his two deputies. Both would be worth a footnote if there were any in this book: Guy Stephenson, the Assistant Director, was the son of the former Director, Sir Augustus Stephenson (his own son was to become Lord Justice Stephenson); the other deputy, F.J. Sims, had 'all the practical qualifications' for the job of Assistant Director, but had not qualified as a lawyer, so he was given the title of Principal Assistant instead (and less pay).

A couple of years after he took office, Mathews had to deal with one of the most notorious crimes of the century. You can see how he handled the case of Dr Crippen in the next chapter of this book.

A 'professional clerk' in Mathews' time was paid £150 a year: the letter sent to one Vincent Evans in 1912 told him he was expected to work from 10.30 in the morning to 5.30 at night, which doesn't seem too bad; he was, however, expected to 'attend earlier, or later, when the public business requires', and to work on all Saturday mornings and occasional Saturday afternoons. He was given holidays of '30 working days annually' (which must mean five weeks); on the other hand, judging by the date of Mr Evans' letter of appointment — 26 December — it seems that the post-Christmas stupor had not yet affected government offices. (Mr Evans stayed in the job for some 37 years, ending up as Deputy Director from 1946 to 1949.)

Sir Charles Mathews was an easy-going man, accused by some of leaning over too far in the direction of complacency. The case of the failure of the Charing Cross Bank, in which blatant and widespread fraud was committed on the public, demonstrated the tolerant view Mathews took of his duties: it was only after strong pressure that he took proceedings. A valuable unpublished history of the Director of Public Prosecutions written in 1984 by two members of the Director's staff, Kenneth Winfield, MBE and Adrian Lee, says Mathews was 'reputed to have been a very kindly man, always keen to improve the lot of his staff'. Certainly the newly-established Departmental Whitley Council, which was set up to deal with negotiations between management and staff, decided at its meeting in July 1920 'to place on record an expression of great regret for the loss occasioned to the department by the death of its esteemed Chief'. Mathews had died in office in January of that year.

During Mathews' last illness, and for the six months after his death before a successor was appointed, Guy Stephenson minded the shop. But he failed to get his father's old job: as compensation for being passed over, Stephenson was given a pay rise of £300 and, after a decent interval, a knighthood.

Sir Archibald Bodkin (1920–1930)

Archibald Henry Bodkin became Senior Treasury Counsel at the Old Bailey in 1908, when his predecessor, Sir Charles Mathews, became Director of Public Prosecutions. By 1920, Sir Archibald Bodkin had become — in the words of the present Director, Sir Thomas Hetherington, 'one of the great prosecutors at the Old Bailey'. Sir Thomas, in his Upjohn Memorial Lecture delivered in 1979, said that Bodkin

> was most meticulous and assiduous in his preparation of a case, and took an active part in directing police enquiries. He was also a vigorous prosecutor, and his rate of success was extremely high. In 1920 it seemed natural that Bodkin, with his great experience, should follow in the tradition of his predecessor and move from the Old Bailey to the office of the Director. It no doubt seemed to those appointing him that his qualities were just those required for the post, and indeed to a great degree they were.

But then Sir Thomas Hetherington drew attention to a criticism of Bodkin which he thought stemmed from Bodkin's tradition and background.

> He did not keep himself fully informed of new streams of thought in relation to crime and the way it should be handled. In particular, he was not aware of developments in the literary and artistic worlds, nor in the economic and social worlds. This may have been because Bodkin [who was born into a family of lawyers] was too fully involved in his own traditional legal world and his own social circle, so that he missed what has been described [by his biographer, Robert Jackson] as 'the leavening influence of contact with the public which was so essential to the proper discharge of his office'.

This criticism of Archibald Bodkin tells us as much about Sir Thomas Hetherington as it does about his predecessor. I shall be exploring Hetherington's views in the last section of this chapter. And in Chapter 3 you can read about two of Bodkin's best known cases, the Campbell incident and the prosecution of *The Well of Loneliness*.

The case which probably led to his downfall was, however, the so-called Savidge affair. To tell the tale I can do no better than quote again from the lecture given by Sir Thomas Hetherington in 1979.

> What happened was that on a summer's evening in Hyde Park, Sir Leo Money, who was an ex-member of parliament and a friend of cabinet ministers, was arrested together with a girl called Irene Savidge for behaving indecently in the park. Two police officers took them to the police station and both Sir Leo and Miss Savidge were charged before the Marlborough Street magistrate. However, after the police had given evidence the case was dismissed. There were immediate allegations from critics of the Metropolitan Police that the officers had committed perjury and that the matter should be fully investigated with a view to their prosecution for that offence.
>
> The papers then came to Bodkin who then proceeded, in his usual way, to direct in great detail the investigation of the case by an officer from New Scotland Yard. He instructed the investigating officer as to the order of interviewing the participants, and what he should say to them. It may well have seemed, from the way he was instructing the police to carry out their investigation, that his aim was to show that Sir Leo and Miss Savidge had after all committed the offence of which they had been acquitted, rather than to discover whether there was evidence that the police officers had committed perjury . . .

The whole thing ended up with questions in parliament and a Tribunal of Enquiry. Bodkin was accused of undue participation in the investigation of a crime and of an attempt to intimidate witnesses. In the result the tribunal acquitted the police and Bodkin of any improper conduct and there the matter rested. However, there is no doubt that the criticism which Bodkin had to undergo at the time — and subsequently — had a very severe impact on him. The challenge to his integrity, unjustified as it may well have been, was a shock to him . . . There is no direct evidence that the Savidge incident led to Bodkin's resignation. Nevertheless, not long afterwards he suddenly summoned all members of his staff to his office one morning and announced that he was departing that afternoon.

Sir Thomas Hetherington also makes two telling comparisons with his own period in office. To explain the shock suffered by Bodkin when his integrity was challenged he says 'it may be that he was less accustomed than more recent holders of the office to the accusation of being politically motivated'. The second point Sir Thomas makes is that Bodkin resigned only a few months before completing the ten years which would have entitled him to his pension. This 'indicates either a lack of worldly wisdom or a happy disregard for worldly wealth. In this,' says Hetherington, 'times have changed'.

Bodkin's biographer, Robert Jackson, says that 'in a sense, Bodkin's life after retirement was a twenty-seven year long anti-climax. It was not that he had lived too long but that, almost without realizing it, he had been projected into a different world, with standards very different from his own'. And Jackson draws attention to Bodkin's obsession with work: it was 'more than a habit . . . it was a disease':

> A more liberal-minded man would have kept himself informed of the new streams of thought on crime and punishment, even if he didn't keep abreast of developments in the literary and artistic worlds. The errors of judgment Bodkin made were largely due to his failure to stand back and see the problems confronting him in the context of a quickly changing world . . . Bodkin was a firm Director who saw himself as the watch-dog of the public, and the knowledge and experience — and prestige — that he handed on have stood his successors in good stead. In the sphere of public morals, his activities are more open to criticism. The common assertion made today [this was 1962, just after the trial of *Lady Chatterley*] that a lawyer should not set himself up as a public censor has much force and it had more force in Bodkin's day.

Sir Edward Tindal Atkinson (1930–1944)

Edward Hale Tindal Atkinson, like two of his predecessors, had been a part-time judge: he was appointed the first Recorder of Southend-on-Sea a year before being made Director. His period in office is described in the unpublished work which I mentioned earlier as one of the least contentious in the history of the department. Even though he was Director for most of the war years, he did not have any really very interesting cases to deal with.

In fact, most of the papers in Winfield and Lee's file refer to staffing arrangements. The professional and clerical staff were all men, of course, including the shorthand-typists (one of them a blind ex-serviceman, which seems a remarkable achievement) and the coal porter. There were also five 'charwomen', as they were described in 1934; by 1942 they had been re-designated 'women cleaners'. One of them was called Mrs Rawbone, which was probably an appropriate name for someone whose hands were presumably never far from a bucket of soapy water.

Sir Edward Tindal Atkinson, as he was by then, retired in 1944 at the age of 66, leaving behind him an organization still firmly rooted in its Victorian origins. His successor was much more interesting.

Sir Theobald Mathew (1944–1964)

Theobald Mathew was Director of Public Prosecutions for almost twenty years, but he was only 65 when he died suddenly in 1964. Unlike three of his predecessors he had not been a Recorder before becoming Director, though his grandfather was a Law Lord, and his father a KC. (Theobald Mathew's own son is John Mathew, QC.)

So it was not perhaps surprising that Theobald Mathew was called to the Bar in 1921. What was unusual was that in 1925 he became a solicitor instead, remaining in private practice until 1941 when he joined the Home Office to become Head of the Criminal Division there. Toby Mathew (as he was called) was the youngest man ever to be appointed Director, and the only solicitor. His familiarity with running an office — both as a solicitor and as a civil servant — gave him a significant advantage over the barristers who had preceded him.

A brief glimpse at the notes made by Kenneth Winfield from the department's internal records illustrates the unprecedented social upheaval which took place during Mathew's period of office. For example:

> 1944 Due to the shortage of male shorthand writers, we noted that we may be forced to employ ladies.
>
> 1947 Electricity was on ration: lights must not be used between 9 a.m. and 12 noon or 2 p.m. and 4 p.m.
>
> 1949 Staff Notice: volunteers required to spend at least one week at agricultural camp to help with the harvest. Under special circumstances, special leave would be granted.
>
> 1950 Copying section under strain due to increased work load. Original exhibits were still being typed out for briefs to counsel, and photocopying was slow because it was a wet process and the copies had to be hung up to dry.
>
> The office moved to 12 Buckingham Gate.
>
> The table tennis club was established.
>
> 1952 To save money, non-professional officers must not make any phone calls without prior permission. The telephone was to be used for urgent business only.
>
> 1953 Departmental firearm, a .25 pistol, no longer wanted: surrendered to police at New Scotland Yard. 14 rounds of ammunition unaccounted for.

The Establishment Officer agreed to act as press officer, giving only the date and hearing place of our cases.

Staff would be allowed to view the Coronation procession from the office windows overlooking Buckingham Palace. They could bring their husbands or wives, or an adult near relative whose relationship had to be stated on the application form.

1956 The 42 hour week was introduced, and the office shut on Saturdays.

1961 Subscriber Trunk Dialling introduced. Costs of telephone calls were to be kept to a minimum, but there was no repetition of the instruction to seek permission before use.

1964 Five Dictaphones were brought into use to alleviate the shortage of shorthand typists.

A Requiem Mass was held for the Director at Brompton Oratòry at 5 p.m. The office was shut at 4.30 to enable staff to attend.

Of Sir Theobald Mathew, his successor Sir Thomas Hetherington said in 1979 that

Sir Theobald had the task of converting an organisation based on Victorian lines, and influenced by Victorian standards, into a modern department, capable of applying modern doctrines to a much greater variety of cases than hitherto. Within a few years of his taking office new regulations substantially increased the categories of offence which had to be reported to him; and there developed the modern trend, which still continues, of incorporating in new statutes a provision requiring the consent of the DPP or the Attorney General to institute prosecutions — thus limiting the right of private prosecution. He would also have found that there were still plenty of the old types of case coming in, such as the classic murders leading to famous trials on the old pattern. In addition, there were during the late 1940's and early 1950's a series of spy cases which deserved, and received, his personal attention. At that time, of course, death was still the penalty for murder, and for that reason each individual murder file was carefully considered by the Director or by his deputy.

Sir Thomas said his predecessor Sir Theobald had 'largely to rethink the principles which the department should apply and to reorganise its structure to meet that purpose'. In this Sir Theobald Mathew had 'succeeded very well', according to his successor. 'In effect it is his legacy which I have inherited in my present post', said Sir Thomas in 1979. 'In my view the foundations and structure are sound.' But he added: 'modernisation and some refurbishing is required'.

Unlike his predecessor Bodkin, Theobald Mathew was content to let his staff do the work of preparing cases for trial. As he had never been a prosecuting counsel, Mathew was not — in Sir Thomas Hetherington's phrase — 'homesick' for the Old Bailey. And Hetherington thinks Mathew was perhaps ahead of his age in recognizing that there should be a distinction between public morality and private morality. *The Times* said of Mathew on his death that he did not regard himself as a guardian of public morals but as an instrument by which the criminal law was enforced. Mathew's obituary continued:

The situations which caused Mathew the greatest difficulty were those in which the fields of law and personal as opposed to obviously public morals overlapped. This sort of situation is perhaps best typified by the law relating to the publication of obscene matter. Mathew's view was that so far as private conduct was concerned a man might damn himself so long as he did so with discretion: he would be answerable to his own conscience and it was none of the state's business. But where a man did not use discretion and thereby came into conflict with the criminal law it was the duty of the Director of Public Prosecutions to consider where to take action. With the law relating to obscene matter this was no easy matter to decide, for who is to say whether a particular publication tends to deprave or corrupt?

The answer was that Mathew had to, notably in his notorious decision to prosecute Penguin Books over the publication of *Lady Chatterley's Lover*. How did he set about reaching his decision? *The Times* explained, and then passed judgment:

> Striving always, as he did, to exclude his personal opinions and views, it was nevertheless necessary for him to make up his mind on some basis: he could and did take advice from Treasury Counsel but they were in the same difficulty. On the one hand the law prohibited the publication of obscene material and it was the Director's duty to act; on the other hand the public and general conception of what was immoral or obscene was in a fluid state and no one could tell the outcome. It may be that Mathew made mistakes in choosing to prosecute some particular work or in choosing some particular form of procedure but it was a measure of his courage that he did not act in such a way that he could be taken to regard the law prohibiting obscene publications as a dead letter. While recognising that his task was well nigh impossible, Mathew nevertheless sought fairly to enforce the criminal law in the state in which it had been entrusted to him.

I shall be taking a critical look at this argument in Chapter 8. Mathew himself was clearly uncomfortable about the whole issue: he had told the Select Committee on the Obscene Publications Bill in 1957 that he strongly deprecated his department being placed in the position 'which apparently it is thought by some persons to occupy already', of being a censor of novels or other literary publications. But as Professor Edwards points out in *The Law Officers of the Crown*, that is really what he was — because if the Director advised that a book should not be prosecuted the chances were that nobody else would attempt a private prosecution.

The prosecution of *Lady Chatterley* — discussed in Chapter 3 — came a full ten years after a lecture Mathew delivered at the University of London in 1950. In his lecture (which, with commendable economy of effort, he repeated when addressing the Law Society in 1952, and at a meeting in London of the American Bar Association in 1957) Mathew explained that the Director was 'responsible for dealing with cases of obscene or indecent libels, exhibitions, and publications so that there may be a common standard for the prosecution of this type of offence throughout the country'. Why, then, did he prosecute Penguin Books under the Obscene Publications Act of 1959? As a test case, perhaps, to see what public opinion would accept in the future? This of course was the one question that Mathew would never answer, as the following extract from his lecture makes clear. Mathew reminded his listeners that the Director of Public Prosecutions

> acts under the general superintendence of the Attorney General who answers for him in parliament, and by the Prosecution of Offences Regulations he is subject to the directions of the Attorney General. However, for reasons that are sufficiently obvious the Director does not state publicly the reasons for his decision in any particular case. He is, therefore, to that extent in a quasi-judicial position with regard to the exercise of his discretion but, although this position is generally accepted in practice, there is nothing to prevent his decision being challenged in parliament, nor does he enjoy immunity from actions for malicious prosecution.

Sir Theobald Mathew went on to deny suggestions that in cases where Parliament had given the Director of Public Prosecutions sole discretion to prosecute, he was therefore independent of the Attorney General and couldn't be told what to do by anyone. Mathew recalled that Parliament was sovereign and the executive was always answerable to it. Parliament had laid down that the Director of Public Prosecutions was to act under the superintendence of the Attorney General, thus ensuring that there was a member of the executive answerable to Parliament for the way the Director did his job. In Mathew's view, 'the Director remains the servant — the proud servant possibly — of the public, through parliament which represents them, and of the executive which, through parliament, is responsible to them, and he is in no sense the master of either'. (I shall be discussing in Chapter 10 the modern relationship between the Director of Public Prosecutions and the Attorney General, under whose 'superintendence' he works.)

But although Mathew considered himself answerable to the executive, he wasn't subservient to it. In the view of Sir Thomas Hetherington, Mathew 'certainly respected the great tradition of the independence of the Director from interference by the executive, as did the Attorneys General with whom he served'. Sir Thomas said in his Upjohn Lecture in 1979 that he had studied papers from which it was apparent that Mathew and the Attorneys of the time were very conscious of the lessons to be learned from the case of John Ross Campbell in 1924, and were determined to avoid any repetition. That case, discussed in the next chapter, involved an apparent attempt by Ramsey MacDonald's Labour government to stop, for political reasons, a prosecution against the editor of a Communist newspaper under the Incitement to Mutiny Act. The government fell soon after and, Sir Thomas Hetherington tells us,

> one of the first things that happened when the new government came in under Stanley Baldwin was that a directive was issued by the new Prime Minister, decreeing that under no circumstances was any member of the Cabinet to bring political pressure to bear on the Attorney General or the Director of Public Prosecutions. That has remained the position ever since.

An example of Mathew's robust approach to any hint of political pressure

was his response to a letter from the Ministry of Housing and Local
Government in 1953. As part of a cost-cutting exercise the Ministry had
been asking local council treasurers whether they thought central
government policies were leading to unnecessarily high rates. One City
Treasurer told the Ministry that the Director was now using local firms of
solicitors as his agents to handle cases in his city, instead of the Town Clerk
as before. This, said the Treasurer, had increased the costs payable to the
Director by the local authority. The Ministry then passed this information
on to Mathew and asked for his comments. They got a very shirty reply
from Mathew, who said he regarded it as important for the proper
administration of criminal justice that he should retain complete
independence in deciding who should act as his agent in any case which
was not conducted directly by his department. For good measure he added
that to use the local authority prosecuting solicitor instead of a private firm
would save less than £10,000 a year over the whole country — which must
have been an insignificant sum, even then.

On the other hand, Mathew put much effort into battling with the Treasury
to get more resources for his own department. By 1957 staff levels were
considered to be too low to cope with increased work-loads, while promotion
prospects within the department were poor. The Treasury's response was
merely to propose that two men should be promoted to more senior grades.
Mathew refused to accept this solution, which would have done nothing
to improve staffing or promotion prospects for most of his staff. Instead
he pressed for, and got, the creation of a new post of Assistant Solicitor.
The Civil Service is, of course, renowned for giving its staff titles which
seem to be in inverse proportion to their seniority: anywhere else a secretary
would be pretty low down in the pecking order and to be a permanent
secretary would be even worse. So it is with the unimpressive-sounding title
of Assistant Solicitor: the man appointed in 1958 was to work directly below
the Deputy Director and to be on the same level as the three Assistant
Directors (who were themselves third in the hierarchy).

Perhaps encouraged by his success, Mathew asked the Treasury for
another Assistant Solicitor position a year later. The Treasury countered
by offering a much more junior post, arguing that what Mathew wanted
would produce an 'undesirable organisational feature'. The Director bided
his time and tried again two years later. The Treasury man replied that he
was afraid 'we still feel that a very strong case indeed would have to be made
for having three Assistant Directors and two Assistant Solicitors side by
side, owing to our fear that this would lead to proposals for upgrading the
former on the grounds of their arguably superior responsibility'.

So the following year Mathew increased the stakes, asking this time for
three new Assistant Solicitors. After a further year he was rewarded with
two more posts, which may have been what he was expecting when he asked
for three.

Mathew was described as a good man to work for. His staff regarded him
with considerable respect and kindliness. Sir Thomas Hetherington said

Toby Mathew was 'a thinking man, he was a kind man, and he was a fair and just man'. He also had an amazing pair of eyebrows, so prominent that they were said to have overwhelmed his face.

It has been said of Sir Theobald Mathew that 'he had been able successfully to keep his finger on the pulse of public opinion, without which no Director of Public Prosecutions can function efficiently':

> There is no point in prosecuting cases if the climate of opinion is such that no jury is likely to convict. The Director, like a judge, must move with the times, and keep abreast of current ideas concerning crime and punishment, economic and social theories, and literally and artistic values . . . If Mathew had continued to operate in the style of his predecessors I suspect that he would not have enjoyed the confidence of the public, and I was aware that I too needed to be alive to new thinking and to move with the times.

The 'I' in that paragraph was Mathew's immediate successor, Sir Norman Skelhorn, in his book *Public Prosecutor*. It is to his career that I now turn.

Sir Norman Skelhorn (1964–1977)

Norman John Skelhorn was called to the Bar in 1931 when he was just twenty-one: he was proud of the fact that he had already had three years practical experience of the law by then. The son of a peripatetic country parson, he practised in Bristol for seven years before moving to chambers in London. After spending the war in the legal civil service he returned to practice in 1945, sitting part-time as a Recorder and becoming a Queen's Counsel in 1954. He devotes the first sixty pages of his book *Public Prosecutor* to reminiscences of the period.

In 1964 — apparently right out of the blue — Norman Skelhorn had a letter from the Home Secretary inviting him to become Director of Public Prosecutions. Skelhorn had set his sights on a full-time appointment as a judge, and realized that to accept the offer would mean giving up any hope of achieving that particular ambition. It would also mean a cut in pay, to a mere £6,185 a year. But what finally convinced him to accept was a feeling that — in his words — 'here was a job in which I could make some real impact'. In his book Sir Norman says the job was one in which he would have the opportunity to influence the standards of prosecution: 'if I exercised that influence rightly, I would be able to give substantial assistance to the administration of justice'. Though he was nearly 55 when he became DPP, and so only five years off the normal civil service retirement age, he was told he could stay on if he wanted to until he was 70. But he eventually decided to retire after 13 years, partly because he still wanted to serve again as a Recorder. 'I am never happier,' he wrote in 1981, 'than when I sit now from time to time in that capacity.' It may even have given him more pleasure than being Director of Public Prosecutions.

When he took on the job, Norman Skelhorn kept the existing structure of the department pretty well unchanged. But, to cope with two increasingly important areas of his work, he added to the two divisions dealing with

London and the rest of the country two more to deal with fraud and complaints against the police. In *Public Prosecutor* he explained a little about how his office was run ('much like any other business, albeit within the framework of strict security') and outlined his policy of prosecuting 'only if . . . there is a reasonable prospect of conviction' (discussed in the section of Chapter 6 entitled 'In the Public Interest'). Beyond pointing out that, contrary to popular belief, he didn't spend all day reading dirty books ('some people think that . . . I was some sort of Director of Public Pornography') Skelhorn gives little away in his book. He describes the notorious cases he had to deal with, but seems to reveal nothing that was not already public knowledge. This, no doubt, is perfectly proper: a retired Director who wrote up his official files into what would then undoubtedly become a best-selling autobiography might find himself falling foul of the very Official Secrets Act under which he would often have advised prosecuting others. But it doesn't make for very interesting reading.

This reticence was even more marked during his years as Director. He gave hardly any interviews, the one notable exception leading to a profile which appeared in *Punch* in November 1976. When I met him at a party to launch the Crown Prosecution Service in 1986, Sir Norman — a small, twinkling eyed, rosy cheeked man, perhaps a little deaf by then — agreed that the reason he had spoken to the *Punch* reporter, David Taylor, was that he felt safe with the magazine: presumably if the profile had turned out wrongly he could have maintained it was not to be taken seriously. He cannot have been the easiest person to interview, and Taylor found him far from forthcoming:

> To even the most straightforward question he seems programmed to pause, to sniff for any syntactical snags or lurking indiscretion, then, after lengthy reflection, will issue a statement both balanced and usually qualified. He does not smoke a pipe, fill in crosswords as he speaks, or doodle, but looks as if he just might at any minute. Off the cuff, he can suddenly turn quite jolly and emits, from time to time, a gurgling laugh. Though by no means a shy man, Sir Norman Skelhorn is persuaded that 'a degree of remoteness is, perhaps, professionally desirable in that it does assist in promoting public confidence in one's impartiality'. Pause, sniff, reflection. 'On the other hand, I think it could be a mistake to be too much of a shadowy figure and certainly the main part of one's function should be understood by the public.'

Skelhorn naturally refused to discuss individual cases in the *Punch* article, though he did make free with his personal opinions. He thought there had been a marked disrespect for law and order, a persistent erosion of standards, and a tendency to blame crime on bad housing:

> Equally, and I must stress that these are personal views and very likely at odds with the official line, I think there is an understandable concern with the way in which we deal with convicted criminals. There is a feeling that we are perhaps too soft. Now, clearly the prisons must seek to reform and rehabilitate. But what I feel is sometimes not sufficiently borne in mind is that the objective is not a tenderness for the prisoner but the best way of

protecting society. Obviously, if you can reform one criminal, society has one fewer to worry about. But what many penologists will not face up to is that there may be those who are not capable of reform . . . I do not, of course, imply that we should go back to the treadmill, but I do suggest that in having prisons made more and more comfortable, the sting of imprisonment is to some extent lost. I am not terribly troubled, personally, as others are when you say this, that you will turn out embittered men. Maybe in some instances you would but, in my view at any rate, it is the protection of society which must come first.

I have always wondered what makes men policemen, what makes them prosecutors. Skelhorn — who was in his life both defender, prosecutor and judge — clearly thought there was a lot to be said for protecting society from criminals, and not much to be said for protecting criminals from society. One lawyer who knew him told me that Skelhorn had difficulty in making up his mind. He took an old-fashioned approach to the men he dealt with in court: 'most criminals bear no animosity to the judge who has sentenced them,' he wrote, 'provided they feel they have had a fair crack of the whip at their trial'. The only abusive letters he ever had followed his decision that a dog, fierce though photogenic, had to be destroyed. But then in England people care about that sort of thing.

Sir Thomas Hetherington (1977–1987)

Thomas Chalmers Hetherington ('Tony' to his friends) had to cope with the biggest change in the Director's role for more than a century. As the ninth holder of the office, it was Hetherington who had to create the Crown Prosecution Service, taking on more than 3,000 new staff scattered throughout England and Wales. I shall be telling you more about the Crown Prosecution Service in Chapter 4, and explaining why Sir Thomas Hetherington no longer holds the view he once expressed that there would be 'disadvantages and difficulties' in creating a national prosecuting agency. His initial doubts dispelled though, Hetherington was in the best position of any Director to cope with the transformation of a few hundred people, most of whom knew each other, into a large modern government department — the first to be run according to the tenets of the Conservative government's Financial Management Initiative. Hetherington said putting together the Crown Prosecution Service had been 'a great challenge' — and one he had enjoyed. His main job initially had been to recruit the senior staff, and he felt he had been fortunate in acquiring some very good people who had lightened the burden of setting up the new service.

Sir Thomas Hetherington was born in Dumfriesshire, the son of a doctor. His family moved south when the young Hetherington was two, and he was educated at Rugby. From there he went on to Christ Church, Oxford, where he decided to read law — more practical he thought, than his original choice of history. After three years in the Royal Artillery he continued to serve part time in the Territorial Army, leaving nearly 20 years later with the rank of major. He was called to the Bar in 1952, and shortly afterwards he joined the legal department of the Ministry of Pensions and National Insurance, intending to stay only for two or three years before returning to private practice. Like others who joined simply to gain experience, he never left: he now regrets he did not have the opportunity to do more advocacy at that time. After working in the Law Officers' Department from 1962 to 1975, Hetherington spent two years as Deputy Treasury Solicitor: as second in command to the government's top legal civil servant, he was following in the path of Sir Augustus Stephenson who — you will remember — went on to combine the jobs of Treasury Solicitor and DPP. Fortunately though, Sir Thomas Hetherington was only expected to do one job at a time: in 1977 he became Director of Public Prosecutions, the first time a career civil servant had been appointed to the post. Perhaps those who appointed him were looking for someone with the administrative skills that would be needed if the Director was to head a national prosecution service (although it is worth remembering that Tony Hetherington — unlike other senior civil servants — had never been responsible for supervising a large staff).

Theobald Mathew had been a civil servant for just three years before becoming Director of Public Prosecutions in 1944. Tony Hetherington had been in the government legal service for 24 years when he was appointed to the job in 1977. He had spent nine of those years as Legal Secretary to the Law Officers, in other words the senior official working for the Attorney General and his deputy the Solicitor General. One of the Attorneys he served was Sir Peter Rawlinson, later Lord Rawlinson of Ewell, who said in a recent BBC interview that Sir Thomas Hetherington had a very sound and sensible assessment of issues:

> The Legal Secretary has to do a great deal of liaison work with, for instance, the Secretary of the Cabinet and the heads of the Security Services: he's a very vital cog in the government legal machine. This calls for qualities far beyond that of merely the lawyer or the administrator — you've got to have a very good idea of the national interest and you've got to have a good broad outlook upon what is sensible to do and what, although it may be legally correct, would be rather too legalistic. I've always thought he had very good judgment in those matters particularly.

Being Legal Secretary was good training for the future Director of Public Prosecutions. Sir Michael Havers described him to me as 'a marvellous administrator'. As you will see in my chapter on the Director and the Attorney — Chapter 10 — the two men speak to one another almost every day and there can be little they say which the Attorney's Legal Secretary does not know about. Working as Legal Secretary taught Tony Hetherington a great deal about the criminal justice system. More important perhaps, the Law Officers' Department — because it is so tiny — is probably the last government department not to have a press officer. As a result, the Legal Secretary is one of the senior officials in government who has no excuse for not speaking to journalists, except perhaps when he is submerged under the crises which seem to occur with increasing frequency — the attempt to stop Peter Wright from publishing his memoirs in Australia and Duncan Campbell's BBC television programme on the Zircon spy satellite being the most recent examples.

It may therefore have been Hetherington's discovery while Legal Secretary that people like me do not actually have two heads which perhaps contributed in part to his decision to open up the office of Director of Public Prosecutions to media scrutiny. As a result, he was better able to cope with the publicity surrounding the launch of the Crown Prosecution Service in 1986 — not all of which was favourable. I thought at the time that, despite Hetherington's experience, someone more skilled than he was in the dubious craft of 'news management' might have managed to present the Crown Prosecution Service rather more attractively. It was a few months later that the Director appointed Janet Naim to be his Head of Press and Public Relations at the Crown Prosecution Service. Before then, Mrs Naim had spent 12 years in the Government Information Service. At the Department of Transport she had a 'major role in the production of below the line publicity'.

Sir Thomas Hetherington's personal decision to allow people to know what was going on in his department was a major change. 'We are a public service,' he told me 'we're acting in the public interest, and I've always thought it right that the public should know the way we tick: it is right that they should know our general policy and how we apply it. We haven't felt able to give details of individual cases, but I think it is right — and this is now generally accepted — that we should be as open as we can.' In Hetherington's words, it was necessary 'not to operate in a monastery'. He said he had deliberately aimed to increase 'media awareness of what goes on here'. In explaining why he had not followed his predecessors' policy of saying 'no comment' at every opportunity, Sir Thomas Hetherington commented that previous Directors had not understood the journalistic conventions — that remarks could be provided on an unattributable basis, or that a background briefing could be given without the risk that the Director himself would be quoted. To help him in this approach Sir Thomas Hetherington imported the Whitehall model of a Private Office, adding to the existing personal secretary (a hand-picked typist, diary-keeper and tea-maker) a Private Secretary (researcher, fixer and mind-reader), a Parliamentary Clerk (to keep track of MPs' questions), a locally recruited Press Officer (who was always careful not to say anything more than he should), and most recently the Public Relations Officer. One of the pitfalls of having a Press Office and being relatively open was that Hetherington was expected by the press to comment whenever, for example, a magistrate criticized the Crown Prosecution Service, which is not something he would do until he had found out the full facts — and then it might be too late for the journalist's deadline.

I wondered whether Tony Hetherington, trained as he had been in a civil service not known for its love of publicity, felt uncomfortable when people like me thrust microphones in his face and demanded instant answers. 'I've been a civil servant all my career,' he said, 'but I've also been a lawyer all my career — so I'm fairly used to the public knowing what I have to say.

I don't find it particularly frightening; I think I did perhaps originally find
it more frightening than I do now.'

In a perfect world, an open approach to the media would encourage
informed comment while precluding ignorant criticism. Things do not always
work out that way, and during the Glenholmes affair, for example — as you
will see in Chapter 5 — Sir Thomas Hetherington had to put up with
accusations of incompetence and calls in Parliament for his resignation. More
frequently though, the accusation was not that he lacked competence: the
charge against him was either that he had failed to prosecute in a case where
people thought there should have been a prosecution (such as the case of
the Essex doctor and the eight-year-old girl, described in Chapter 9) or, more
commonly still, that a particular prosecution which resulted in an acquittal
should not have been brought in the first place. 'The only cases anyone seems
to be interested in are the ones we've lost,' mused Sir Thomas, ruefully. 'But
actually we do win quite a few you know.' I wondered how he felt when his
decisions were publicly criticized. 'No-one likes public criticism,' he said,
'but there are many cases that are acquitted for reasons which have only
come out during the trial: so when one of my officers was deciding whether
to go ahead, he or she did not in fact know all the factors that ultimately
emerged. What I do not like is when a case is thrown out by the judge 'at
half time' or if magistrates decide there is not a case to be committed. That
does suggest to me that something has gone wrong — and I like to know
why.' The doctrine that an acquittal only amounts to a misjudgment if the
case has been thrown out before the defence gets up to speak clearly gave
Sir Thomas Hetherington some comfort. On that basis he felt he had not
done too badly — despite verdicts of not guilty for Jeremy Thorpe, Clive
Ponting and the Cyprus servicemen. I shall have more to say about these
cases in the next chapter.

As you can see already (and I shall be explaining this more fully in Chapter
5), the Director of Public Prosecutions takes very few prosecution decisions
himself. He decides only the most difficult and sensitive cases, but naturally
enough these are the ones where a misjudgment — real or perceived —
is likely to provoke the biggest outcry. Lady Hetherington said her husband
got 'a little hurt when the press get at him'. But she thought press criticism
hurt her more than it hurt him. 'And he is able to just go on to the next
case, because he's so busy that he has to do this,' she said in an interview
to mark her husband's sixtieth birthday. 'I don't think you could do the job
if you begin to worry about every single case that you take on,' she added.

Hetherington acknowledged that he did feel 'a bit irritated' by an acquittal
if, on his view of how the evidence had turned out in court, he thought there
should have been a conviction — particularly if a great deal of work had
gone into the case. 'But I quite rapidly forget about that case — in the sense
that I don't go away and worry about it. I put it down to experience, and
to that extent I do remember it, because next time I get a similar case I
would remember what happened last time.'

In general, Sir Thomas Hetherington supports the jury system. However, he was one of those who argued in favour of complicated fraud trials being conducted by a judge with two assessors, rather than by a judge and jury. This proposal was put forward by Lord Roskill's committee on fraud trials but rejected by the government in 1986. Hetherington was in favour of plans to abolish peremptory challenge — the defendant's right to object to potential jurors without giving reasons — and he supported moves to reduce pressure on the Crown Court by taking away the right to jury trial in certain cases.

As well as being criticized for losing cases, Sir Thomas Hetherington — like all Directors — was also attacked for not bringing prosecutions. Cases involving police officers proved particularly difficult. There were 26 cases in the 1970s involving complaints of deaths in police custody: giving evidence to a House of Commons Select Committee in 1980, Hetherington said that in each of the 26 cases the decision not to prosecute was reached because there had not been enough evidence. Hetherington said he had looked at three of the 26 cases personally, and was fully satisfied that there was no need to question witnesses further or make fresh inquiries.

One such case involved the death of Liddle Towers, shortly after his release from police custody. 'We had no doubt about how Towers sustained the injuries which resulted in his death,' Hetherington told me. 'There we decided however that the evidence was not strong enough to justify criminal proceedings against a police officer.' Another similar case was that of Blair Peach. 'In that case, where death was caused after a group of police officers had been in physical contact with a crowd of people including Blair Peach, there was no doubt Blair Peach had been hit over the head, in what was almost certainly an illegal act,' Hetherington said. 'But we did not have the evidence against any identifiable individual, and you can't prosecute the Metropolitan Police.'

In 1981, Hetherington told the then legal correspondent of *The Times*, Marcel Berlins, that there had been no prosecution in this and other similar cases because it was impossible to tell which of several police officers had committed the crime:

> That was very much the Blair Peach position. I am not absolutely certain he was hit on the head by a police officer, but I think it is probable that he was. There was no evidence as to which one, literally no evidence, and no evidence really as to what the weapon was, except that it was a blunt instrument.

Hetherington had looked into the possibility of prosecuting for conspiracy to pervert the course of justice, but there was no evidence for that charge either. The police officers under suspicion had all remained silent, as they were entitled to do.

A more recent example was the decision late in 1986 not to prosecute anyone over the death in police custody of John Mikkelsen, a Hell's Angel. Seven officers from the Metropolitan Police, including a Chief Inspector, had been suspended after an inquest jury returned a verdict on Mikkelsen of unlawful killing. This means, of course, that the jury thought Mikkelsen's death resulted from manslaughter or murder. Since he died in police custody, the inference to be drawn from the verdict was that Mikkelsen had been killed by one or more police officers. But the Director announced there would be no prosecution — because of lack of evidence. (Later, the verdict of unlawful killing was quashed by the High Court after legal action taken by police officers, and at a new inquest another jury returned a verdict of misadventure.)

I asked Sir Thomas whether he found cases like these frustrating. 'I always find it unsatisfactory where it's quite clear an offence has been committed and one can't identify the culprits, such as in a riot, for example. But clearly we are professional people: we have to take a professional view of it. We regret it, but we move on to the next case.'

You will remember that Hetherington thought Sir Archibald Bodkin, who had been Director in the 1920s, was out of touch with contemporary developments in the literary and artistic worlds. But Hetherington said in the Upjohn Lecture I mentioned earlier that it was too easy to criticize Bodkin for taking an excessively prudish view in prosecuting the publishers of a book about lesbianism:

> It is apparent from the reaction of others at the time, although I must concede that public opinion was perhaps not entirely informed, that [Bodkin] was acting in accordance with the view which the public as a whole took of the subject matter. That being so, it can be said he was regarding himself, as I think all Directors must regard themselves, as the servant of the public and was attempting to fulfil the public's wishes in the application of the criminal law.

So did Sir Thomas Hetherington see himself as deciding what was fit for the rest of us to read or watch?

> I certainly don't see myself as a guardian of public morals. Clearly the way we exercise our policy in prosecuting pornography does have its effect: if we decided not to prosecute anyone under the Obscene Publications Act that would be wrong, because that statute is law and must therefore be operated. Clearly we do take account of public opinion, we look to see what the public are thinking about cases of that nature, in deciding whether to prosecute. And of course there's a very good reason for that, because if we prosecute cases which the public as a whole do not think should be prosecuted, we're going to get jury acquittals, or we're going to get magistrates throwing out the cases, and that would be bad.

Tony Hetherington does not try to create a public image for himself: he does not deliberately dress to impress. It is almost as if he could not quite believe he really was the Director of Public Prosecutions. He is unstuffy and the very opposite of pompous; he deals politely with pomposity and obsequiousness in others but is not taken in by it for a moment. Perhaps his best defence against the many criminals, and indeed terrorists, from whom he must still be at grave personal risk was that few of those who met him in the street or saw him having a drink in the pub with his staff would gather from his outward appearance that they were looking at the DPP: like George Smiley, he merged into the crowd. He struck me as charming, kind, firm — and perhaps a little shy, an impression confirmed by the Attorney General, Sir Michael Havers. 'Although he's transformed the public image of the office, because he has been so much more open about it, I've always thought of him in fact as a slightly shy man,' Sir Michael told me, adding hastily that he saw no harm in that at all.

Hetherington's own office, too, was modest and unassuming: white walls, restrained but tasteful period furnishings, not enough room even for a conference table (characteristically, he allowed the room he had previously used for meetings to be taken over by the enlarged press office in 1986). There were a few law books in the book case, some more on his desk, and a secure cabinet for files: clearly, though, most of the papers that are sent to the Director of Public Prosecutions do not stay very long in his own office, if indeed they ever get there. The Director's office has a fine bow window dating back to the original construction of the building in 1836; fortunately the substantial rebuilding of the offices in 1972 did not involve installing the noisy and intrusive air conditioning which even Ministers have to put up with at the Home Office down the road.

Sir Thomas Hetherington announced in September 1986 that he would be retiring a year later, having stayed on a year beyond the normal civil service retirement age of 60 to see the Crown Prosecution Service through its first year. Speaking to me with a full year to go, I asked him whether he was planning to follow other senior civil servants into a lucrative job in the private sector. 'I haven't decided to take up any lucrative job,' he said then, 'and in fact nobody's offered me anything.'

He did say he had agreed to deliver a series of lectures on investigating insurance fraud for the United Nations Asian and Far Eastern Institute in Japan. He also planned to write a book on his personal impressions of the prosecution system, starting with his time as a prosecutor in the Ministry of Pensions and National Insurance.

Sir Thomas said he hoped to involve himself more in local affairs: his daughters had all been to one of the local schools near the family home in Surrey and he had been asked to be a governor of the school. It did not sound to me as if that would keep him fully occupied. He agreed, and said he would try and find a part-time job: 'clearly I'm not just going to retire to my garden,' he said, 'it would drive my wife mad apart from anything else'. Not so, of course: Lady Hetherington said she was very much looking forward to seeing more of husband on his retirement.

Tony Hetherington added that he was looking forward to spending time tracing his family history. He thought it would be fun to find out more about his antecedents, as he put it. 'My father was a Scottish doctor,' he said, 'and my great-grandfather was a fairly eminent Scottish cleric: his books are particularly unreadable. My father's great-grandfather was an agricultural labourer in Dumfriesshire. On my mother's side, again there is a long history of Scottish professional tradition: my grandfather on that side was a lawyer.'

Sir Thomas and Lady Hetherington have four daughters. One became a nurse, two trained as teachers and the fourth was called to the Bar. She is not in practice though: despite the inevitable ribbing that must come from 'joining daddy's firm', the boss's daughter followed the example of her distinguished father and joined the Crown Prosecution Service.

THREE

The Case of the Century

Writing about past Directors' triumphs and failures is not easy. Their files are normally 'closed' to the public for 75 years. To look at them I would have had to meet the most remarkably stringent conditions, imposed by the government and outlined in a letter from the Cabinet Office. Not only did they want me to submit my manuscript for 'official clearance', not only was I to keep it secret until then from my publishers and any typist not 'provided for by the Government Service', not only would I have had to agree, as a condition of publication, to leave out bits 'not acceptable in the public interest', but also my publishers would have had to undertake to 'indemnify' Her Majesty's Government, its servants, or agents, against liability in respect of any claims which might be brought for defamation'. Needless to say, this was not on.

And fortunately it is not necessary. To understand the present you must first study the past. Seventy-five years have now elapsed since one of the most notorious crimes of the century. Now, as the newspapers used to say, the truth can be told: not only about Dr Hawley Harvey Crippen, MD, but also about Sir Charles Mathews, whom you will remember from the previous chapter as the first independent Director of Public Prosecutions. The case of Dr Crippen is the first in a series of prosecutions I want to tell you about, cases which have kept the newspapers in business over the years. I have tried to restrict this chapter of *causes célèbres* to cases which throw light on the Director of Public Prosecutions and his work. But I will leave it to you to decide which one the papers would be justified in calling 'the case of the century'.

Dr Crippen

Certainly the newspapers were not slow to write about Crippen as he waited to stand trial for the murder of his wife, and indeed after the *Daily Chronicle* strongly hinted that Crippen had bought a deadly poison, hyoscin, from a chemist's shop in London shortly before his wife was last seen alive he tried to have the editor committed to prison for contempt of court; it had also made the even more damning assertion that Crippen had admitted killing his wife, though the paper said he had denied actually confessing to her murder.

The newspapers of today still love a good murder, though that splendid legal writer John Mortimer, QC says in his introduction to the collected Penguin series of *Famous Trials* that the great murders of the past come from the vintage years before the last war:

> High above the great British contributions to world civilisation, the plays of Shakespeare, the full breakfast, the herbaceous border and the presumption of innocence, must rank our considerable achievement in having produced most of the best murder trials in the long history of crime . . . Colour supplements devoted to *nouvelle cuisine* have failed to make any great change in the English Sunday, which goes with a joint in the oven, the all-pervading smell of boiled cabbage, and an account of charred remains found in a burnt-out Ford Popular as described on page one of the *News of the World*.

The one thing everyone knows about Crippen and his mistress Ethel le Neve is that they were discovered, in disguise, on a ship bound for Canada, as the result of a message sent by wireless. Alas, not so. It was a newspaper again, this time the *Daily Mail*, which clinched it. Crippen and le Neve boarded the *Montrose* in Antwerp on 20 July 1910. The ship's captain, Commander Kendall, had already been told by the Thames police when he left London the previous week to look out for the two fugitives, one of them a woman disguised as a boy, but while waiting in Antwerp he had bought a continental edition of the *Mail* which included their photographs. Then he spotted them on board. 'When I saw the boy squeeze the man's hand I thought it strange and unnatural,' Commander Kendall told the police, 'and it occured to me at once that they might be Crippen and le Neve.' It was on 22 July that he sent for his Marconi operator and instructed him to send a message to the ship's home port of Liverpool. Chief Inspector Dew of Scotland Yard overtook the *Montrose* in a faster ship and, after further wireless messages between the two vessels, he boarded the *Montrose* off Quebec to arrest Crippen and le Neve. It was the last day of July.

By then, events in London had already moved fast. On 26 July the DPP had opened a new file. The following day, he had received an Opinion from two barristers with chambers at the Temple, R.D. Muir and Travers Humphreys, which he immediately forwarded to New Scotland Yard and the Home Office. The original document, in Muir's handwriting, is in the Public Record Office:

> 1. In our opinion Crippen can be lawfully arrested upon a warrant issued in England against him for a crime committed in England if he is found within the territorial waters of Canada on board a British ship.
>
> 2. In our opinion he would if so arrested be still in lawful custody if conveyed from that British ship to another British ship in one of the boats of either of those British ships.
>
> 3. In our opinion he could be brought to England for trial on either of those

British ships. He would have no right to object to the fact of the absence of surrender proceedings in Canada.

4. Our opinion applies equally to Neve [sic].

Richd. D Muir
Travers Humphreys

Temple 27 July 1910

This Opinion, with its support for every detail of what presumably were plans being made by the police, must have come as music to their ears. It reminds us though of a simple but important fact, valid then and equally so more than 75 years later. When the Director is asked for advice by the police and, of course, when he himself has to decide whether there is enough evidence to support a prosecution, he does not have to make his mind up in a vacuum. He has direct access to advice from the best counsel he knows, counsel who are handling similar cases day by day in the courts. They may not always be right; but at least he has done his best to get advice, and that counts for a lot in the law.

Crippen instructed a London solicitor, Arthur Newton, who had offices in Great Marlborough Street. The crime writer, Jonathan Goodman, described him in a recent BBC radio programme called *Dr Crippen's Trial* as 'another of the villains in the case . . . an infamous solicitor who seemed to have gone out of his way to find the shady people of the world, and the criminals who were likely to be written up'. Newton sent a cable to Crippen in Canada as soon as he was arrested, claiming falsely that Crippen's friends had asked Newton to represent him. Crippen's cable in reply was acknowledged by Newton on 3 August in a letter which has found its way into the DPP's file at the Public Record Office. Addressing their letter boldly to 'Dr Crippen, The Prison, Quebec, Canada', Newton's firm stressed 'the importance of agreeing with our advice not to say a single syllable under any pretence whatsoever to anyone' about the case. 'As far as we can see,' they told Crippen, 'there is really no evidence against you at all; although the newspapers are anxious to try you beforehand.' *Plus ça change*. Despite their cautiously worded optimism, Arthur Newton & Co ended their letter by hoping that Crippen will 'keep up a good heart,' reminding him tactfully that they had 'a very long and varied experience extending over many years in matters of this kind'.

Crippen and le Neve were brought back to London and committed for trial at the Old Bailey. It was on 6 October that the Assistant Director of Public Prosecutions, Guy Stephenson, sent a note to the Director saying that following

> a lengthy consultation at the Temple last evening, Muir rang me up on the telephone and said that, after carefully considering every aspect of the matter, he and Humphreys had come to the conclusion that Crippen and le Neve ought to be tried separately . . . I told him I was *strongly* disposed to agree with his view, on the ground that the great point was to secure

a conviction of Crippen, and that the result of the proceedings against le Neve was of very little importance.

Sir Charles Mathews wisely agreed; Crippen was tried for murder (and convicted); le Neve was tried a few days later as an accessory after the fact (and acquitted).

Before the trials Mathews, as the first Director to be independent of the Treasury Solicitor's department and the Home Office, was busily laying down some ground rules for his new department. First, who was to appear in court for the Crown? Normally the Attorney General would have taken the case, but with so much at stake we can surmise that having the case opened by a politician is the last thing the Director would have wanted. So he shrewdly told the Attorney that the case

> does not seem to me to be a very difficult one and, in my opinion, it would be safe in the hands of Muir and Travers Humphreys, whom I intended to instruct, but of course it has excited very considerable interest and very wide publicity and you might be better satisfied if you were to take it into your own hands . . . Perhaps I ought to say that the expense, thus far, has been very considerable, but I am sure this is not a matter which you ought to consider at all where the interests of justice are at stake.

When the Attorney, Sir William Robson, said in reply that Muir and Humphreys would suffice, 'especially in view of the great expense', Guy Stephenson, the Assistant Director, wrote a note on the envelope telling his chief clerk to put the letter with the papers as it was 'a useful precedent'.

Arranging for the prosecutor he wanted seems reasonable enough. But Mathews also chose the judge. He wrote to Lord Alverstone, the Lord Chief Justice, saying he 'ventured to submit it would be of great public advantage' if Alverstone could arrange to preside at the trial. In writing this letter Mathews was only responding to an offer made by Alverstone himself in earlier correspondence, but some idea about what he must have been thinking of can be found in a remarkable letter to the Director from James Mellor — the man who, as Master of the Crown Office at the Royal Courts of Justice, kept the Lord Chief Justice's diary:

> My dear Sir Charles
>
> I told the Chief Justice he ought to try Dr Crippen — it is to me a most interesting case and one in which I think an inexperienced judge might possibly give some misdirection which would be a public calamity. On the other hand the enormous weight of prejudice in the public mind, of which I think there are many indicators, is very much against the prisoner, and it is of the utmost importance that he should be protected in the eyes of the public, and of the Jury taken from them, by the judge who tries the case. This is just one of the criminal cases that I think the LCJ ought always if possible to try — he told me if you thought so too, he would do it — though he is not at all fond of the New Old Bailey as sitting there usually makes him ill.
>
> Yours v. sincerely
> James N. Mellor

The case of Dr Crippen was handled with impressive speed — perhaps the most striking difference from the trials of today. Crippen was arrested on 31 July; after an inquest and committal proceedings at Bow Street Police Court his trial was held from 18 to 22 October; the appeal was heard (and dismissed) on 5 November; and on 23 November he was hanged. The last letter on his file, made all the more morbid by the black-edged paper used during court mourning for Edward VII, is doom-laden in its archaic drafting and lifeless prose:

SECRETARY OF STATE
HOME DEPARTMENT

WHITEHALL
19th November, 1910

Sir,
    I am directed by the Secretary of State to acquaint you that, having had under his consideration the case of Hawley Harvey Crippen, now lying under sentence of death in Pentonville Prison, he has failed to discover any sufficient ground to justify him in advising His Majesty to interfere with the due course of law.

I am, Sir,
Your Obedient Servant,
E. Blackwell

Frederick Seddon, Poisoner

Working at the BBC, I get letters now and then from people complaining about miscarriages of justice. It is rather the same for the Director of Public Prosecutions. The people who write to me, (or, even worse, ring me up) have sometimes got to the point where their obsession with some minor dispute many years ago has completely taken them over. I expect that the DPP gets his fair share of these letters too, but not all of them turn out to be a complete waste of time.

In October 1911, a man signing himself F. E. VonderAhe wrote to 'the Public Prosecutor Sir Charles Mathews' about his cousin, Miss Eliza Mary Barrow, who had died suddenly the previous month at the age of 48. In the months leading up to her death, Miss Barrow had made over her money and investments — some £4,000 in all — to her landlord, Frederick Seddon, who was an insurance superintendent. In return he said he had promised to pay her an annuity of £72, and to let her live in his house in North London rent-free.

Early in September 1911 Miss Barrow had been taken ill with an attack of acute gastro-enteritis. She died within a fortnight and Seddon hurriedly arranged for her to be buried in a common grave at Finchley — even though there was a family vault at Highgate Cemetery.

Four days later Mr and Mrs VonderAhe, who lived only a short distance away, learned to their amazement that Miss Barrow was dead and buried.

When Mr VonderAhe visited Seddon's house in Islington to ask why he had not been told of her death, Seddon claimed there was a letter in the post. His attitude prompted Mr VonderAhe to write to Sir Charles Mathews in the hope that he might 'see some way of clearing up what appears to me a matter of public as well as private interest and a case around whch there is some mystery.'

Mathews received the letter on 23 October 1911. On the same day, he wrote to the Assistant Commissioner of Police at Scotland Yard, enclosing the letter from VonderAhe and asking for an 'enquiry to be made into the truth of its contents'. What particularly struck him was that Miss Barrow seemed to have 'died so quickly after the making of her will, and to have been rather quickly buried after her death'.

The Director's file shows how he was not afraid to use his influence to ask banks, including the Bank of England and the Post Office Savings Bank, to disclose confidential information 'in the interests of justice' about Miss Barrow's affairs. It also contains his correspondence with the Coroner, George Cohen, who sent this letter to the Director on 11 November.

> I have arranged for the exhumation to take place as secretly as possible and the doctors whose names I mentioned to you have agreed to carry out the examination.
>
> There is a fee of £10.12.0 to be paid and unless this is paid in advance the Superintendent of the cemetery would have to place the matter before his Board, some of whom are neighbours of . . . [sic] So I told him I would send him my cheque on Monday evening. I should therefore be pleased to hear that I am right in making this payment on your behalf. Unfortunately there are 16 bodies on top of the one we want and the fee for moving each body is 10 shillings with an additional fee, irrespective of the number of bodies moved, of £2.2.0.

The Coroner got his cheque. Miss Barrow's body was exhumed. A doctor examined the remains and decided she had died from acute arsenic poisoning. Seddon was arrested the same day on a charge of murder.

When his trial opened at the Old Baily the new Attorney General, Sir Rufus Isaacs, appeared for the Crown. It was then customary for the Attorney to lead the prosecution in poisoning cases. With him were R.D. Muir and Travers Humphreys (who you will remember from the Crippen case); defending Seddon was the great Marshall Hall.

The prosecution evidence was highly circumstantial. There was nothing to prove Seddon administered arsenic to Miss Barrow, merely a suggestion that his daughter may have bought a packet of Mather's Chemical Fly-papers, which worked by poisoning the flies: remarkably it transpired that one of these fly-papers, boiled in water, would yield enough arsenic to kill somebody.

Despite the unsatisfactory evidence Seddon was convicted by the jury. His appeal was rejected by three judges in the Court of Criminal Appeal, presided over by Mr Justice Darling.

A book of *Lord Darling's Famous Cases* by Dudley Barker reveals an unusual aspect of the trial. The judge was just about to put on the notorious 'black cap', part of the morbid ritual of passing the death sentence. Then, speaking from the dock, Seddon

> disturbed the judge greatly. He let him know quite certainly that they were both members of the brotherhood of Freemasons who are sworn to help each other in extremity. 'I declare before the Great Architect of the Universe,' he proclaimed, 'that I am not guilty, my lord.'
>
> The chaplain stood by the judge's side as with obvious signs of distress he assumed the black cap. For a moment he was so overcome with emotion that he could say nothing and when he did pass sentence sobs shook his voice . . . 'From what you have said,' continued his lordship, 'you and I know we both belong to one brotherhood . . . but our brotherhood does not encourage crime: on the contrary it condemns it. I pray you again to make your peace with the Great Architect of the Universe.'

Seddon was executed — still proclaiming his innocence — in April 1912.

The file shows the close attention that the Director paid to the case from the very beginning. He wrote profuse letters of thanks afterwards to the Attorney General for conducting the case, and to the police whose officers had managed to track down 33 £5 notes which Miss Barrow had hoarded but which Mr or Mrs Seddon had spent. There is also a complaint to the Law Society on the file, alleging that Seddon's solicitor had leaked to the press letters Seddon had written to his wife from the condemned cell. The solicitor was also said to have pocketed the manuscript of Seddon's memoirs which he said he would publish to recoup unpaid fees. But the Law Society decided there was not enough evidence to take any action.

The Campbell Incident

John Ross Campbell was the acting editor of a Communist newspaper called the *Workers Weekly*. In July 1924, six months into the first Labour government, it printed an article which, in effect, was an invitation to the armed forces not to fight in any war which might involve the killing of fellow workers. This article was shown to the Director of Public Prosecutions, Sir Archibald Bodkin, who consulted Travers Humphreys, by then Treasury Counsel at the Old Bailey, and the Attorney General, Sir Patrick Hastings. Bodkin decided to prosecute Campbell under the Incitement to Mutiny Act 1797 and Hastings gave the necessary consent. Bodkin then went off on his holidays while the police raided the offices of the *Workers Weekly* and arrested Campbell.

A few days later, after uproar in the House of Commons, the Labour Prime Minister Ramsay MacDonald summoned the Attorney General and the Assistant Director of Public Prosecutions, Sir Guy Stephenson, to his room. Sir Thomas Hetherington takes up the story:

> What precisely happened at that meeting is not clear. But what is apparent is that at the end of it the Assistant Director and the Attorney General were left in no doubt that the Prime Minister considered that no prosecution should have been brought against a Communist without his personal permission. He regarded it as a political matter in which he and the Cabinet

had the overriding say. Bodkin was summoned back from holiday; and in due course an application was made to withdraw the warrant — on the grounds apparently that Campbell was only temporary editor at the time and was not his own master, and anyway he had a first class war record.

Later in the day of the meeting in Ramsay MacDonald's room, 6 August, the Attorney General Sir Patrick Hastings reported to ministers on what had happened. He later told MPs that he 'left the Cabinet meeting with a decision at which I had arrived interfered with by nobody'. John Edwards charitably adds in his 1964 book *The Law Officers of the Crown* that 'there is no reason to suppose that Hastings did not reach his decision to discontinue the prosecution by the exercise of his independent judgment'.

Twenty years on, I find Professor Edwards is not so sure. As if to answer my unspoken accusation of naïvety, he admits his previous interpretation of Hastings' stance 'appears to have been too charitable'. New evidence showed Edwards that he was a compliant Attorney General anxious to do the bidding of his political colleagues:

> In effect, the Ramsay MacDonald government, through the Cabinet, asserted its right to interfere with decisions to prosecute political cases and, by his silence, Hastings must be deemed to have conceded that right. His subsequent protestations to the contrary . . . ring hollow in the light of his acquiescence in the formal decision of the Cabinet . . . Neither does it affect the basic issue of the Law Officers' independence that, since the Cabinet decided to adopt the same option as that which Hastings had chosen to follow, there was in fact no political interference in the Campbell case.

Worse still, Ramsay MacDonald lied to the House of Commons about what had happened. When Parliament returned at the end of September, the Prime Minister said

> I was not consulted regarding either the institution or the subsequent withdrawal of these proceedings. The first notice of the prosecution which came to my knowledge was in the press. I never advised its withdrawal but left the whole matter to the discretion of the Law Officers, where that discretion properly rests.

A week or so later, MacDonald tried to wriggle out of the pit he had dug for himself. As A.J.P. Taylor puts it:

> MacDonald . . . denied that he had been consulted in any way; then denied that he had denied it. Hastings gave good reasons for dropping the prosecution, but there can be little doubt that they were excuses. Protests from Labour backbenchers were the decisive factor, and the Communists had ground for claiming that 'for the first time the course of justice in the Law Courts had been changed by outside political forces into a triumph for the working classes over the capitalist classes'.

This gave Conservative MPs the opportunity they had been waiting for. A vote of censure was carried in Parliament, and the Labour government fell. The Campbell incident was by no means the only factor in its defeat, but it and the Zinoviev letter were held to blame at the time.

Stanley Baldwin became Prime Minister in November 1924, and disclosed that on 6 August the Labour Cabinet had decided that 'no public prosecution of a political character should be undertaken without the prior sanction of the Cabinet being obtained'. Despite evidence that previous Conservative Attorneys General had behaved in just the same way, Baldwin was able to say that 'such an instruction, in the opinion of the government, was unconstitutional, subversive of the administration of justice, and derogatory to the office of Attorney General. His Majesty's government have therefore given directions that the instruction be excised'.

It feels rather uncanny to be writing early in 1987 about a man called Campbell whose weekly paper was raided with the approval of the Attorney General. It is stranger still to be discussing the extent to which an Attorney General can properly discuss politically sensitive subjects with his Cabinet colleagues, while maintaining that in criminal proceedings he acts totally independently. Those were, of course, the issues in the Second Campbell Incident, which I shall be discussing in the last section of this chapter.

The Well of Loneliness

You may remember from the last chapter that Sir Archibald Bodkin, Director of Public Prosecutions in the 1920s, was a bit of a prude. Even the slightly *risqué* picture postcards sold at seaside resorts used to annoy him. Imagine his feelings then when he saw a review in the *Sunday Express* of a book about lesbianism by the novelist Radclyffe Hall. Unnatural and horrible, thought Bodkin as he read about *The Well of Loneliness* — or so his biographer Robert Jackson tells us.

When Bodkin got into the office the next day, he arranged a meeting with the Home Secretary — after which instructions were given that all copies of the book should be seized. The police removed copies from the publishers, Jonathan Cape, and from the London office of the French company which had printed the book. Bodkin then began proceedings at Bow Street Magistrates Court to have these copies destroyed.

What outrageous obscenities were to be found in *The Well of Loneliness* then? None that a modern reader would notice. True, there is a certain amount of kissing, but the most explicit line in the book hardly enlightened readers who had discovered from all the publicity that sexual relations between women were in fact possible and began to wonder what it is that lesbians actually *do*: 'Those who turned to the book in prurient anticipation or even in a spirit of honest enquiry . . . often retired baffled,' writes Alison Hennegan in her introduction to the Virago edition, ". . . and that night they were not divided' is all Radclyffe Hall has to say about the actual consummation of her heroine's first affair'.

The heroine is actually named Stephen by parents who had assumed their unborn child would prove to be a boy. What's more, she turns out to have all the characteristics of an ideal male: she is tall, with large hands and feet;

she is well co-ordinated, fit and muscular. Her figure is 'handsome in a flat, broad-shouldered and slim flanked fashion'; she soon takes to wearing tailored suits and neckties; eventually she has her hair cut short, like a man's. Put like this, it all seems rather crude: Hall's notion that such women were born to be 'inverts' is out of keeping with modern views of lesbianism (a word that is never mentioned in *The Well of Loneliness*). It also strikes the modern reader as rather wet, although this is, of course, a man's reaction, and thus immediately suspect: the book still sells well, and Alison Hennegan says innumerable girls and women — in fact and fiction — have turned to *The Well of Loneliness* for enlightenment and support. ('Tremulous daughters have given it to their mothers, preparing the ground for revelations yet to come,' writes Hennegan, 'mothers have given it to their daughters to indicate that personal revelations will be sympathetically received. Close female friends have given it to each other as a delicate hint that friendship could include yet more . . .').

But in 1928, what apparently worried the authorities most of all was the book's suggestion that because some women — notably those who had been ambulance drivers at the front during the 1914-1918 war — were homosexually inclined, lesbianism should be recognized and accepted. To the Director of Public Prosecutions, this was just not on.

Robert Jackson, in his biography of Bodkin, reminds us that Jonathan Cape was a publisher of the highest repute and Miss Hall — who was christened Marguerite but in adult life called herself John — was a much admired writer who had dealt seriously with an unusual and important subject. But by the time the hearing opened the Chief Magistrate, Sir Chartres Biron, had read *The Well of Loneliness* and agreed with the Director of Public Prosecutions that the book was obscene:

> The court was crowded and more than forty eminent men in literature, science and medicine were ready to give evidence for the defence, but Biron refused to hear a single one of them. 'How can the opinion of a number of people be evidence?' he asked Norman Birkett, KC, who appeared for Capes.
>
> 'The test of obscenity is not the magistrate's personal opinion but the view of reasonable men,' replied Birkett tartly.

But Birkett was not allowed by the magistrate to call any of the 'reasonable men' he had lined up, including literary critics, academics, ministers of religion, social workers, doctors and librarians. Instead, a Chief Inspector from Scotland Yard gave evidence that 'the whole theme of the book is objectionable' and in due course Biron decided the book was obscene, although it had 'some' literary merit. He ordered all seized copies of the book to be destroyed.

The publishers decided to challenge this blot on their reputation and appealed to the London Sessions where the case was heard by a full bench of 35 Justices of the Peace. Robert Jackson tells us that Bodkin

> regarded it as of first importance that the conviction should stand and persuaded the Attorney General, Sir Thomas Inskip, whose chief interest

outside professional work and the House of Commons was Sunday Schools, to appear for the Crown before the London Sessions Appeals Committee . . . Inskip was not merely representing the Director's view, but his own, when he said the book was more subtle, demoralising, corrosive and corruptive than anything that was ever written. The chairman, Sir Robert Wallace, came down heavily against the book . . . A dangerous and corrupting book, he said. Disgusting when properly read. A book prejudicial to the morals of the community.

And he upheld the conviction. *The Well of Loneliness* remained banned until 1948, although determined readers had managed to import copies from France and the United States before then.

The case has an amusing sequel: after it was over, Bodkin called in every copy of the book that had been issued to those involved in the prosecution, and insisted that they should be burned in his presence. Sir Thomas Hetherington takes up the story in his Upjohn lecture:

> It appears that no Director is infallible, because when I began to make enquiries about this case for the purpose of this lecture, one copy of the original issue was discovered in my library. It was very dusty and it was quite apparent that no one had bothered to look at it for many years.

When *I* began to make enquiries about the book, I discovered it had been hidden away again. But Stuart Orr, the Director's Records Officer, unearthed the rare and valuable first edition (although it was in fact the third printing) so it could be photographed for the book you are reading now.

There are two things left to be said about this case. One adds nothing to our knowledge of obscenity, but tells us a great deal about Sir Thomas Inskip, the Attorney General who appeared for the Crown in the ill-fated appeal. It was in another case that Inskip, who you will remember came from a rather sheltered background, informed the Law Lords when he was appearing before them that 'roulette was played with cards'. As one writer put it in a classic line, Inskip then had the indignity of 'suffering a devastating monosyllabic correction from the Woolsack'.

The other point is rather more serious. You may think that people who publish books about homosexuality are no longer prosecuted. How is it then that nine directors of a London bookshop called 'Gay's the Word' were sent for trial at the Old Bailey in the autumn of 1986, charged by HM Customs and Excise with importing indecent or obscene books? A few weeks before the hearing, more than a hundred charges were dropped and the case never came to trial, but only after a long and expensive campaign by the defendants. If the case had gone to the DPP instead, it seems unlikely that charges would ever have been brought.

10 Rillington Place

In the late 1950s, when I was still young enough to be taken to school by my mother, we used to walk past a street called Ruston Close. One day, pedantic as ever, I remarked on the fact that it was in a different postal district from Ruston Mews, just across the main road. It was then that my mother told me a rather more interesting fact about Ruston Close. That was not what the street had always been called. A few years earlier the residents had asked for it to be re-named. The street was originally known as Rillington Place.

It was hardly surprising that the residents of this shabby cul-de-sac in the Notting Hill area of West London were embarrassed by their address. Imagine telling someone you lived at 10 Rillington Place. 'Oh yes,' would come the reply, 'that was the house where eight bodies were found.' Or perhaps they might say that two of the previous tenants of the house had been hanged for murder — three years apart. They might even have mentioned the remarkable coincidence that — in the eyes of the law — *two* necrophiliac stranglers who disposed of their victims' bodies in exactly the same way had unknowingly lived in the same small house, at the same time.

The first was Timothy John Evans, a semi-literate van driver. Ludovic Kennedy, whose book *10 Rillington Place* had a dramatic effect on how the case was seen by the authorities, said Evans was 'in the literal if not the generally-accepted sense of the word, half-witted. This is the most important single thing to remember about Evans, that he had the body of a man and the mind of a child . . . His most outstanding characteristic was his ability to lie. There can have been few people who lied as consistently and imaginatively as he did'.

It was his capacity to lie which led to his death. Evans was charged with the murder of his wife Beryl and baby daughter Geraldine, whose bodies were found at 10 Rillington Place in December 1949. He confessed; he was convicted of Geraldine's murder; and he was hanged.

But Ludovic Kennedy demonstrates that the confessions Evans was said to have made to the police were clearly false. Kennedy also goes to great lengths to explore the 'brain-washing' techniques he says the police used against Evans.

Evans's trial was for Geraldine's murder alone: the prosecution had chosen to take that indictment first. Leading counsel for the Crown was Christmas Humphreys, whose father Travers we met in the Crippen case earlier in this chapter: both father and son went on to become distinguished judges. Christmas Humphreys made much of the fact that Evans was a liar. To be fair, he could hardly have known what, with hindsight, seems self-evident — that Evans was not lying when he said the principal prosecution witness was, in fact, the murderer. That man was John Reginald Halliday Christie.

Christie left 10 Rillington Place in 1953. His landlord then allowed one of the other lodgers in the house to use Christie's old kitchen. The lodger, Mr Beresford Brown, did a bit of clearing up in the kitchen, and looked around for somewhere to fix a bracket for his radio. The crime writer F. Tennyson Jesse tells us what Mr Brown did next:

> He tapped a wall and it sounded hollow, so he tore off some ragged wallpaper. Through a gap in the rough boards behind, which proved to be part of a door to what had once been a coal-cupboard, he saw a woman's

naked back. He rushed out of the house for the police . . . When she was lifted out of the cupboard, another body wrapped in a dark blanket came into sight, and behind that a third . . . Later that night the police . . . saw the outlines of a body, buried in rubble, under the boards of the ground-floor front room. A guard was set until morning, when the body of Mrs Christie was uncovered.

After searching the house, police officers found the bones of two more women buried in the back garden, making six bodies in all. A human thigh bone had actually been used as a fence prop; but, as Miss Tennyson Jesse says, 'Christie knew that people saw what they expected to see, and . . . no one would have expected to see a femur in a fence'.

The police then announced that they were 'anxious to trace' Mr Christie, because — in their words — they believed 'he may be able to assist them in their enquiries'. A week later an alert constable spotted him standing near Putney Bridge: 'I recognised him as John Christie, wanted for interrogation in a certain matter,' the officer reported later in the approved textbook manner. 'I asked him if he was willing to come to Putney police station with me for interrogation, and I then arranged to take him there.'

Christie, like Evans, was put on trial in No 1 Court at the Old Bailey: the charge against him was that he had murdered his wife. Because this case was one of public importance the Attorney General, Sir Lionel Heald, led for the prosecution. The jury were out for over an hour, and when they returned Christie was found guilty of murder and sentenced to death.

It was at this point that people could ask publicly what many had thought since the day of Christie's arrest: *was Evans innocent?* The Home Secretary, Sir David Maxwell Fyfe (who was later to become Lord Chancellor Kilmuir) asked Mr John Scott Henderson, QC to take a fresh look at the Evans case. The inquiry opened on 6 July and had to report before the date fixed for Christie's execution, 15 July 1953.

Ludovic Kennedy points out that no satisfactory reason has ever been given for rushing the report through before Christie's execution. (It was not *Christie's* conviction that was in doubt, and it was too late to do anything for Evans.) As Kennedy says in *10 Rillington Place*:

> How Mr Scott Henderson or anyone else could have been expected, *in ten or eleven days*, to read, study and analyse all the relevant documents in this enormously complicated matter, examine and take notes from the material witnesses, sift out the trustworthy from the untrustworthy evidence (in Evans's and Christie's case no easy matter), weigh up *and reflect on* all the pros and cons, then write and present a report which made any sense at all, passes all comprehension. Yet this is what Sir David Maxwell Fyfe expected Mr Scott Henderson to do, and what Mr Scott Henderson attempted to do . . . With supreme confidence in his own powers of analysis and deduction, Mr Scott Henderson concluded that 'for reasons of overwhelming cogency' no miscarriage of justice had occurred.

Kennedy then proceeds to take Scott Henderson's report to pieces. He quotes the Labour MP, Reginald Paget, QC, (now Lord Paget) as telling the Commons:

> We are not attacking this report merely because this report does not disclose the truth. We are attacking the report because we say that it deliberately conceals the truth. We are attacking this report not because it is mistaken but because, we say, it is dishonest.

As a result of Parliamentary criticism, Mr Scott Henderson wrote a supplementary report which reinforced his earlier conclusion. He sent it to Sir David Maxwell Fyfe, a man who had told the House of Commons in 1948 that there was 'no practicable possibility' of error in a murder case: anyone suggesting otherwise — he had said — was 'moving in a realm of fantasy'.

But the man who had actually had to confirm the death sentence on Timothy Evans was Maxwell Fyfe's predecessor, the Labour Home Secretary James Chuter Ede. It was he who told the Commons in 1955 that he thought the Evans case showed that

> a mistake was possible, and . . . a mistake was made. I hope that no future Home Secretary, while in office or after he has left office, will ever have to feel that although he did his best and no one would wish to accuse him of being either careless or inefficient, he sent a man to the gallows who was not 'guilty as charged'.

Ludovic Kennedy's book was first published in January 1961. Despite the considerable political pressure that resulted, it was not until August 1965 that the Home Secretary, Sir Frank Soskice, decided to order a new enquiry under a High Court Judge, Sir Daniel Brabin. Unlike Scott Henderson's report, this was no rush job: the Brabin report was not published until October 1966. It was greeted with some astonishment. Brabin came up with what Ludovic Kennedy calls 'the novel idea that while Evans had probably *not* murdered the baby (for which he was hanged) he probably *had* murdered the wife (for which he hadn't even been tried)'.

As Kennedy says, this strange theory seemed aimed at pleasing everybody: 'yes, we had done Tim Evans wrong, [Brabin] appeared to say, but only on a legal technicality: the law could breathe again'. But the new Home Secretary, Mr Roy Jenkins, was not prepared to take Brabin's accusations as standing in the way of justice, and he asked the Queen to grant Evans a posthumous free pardon.

And what of the Director of Public Prosecutions, Sir Theobald Mathew? What role did he play in what many people now see as a classic miscarriage of justice? For once, there seems to have been no criticism of the Director's actions. There was, on the face of it, a cast-iron case. It was only after Christie's killings became known that people began to look closely at the statements Evans was said to have given the police. Whether it would have been proper or even possible for the Director to have added his voice to those who were saying in 1953 that an innocent man had been hanged is far from clear, but for once it is the Home Office and their man John Scott Henderson who come out of the case badly.

Worst of all was, of course, capital punishment. If Evans had still been alive after Christie had been found guilty of murder there seems little doubt that his own conviction would then have been regarded as unsafe. Evans would probably have persuaded the Court of Appeal to set aside his conviction, and he would have ended up with a useful sum from the Home Office to compensate him for three or four years in prison. Had he lived, Evans would now just be approaching retirement age.

Rillington Place is no more; nor is Ruston Close. The street with two names is long since demolished, and in its place stands Bartle Road, perhaps named after Bartlett's Iron Foundry which adjoined Rillington Place many years ago. The exact spot where 10 Rillington Place once stood is hard to remember — which is perhaps just as well.

Nina Ponomareva, Soviet Shoplifter

Nina Ponomareva visited London in 1956 as part of a Russian athletics team. It was a time when attempts were being made to improve cultural and sporting links between Britain and the Soviet Union. She was alleged to have stolen a hat from a famous West End store, which duly started a private prosecution. Miss Ponomareva failed to appear in court, and a warrant was issued for her arrest. She had, in fact, left the country by then.

At this stage the private prosecution was taken over by the Director of Public Prosecutions, Sir Theobald Mathew. It was assumed this had been done so that the Director could drop the charge in response to pressure from the Soviet authorities. In fact, he did not. It was announced that the Director, with the support of the Attorney General, proposed to proceed with the prosecution if Miss Ponomareva returned to Britain (which in fact she never did).

There were two reasons for this. First, Mathew valued the right of private prosecution and was very hesitant to destroy that right by taking over a prosecution just so as to drop it. He considered that, unless there was an overriding public interest in preventing the case from going ahead, then either the private prosecutor should keep the case or — if it was to be taken over by the Director — the prosecution's case should at least be presented to the court.

Secondly, the case had gone to the Attorney General, Sir Reginald Manningham-Buller, who consulted the Foreign Secretary on the effect continuing the prosecution would have on relations between Britain and the Soviet Union. The decision not to stop the prosecution followed that consultation. It was said at the time that the Attorney had asked his government colleague for advice, not instructions. Sir Thomas Hetherington says it is perfectly proper to ask for advice, but not to act on the directions of a minister or the goverment as a whole. And Professor Edwards says this practice is constitutionally correct, while conceding that 'the demarcation between seeking advice and a duty to act on that advice may be a tenuous one at times'.

Some people would argue that the distinction is so tenuous as to be non-existent. Suppose for a moment that the Foreign Office advice had been something like 'we think that if Ponomareva is convicted the Russians will bomb Bow Street and there will be total devastation in central London — but of course it's your decision, old boy'. Surely any Attorney would then have been able to say, without the need for *instructions* from anyone, that in his own personal view a prosecution would not be in the public interest. An Attorney General does not need a gale warning to tell him which way the wind is blowing.

In the Ponomareva case, we do not know what advice the Foreign Secretary offered. It seems reasonable to suppose he would have preferred the prosecution to have been withdrawn, and if this was so then the fact that this did not happen does suggest a certain independence of mind in the Attorney's chambers — despite the theory I have just put forward. But it may have been that the Foreign Secretary knew perfectly well that Miss Ponomareva would never be seen here again, and thought it politic not to be seen as interfering with the course of justice.

Lady Chatterley's Lover

It seems strange to think that when *Lady Chatterley's Lover* was first published in this country schoolboys were punished for reading it. Now *Lady Chatterley* is part of the school syllabus. The Penguin edition, which has been reprinted many times, is dedicated by the publishers to the nine men and three women who found Penguin Books not guilty of breaking section 2 of the Obscene Publications Act 1959 when the company was prosecuted at the Old Bailey in 1960.

Sir Thomas Hetherington says in his Upjohn lecture that the then Director, Sir Theobald Mathew, was apparently very hesitant about prosecuting the book's publishers:

> He was in many ways ahead of his times in his own thinking. But . . . he did in the end feel that he ought, as a servant of the public, to accept what he believed to be the prevailing climate of public opinion. There is evidence too that his colleagues in the department regarded the book as eminently deserving of prosecution. One officer emphasised the importance of the trial with these words: 'For if the prosecution fails the obscene version will be offered openly and persuasively to every child or teenager who has three and sixpence [17½p] in his or her pocket. That is a fearsome thought.'
>
> Mathew, unlike Bodkin in the *Well of Loneliness* case, had difficulty in getting enough copies of the book for prosecution purposes. One organisation which was asked to copy the book was very reluctant because they felt that the copying process would have to be undertaken by a staff composed mainly of young girls. There might be serious objections to their putting it in the hands of those young members of staff.

It is hard to believe that this was as recently as 1960. The Beatles, the Rolling Stones and the pop/sex/drugs culture were just a few years away. Yet the proposal to publish an unexpurgated paperback of D.H. Lawrence's famous novel provoked a criminal prosecution.

The Obscene Publications Act of 1959 had just re-defined obscenity. It said that a publication was obscene if its effect, if taken as a whole, was 'such as to tend to deprave and corrupt' people who were likely to read it. No longer would an entire work be condemned because a small part of it was objectionable. And no longer was the court to consider what would happen if, for example, the book was to fall into the hands of a precocious 14-year-old schoolgirl: the readership was to be the actual, or at least the predictable, reading public.

Section 4 of the Act added that a person who had published an obscene article would not be convicted if 'publication of the article in question is justified as being for the public good'. Publishers of books and magazines could use this defence if publication 'is in the interests of science, literature, art or learning, or other objects of general concern'.

The boundaries of obscenity were therefore far from clear at that time, and from the Director's point of view a test case was not entirely unreasonable. I have already referred in the previous chapter to the problems Mathews faced in deciding whether to go ahead with the prosecution, but paradoxically anyone who rejoices in the freedom of the press must thank the Director for what he did. As Robertson and Nicol say in their book on *Media Law*, the trial 'enabled the full force of the reformed law to be exploited on behalf of the recognised literature. The book fell to be judged, not on the strength of its four-letter words or its purple passages, but on its overall impact, as described by leading authorities on English literature'. And, of course, once Penguin Books had been acquitted, they had a cast-iron guarantee from the courts that they could publish *Lady Chatterley* without any fear of further legal action.

The Moors Murders

As Director of Public Prosecutions, Sir Norman Skelhorn sat in court for the first three days of the trial of Ian Brady and Myra Hindley; knowing the strength of the evidence to be called for the Crown, he remembers wondering how such wicked people could look so ordinary. He was also worried about the main prosecution witness, Hindley's cousin David Smith, who had previous convictions for violence and apparently stood to gain financially from a conviction: a newspaper had offered to buy his story if Brady and Hindley were found guilty.

Smith had contacted the police early one morning in October 1965. The night before, Hindley had invited him back to the house she shared with Brady outside Manchester. Earlier that evening, Brady had picked up a 17-year-old boy named Edward Evans and brought him home. When Smith arrived he saw Evans on the sofa: he was still alive, but Brady was smashing the boy's head in with an axe. Hindley was watching.

The police responded to Smith's call, found Evans' body, and in due course charged both Brady and Hindley with his murder.

In Hindley's car the police found a so-called 'disposal plan' for the dead boy's body. It included the cryptic reference 'Tick, Place P/B'. When asked,

Brady said this referred to Penistone Burn, where a payroll snatch had been planned for the following week. But a few days later an observant policeman found a cloakroom ticket tucked behind the spine of a religious book belonging to Hindley. The ticket turned out to be a receipt for two suitcases which had been deposited at Manchester Central Station the evening before Evans's death.

In the words of Sir Norman Skelhorn:

> If 'Tick' referred to ticket and 'P/B' perhaps to prayer book . . . there was the closest possible connection between the death of Evans and what was in the suitcases. And it was the contents of the suitcases that turned what might otherwise have looked like a particularly unpleasant murder investigation into one of the horror stories of our time.

The suspicion was that Brady had planned the killing in advance and did not want what was in the suitcases to be discovered in any police investigations. This would hardly have been surprising. Inside the suitcases police officers found evidence linking Brady and Hindley to the murders of two young children.

Nearly a year earlier, on Boxing Day 1964, 10-year-old Lesley Ann Downey had disappeared without trace from a local fairground. The previous year, in November 1963, 12-year-old John Kilbride had gone missing from a market near his home. In the suitcases at the station the police found a photograph taken by Brady of Hindley posing on John Kilbride's grave. There was another photograph of where Lesley Ann Downey had been buried. The bodies of both children were found on Saddleworth Moor, outside Manchester.

It was clear from other photographs in the suitcase that the two children had been sexually abused, as had Evans. Most horrifying of all, there was a tape-recording in which the little girl could be heard pleading to go home.

At their trial in April 1966 both Brady and Hindley pleaded not guilty to all three murders. Sir Norman Skelhorn wrote in his memoirs:

> It seemed hardly possible to me on the evidence that a jury would fail to convict Brady of all three murders, but there could be some argument about the extent of Hindley's participation, particularly in the third killing . . . She was younger than Brady — he was aged 28 at the time of the trial — and apparently besotted with him. It could have been that she had acted under his influence. It was significant to me, however, that she reacted calmly to the same brutal events that turned the stomach of a young man with an admitted record of violence. When Smith called the police he was found to be shaking; when Hindley opened the door to them two hours later she behaved as though nothing was wrong.

Brady was convicted of all three murders; Hindley of two. She was acquitted on the Kilbride charge, but found guilty of harbouring Brady, knowing he had murdered the boy. They were both sentenced to life imprisonment. Only Hindley appealed; only Hindley has sought release on licence. Sir Norman Skelhorn seemed to think they should both have been hanged.

There was a bizarre sequal to the case at the end of 1986. John Kilbride and Lesley Ann Downey were not the only children to have disappeared in Manchester at that time. Pauline Reade, aged 16, had vanished without trace on her way to a dance in July 1963. Twelve-year-old Keith Bennett had gone missing as he made his way to his grandmother's house in June 1964. Though it was suspected that they, too, were victims of the Moors Murders, their bodies were not found in 1965, despite a widespread search of the moors.

But in 1986 the case was reopened by Greater Manchester police. Myra Hindley, apparently moved by a letter from Keith Bennett's mother, decided to help the police resume their search for the two missing bodies. The inquiry was led by Detective Chief Superintendent Peter Topping, Head of Greater Machester CID, and it was not an immediate success. In a blaze of publicity, he brought Myra Hindley back for a day to the bleak and featureless moors in the hope that she would recognize areas she had visited briefly more than two decades earlier. Dogs trained to find recently dead victims were used in the unlikely hope that they might find skeletons buried more than 20 years before. Hindley said later that 'this visit was frustrated by the enormous press interest and by the weather'.

Her remarks came in a statement issued through her solicitor in the spring of 1987. She explained that she had made a voluntary statement to Mr Topping a few weeks earlier, in February 1987. 'In this statement,' said Hindley, 'I admitted my role in these awful events and said that I considered myself to be as guilty as my former lover, Ian Brady, although our roles were different. Later I was taken to the moors secretly, and out of the glare of publicity I was able to be far more specific about the location of graves and I now believe that I have done all I can in helping the police in this respect . . . I want nothing more than to help the police find the bodies so that their poor relatives can at last have the comfort of giving them a Christian burial.'

The statement Hindley made through her solicitor was not specific about her role in the deaths of Pauline Reade and Keith Bennett. She clearly went into much greater detail when she spoke to the police over four days in February. As a result of her statement, and two days Hindley spent on the moors in March 1987, police officers began digging again.

It was clearly right that the police should have tried to clear up unsolved murders. And Hindley seemed right in thinking that finding the bodies would give comfort to the bereaved relatives — although the abortive search in 1986 must have dashed their hopes cruelly. But there was some confusion at the time over what would happen if and when the bodies were found.

Any further prosecution of Ian Brady seemed unthinkable. He had made no confession. The chances of evidence remaining on the moors after more than 20 years seemed remote. Hindley's word would not have carried much weight. But most important of all, Brady was in a secure psychiatric hospital: he was said to be clinically insane. A glance at the Code for Crown Prosecutors — which I will be discussing in Chapter 7 of this book — makes it clear that if the reports of Brady's medical health were accurate he would not be prosecuted.

Hindley was in a rather different position, but any prosecutor would think long and hard about prosecuting one conspirator without the possibility of even interviewing the other. And the Code I have just mentioned says 'the Crown Prosecutor should be slow to prosecute if the last offence was committed three or more years before the date of trial, unless, despite its staleness, an immediate custodial sentence of some length is likely to be imposed'. Now it is quite true that some prosecutions, notably for murder, have been brought many years after the event. In 1987, a prison officer went on trial at Nottingham Crown Court accused of murdering his first wife in 1965, by pushing her down the stairs. (She had died from her injuries after the fall and an inquest had recorded a verdict of accidental death.) But in that case the defendant was at risk of receiving 'an immediate custodial sentence of some length'. If Hindley was to be prosecuted a second time, a conviction would make no difference to her sentences of life imprisonment.

But, of course, Detective Chief Superintendent Topping knew exactly what to do. He sent the papers to the Director of Public Prosecutions.

The Confait Case

One night in April 1972, fire broke out in a house at Doggett Road, Catford, in south-east London. In a room on the first floor, firemen found the body of a man called Maxwell Confait. He was a transvestite homosexual prostitute. A couple of days later, the police arrested three boys: Colin Lattimore, Ronnie Leighton and Ahmet Salih. All three were interrogated, made statements and were charged with murdering Confait and then setting fire to his house.

Lattimore was 18, but he had been diagnosed as educationally sub-normal and was said to have had the mental age of an eight-year-old. Psychiatrists who examined him were to say he was highly suggestible — 'so that the slightest indication of the expected answer will produce it'.

Leighton was 15. Though brighter than Lattimore, he was said to be 'borderline subnormal', and 'really an immature, inadequate, simple dullard'.

Salih was reasonably intelligent, but he was only just 14.

In November 1972, the three went on trial at the Old Bailey. Salih was no longer accused of murdering Confait: the DPP had dropped the charge earlier. However, Lattimore was convicted of manslaughter on the ground of diminished responsibility, Leighton was convicted of murder and all three boys were convicted of arson. The judge ordered Lattimore to be detained under the Mental Health Act without limit of time, Leighton to be detained during Her Majesty's pleasure, and Salih to four years' detention at a place approved by the Home Secretary.

In July 1973, the Court of Appeal refused all three leave to appeal.

But their families were still convinced of their innocence, and began a long campaign to have them freed. Early in 1974, they enlisted the support of the newly elected Labour MP for Lewisham, Christopher Price. He, in turn, directed his efforts at the new Home Office Minister, Alex Lyon.

The crucial question was the time at which Confait died. On this, the doctors who gave evidence at the trial were remarkably vague. But Lattimore, who was alleged to have admitted strangling Confait, had a watertight alibi for the night of Confait's death. Independent witnesses could vouch for Lattimore's movements from 6 pm to 11.40 pm, and another independent witness had seen him at home at 11.45. His father spoke to him at 12.35 am.

At the committal hearing before Woolwich magistrates, the doctors' evidence, based on the extent of rigor mortis, put the time of death at between 6.30 and 10 pm. But before the Old Bailey trial, Lattimore had to disclose his alibi, under provisions introduced in 1967 to thwart criminals who sprang a false alibi on the prosecution at the last moment and left the police no time to check it. Christopher Price and Jonathan Caplan, in their book *The Confait Confessions*, say

> it was never contemplated when this change went through that it would also favour the prosecution in providing a chance to blur the edges of its evidence when that was found to be in conflict with a disclosed alibi. Colin, Ronnie and Ahmet were caught by this disclosure, which alerted the prosecution to its only chance of a guilty verdict. If the alibi had not been disclosed, the evidence about the time of death would have remained as clear and unequivocal as it was at Woolwich Magistrates Court.

After much pressure, the Home Secretary, Roy Jenkins, referred the Confait case to the Court of Appeal in June 1975. His letter to court says that if Confait's death took place 'some appreciable time before midnight, it appears that the evidence of the boys' whereabouts would assume greater importance, and that doubt would be thrown on the accuracy of their statements of admission to the police, the truth of which they denied at the trial'.

When the case came to the Court of Appeal in October 1975, it was indeed established by further medical evidence that Confait's death took place 'some appreciable time before midnight'. Giving the judgment of the court, Lord Justice Scarman (as he then was) said the effect of the medical evidence had been 'to destroy the lynch-pin of the Crown's case and to demonstrate that the version of the events contained in the admissions relied upon by the Crown cannot be true'. While it was still possible that the boys' confessions to arson at 27 Doggett Road could have been correct, Lord Justice Scarman said their statements could not 'be regarded as sufficiently reliable evidence, standing as they do, alone, to justify the convictions for arson which were based solely upon them'. He released them immediately.

And then the questions started. How could these boys have confessed to a killing they had never committed? And how could the Director of Public Prosecutions, Sir Norman Skelhorn, have authorized their prosecution?

In the hope of finding answers to those questions, the Home Secretary and the Attorney General appointed Sir Henry Fisher to hold an inquiry into the circumstances leading to the trial. As Christopher Price wrote shortly after his appointment, 'The honourable Sir Henry Arthur Fisher is probably one of the dozen most intelligent adults in Britain and has enjoyed a glittering and diverse career'. He shocked the legal establishment in 1970 by resigning after two years as a High Court judge to become a director of a merchant bank.

The Inquiry was held in private and Sir Henry Fisher published his report at the end of 1977. He found that Confait certainly died before midnight and probably before 10.30 pm on 21 April 1972. He accepted Lattimore's alibi and found that he had no part in the killing. He found that Leighton and Salih could have taken part in the killing, and that all three boys could have set light to 27 Doggett Road. Nor could the confessions have been made unless at least one of the boys had been involved in the killing and arson. Sir Henry Fisher thought the most likely explanation was that Lattimore's confession to having taken part in the arson was true, but that he had been persuaded by Leighton and Salih to confess falsely to having taken part in the killing. Fisher also found on the balance of probabilities that the confessions of Leighton and Salih to having taken part in the arson were true, and that although their answers on the killing were falsified to incriminate Lattimore both Leighton and Salih had been involved in the killing.

Fisher also found breaches of the Judges' Rules which (before the introduction of the Police and Criminal Evidence Act 1984) governed police interrogation of suspects. He found that the questioning of Lattimore was unfair and oppressive. Detective Chief Superintendent Alan Jones could see Lattimore was mentally handicapped (he put the boy's mental age at 14) but did not wait until someone else, such as a parent, could attend the interrogation.

He was also critical of the lawyers, and in particular the man in the DPP's office responsible for the case, Doiran Williams. Sir Henry says that

> so far from trying to make the time of death more precise . . . Detective Chief Superintendent Jones, Mr Williams — so far as he was aware of the problem — and Mr [Richard] Du Cann (Treasury Counsel who conducted the prosecution case at the trial) made every effort to keep it as vague as possible. The reason for this was that they were concerned to establish a case which rested wholly or mainly on confessions which could not be entirely true unless the time of death was outside the brackets given by Dr Bain, the police surgeon, and Dr Cameron, the pathologist.

Sir Henry Fisher said he had some sympathy for Mr Williams. 'He was under great pressure of work. The police report did not bring to his attention the difficulties in the case. According to Sir Norman Skelhorn he did all that was expected of him.' But Sir Henry could not absolve Mr Williams from criticism, and said he should have recognized the need for further enquiries.

Fisher said later:

> I accept that Mr Williams is an experienced and conscientious officer. I

believe that he did as much as under prevailing practice was expected of him. Sir Norman Skelhorn did not criticise him . . . The scrutiny which Mr Williams provided in this case fell short of the scrutiny which I believe is required and which (in theory at least) the procurator fiscal would carry out under the Scottish system . . . If I am right in thinking that Mr Williams did as much as under prevailing practice was expected of him, then I am driven to the conclusion that the practice was unsatisfactory.

Fisher went on to say that the Confait case illustrated the need for 'an analysis and evaluation of a case by a legally qualified person at as early a stage as possible':

The purpose of such evaluation should be not only to judge the narrow question of whether there is evidence to support the prosecution's case, but to look into the strength and weakness of the prosecution's case in an objective way to determine whether continued prosecution is justifiable.

This could almost have been a blueprint for the Crown Prosecution Service — as you will see in Chapter 4.

The story was not yet over. In January 1980 Sir Thomas Hetherington received 'new information' about the case. He ordered a further police investigation and took advice from counsel. As a result, the Attorney General, Sir Michael Havers, told the House of Commons in August 1980 that he was satisfied Confait had died even earlier: before midday on Friday 21 April. The Attorney went on:

I am also satisfied that if the evidence now available had been before Sir Henry Fisher he would not have come to the conclusion that any of the three young men was responsible for the death of Confait or the arson at 27 Doggett Road. Counsel have advised, and the Director of Public Prosecutions and I agree, that there is insufficient evidence to prosecute any other person.

The further information apparently related to two men, each of whom claimed to have seen the other kill Confait, but not to have been involved himself.

In 1981, the Home Office offered Lattimore, Leighton and Salih a total of £65,000 in compensation for their wrongful imprisonment.

The Confait case must be the best documented and most authoritative attack on the work of the Director of Public Prosecutions and his staff to date. But as Director, Sir Norman Skelhorn had ultimate responsibility for the case; and Sir Henry Fisher was 'driven to the conclusion' that the way his staff operated was 'unsatisfactory'. I looked eagerly to see how Skelhorn would respond to Fisher's criticism in his autobiography. There are two sentences:

In view . . . of the developments that have now taken place, resulting from fresh evidence having come to light — which was apparently not available either at the time of the prosecution or at the time of Sir Henry's inquiry — I do not think that any useful purpose would be served by now dealing with these matters. Sir Henry's report was of course published appreciably

later than my retirement, but in so far as he suggested possible revision
of procedures, both by the Department and by the police, I feel sure that
they will have received careful consideration.

In other words: no comment.

The *Oz* Trial

Sir Norman Skelhorn said that in bringing prosecutions under the Obscene
Publications Act 1959, it was necessary to outguess the jury. But one case
where he thought the chances of conviction were good was the prosecution
he brought against the publishers of *Oz*.

Oz was an 'underground' magazine, although it was published quite openly.
According to Tony Palmer in his book *The Trials of Oz*, the underground
press existed because it believed that proper newspapers either ignored
what was really happening or else distorted it. This was 1971, and the
underground press seemed a phenomenon of its time. One former
underground paper has survived: *Time Out*.

In his memoirs, Skelhorn denied that his decision to bring a prosecution
over the '*Oz* School Kids Issue' was politically motivated: he said he would
have applied the same test of obscenity to an 'Establishment' newspaper.
He described issue number 28:

> The cover, front and back, showed a number of naked young women, at
> least four of whom appeared to be engaged in lesbian activity. On page
> 10 there was a drawing of a schoolmaster with his trousers down, playing
> with himself sexually while groping a young boy, presumably one of his
> pupils. On page 14 two short essays advocated that we should have the
> same sexual freedom as animals, including the right to copulate in public.
> Following this was a cartoon in six strips showing the lovable Rupert Bear
> sexually inspecting and then assaulting an elderly lady! On page 28, under
> the heading 'Suck,' there was what I suppose was meant to be an extract
> from an imaginary book about oral sex, in which a girl places an ice cube
> in her mouth to increase the man's pleasure . . .

Was that obscene? It took Judge Argyle and an Old Bailey jury five weeks
to find out: the longest obscenity trial in history. That was because the defence
were allowed to call expert witnesses to show the magazine was not obscene,
something the Court of Appeal decided later was wrong. Expert evidence,
it said, could be called to establish the defence of public good under section
4 of the 1959 Act, but the question of obscenity had to be left to the jury.

In the end, the *Oz* publishers, Richard Neville, James Anderson and Felix
Dennis, were found not guilty by the jury of conspiring with a number of
young people 'to produce a magazine containing divers obscene, lewd,
indecent and sexually perverted articles, cartoons, drawings and illustrations
with intent thereby to debauch and corrupt the morals of children and young
persons within the Realm and to arouse and implant in their minds lustful
and perverted desires' — which must have come as a relief because as a
common law conspiracy the maximum penalty was life imprisonment. But
the jury went on to find them guilty of publishing an obscene article, sending

obscene articles through the post and possessing obscene articles for gain. In all cases the obscene articles were *Oz*, issue number 28.

The defendants were then kept in custody 'for medical reports' awaiting sentence. While in prison they were forcibly shorn of their shoulder-length hair (fashionable at the time). Then Neville was given 15 months imprisonment, Anderson got 12 months, and Dennis was sent to prison for nine months.

The defendants appealed. John Mortimer, QC argued successfully that Judge Argyle had misdirected the jury on the narrow meaning of 'obscenity' in the 1959 Act: Judge Argyle had widened the meaning to include what was 'repulsive, filthy, loathsome, indecent or lewd'. The Court of Appeal also said the judge had failed to direct the jury adequately on the defendants' argument that, far from tending to deprave and corrupt, certain things in *Oz* were so disgusting as to deter people from following their example. The appeals against conviction under the Obscene Publications Act were allowed, but the convictions for sending obscene articles through the post were upheld because of the much wider meaning given to 'obscene' in the Post Office Act 1953.

Sir Anthony Blunt

No thriller writer would have dared write a novel in which the principal character was a spy who worked for the Queen at Buckingham Palace for fifteen years *after* he had confessed to treason. People would not have believed it possible. But this is the story of how it happened.

Anthony Blunt had been a contemporary of Guy Burgess, Donald Maclean, and Kim Philby at Cambridge before the war. Like them he was recruited at that time by Soviet intelligence. In November 1979 the Prime Minister, Mrs Margaret Thatcher, told the House of Commons that Blunt worked for the Security Service MI5 between 1940 and 1945: during that time he regularly passed to the Russians any information he had come across which he thought would interest them. 'There is no doubt,' she added, 'that British interests were seriously damaged by his activities.' What Mrs Thatcher did not confirm was whether or not Blunt had stopped working for Soviet Intelligence in 1945, so one may assume his spying continued for some time after then.

Blunt first came under suspicion in the enquiries which followed the defection of Burgess and Maclean in 1951. Despite interrogation he persisted with his denials and no evidence against him was obtained.

But early in 1964, MI5 received new information. Mrs Thatcher chose not to tell the Commons in 1979 where it had come from. But the judgment of Mr Justice Powell delivered in the Supreme Court of New South Wales in March 1987 fills in the gaps. This was, of course, the decision in which he rejected an attempt by the Attorney General, Sir Michael Havers, acting on behalf of the British government, to stop another MI5 officer called Peter Wright from publishing his memoirs in Australia. Mr Justice Powell, deriving his information from books such as Chapman Pincher's *Too Secret Too Long*, and *Conspiracy of Silence* by Penrose and Freeman, said an American called Michael Straight — who had also been at Cambridge with Philby, Burgess and Maclean — told the FBI about Blunt in 1963, which in due course passed the information on to MI5.

Wherever the information had come from, Mrs Thatcher told the Commons that 'it did not . . . provide a basis on which charges could be brought' (15 November 1979) and that it 'was not usable as evidence on which to base a prosecution' (21 November 1979). Quite why this should be is not clear. Perhaps it was hearsay, perhaps Straight was not prepared to come to Britain: the DPP's file apparently contains no record of whether anyone actually looked at the evidence. However, Peter Wright, who as a senior MI5 officer was in a position to know, says the Prime Minister's statement was 'substantially false': David Hooper, who was legal adviser to his proposed publishers Heinemann, reports Wright's affidavit evidence to Mr Justice Powell's court in his book *Official Secrets*. Mr Write swore that:

> the briefs MI5 had prepared for the Prime Minister concerning Blunt . . .
> were untrue. To say Blunt had done no damage was poppycock and it was
> wrong to say there was no usable evidence against him.

But the Prime Minister *was* saying there was no usable evidence against Blunt, and on that basis her options were limited. Mrs Thatcher said it would have been possible to wait for further evidence, but MI5 had already been making enquiries about him for 13 years. Alternatively, they could have confronted Blunt with Straight's statement, but this might have given him information which he could have used to help others.

MI5 therefore decided that Blunt should be given immunity from prosecution, provided he confessed and agreed to co-operate in further investigations. Immunity was, in fact, granted by the Attorney General, Sir John Hobson, who decided that the deal would be in the public interest. Blunt duly confessed, but of course his confession could not then be used against him because it had been obtained as the result of an inducement.

MI5 had approached the Attorney General through the Director of Public Prosecutions' office. There was, in fact, no Director in April 1964: Mathew had died in February and Skelhorn did not take over until May. The Prime Minister was careful not to reveal who it was in the Director's office who had agreed with the Attorney that Blunt should not be prosecuted (there was no Acting Director as such). But Mrs Thatcher pointed out that immunity in exchange for co-operation was ultimately a matter for the Attorney General, who could consult his ministerial colleagues but was not bound by their advice.

According to the Prime Minister's statement, the Director-General of MI5 met the Home Secretary, Henry Brooke, in March 1964, and told him he would be discussing with the Director of Public Prosecutions (presumably when one had actually been appointed) how to conduct the interview with Blunt, bearing in mind MI5's need to obtain as much intelligence as possible about Soviet penetration. This appears not to have happened: Sir Norman

Skelhorn points out in his memoirs that the question of granting Blunt immunity 'was dealt with in the interregnum' before he became Director, and he only became aware of it 'at a considerably later date'. Nevertheless the incident suggests a close relationship between the Security Service MI5 and the Director of Public Prosecutions, a relationship which is still just as close today. MI5's legal adviser, a barrister who cannot have been very happy to see his name in the newspapers at the beginning of 1987, drops in to see the Director from time to time. Occasionally the Director will be told a suspect is to be interrogated by MI5, and that if and when there is evidence of a criminal offence, then the police Special Branch will be brought in to take statements for the Director to consider. That happened in the case of Michael Bettaney, the MI5 man who was himself convicted under the Official Secrets Act.

After Anthony Blunt had been granted immunity from prosecution, he admitted passing information to the Russians during the war. In 1951 he said he had used his old contact to assist Burgess and Maclean to defect. He said he had also once helped Philby to contact Russian intelligence. Among the MI5 officers who interrogated Blunt was Peter Wright.

In later years Sir Peter Rawlinson, Sam Silkin, and Sir Michael Havers were told what had been done and as Attorneys they agreed that — in view of the immunity granted to Blunt to obtain his confession — there were no grounds on which he could be prosecuted.

The next part of the story is, on the face of it, the most remarkable of all. Blunt had been appointed Surveyor of the King's Pictures in 1952. He was awarded a knighthood in the Royal Victorian Order in 1956. He was still Surveyor of the Queen's Pictures in 1964, when he confessed to spying for Russia. What was the Palace to do? Nothing, said MI5. To sack him would have been to have tipped off the Russians. Quite why that should have mattered is not clear: Blunt had, after all, left MI5 nearly 20 years earlier. But the Queen agreed to keep the traitor in her midst. Could this have been simply to spare MI5's blushes?

The unmasking of Anthony Blunt (by the BBC journalist Andrew Boyle) had one major consequence. At the time, in November 1979, the newly elected Conservative government was in the process of replacing the Official Secrets Act with a new and much more tightly drawn Official Information Bill. This was said to be the armalite rifle which would replace the old blunderbuss passed in 1911. But it emerged that under the proposed new law it would have been an offence for a journalist to have revealed Blunt's treachery. Faced with this criticism the government withdrew its bill, and in the years that followed it responded to constant criticism of the Official Secrets Act by saying that attempts to reform the law had not found favour with Parliament. One can only speculate on whether some of the unsuccessful prosecutions under the Official Secrets Act which you can read about in the following pages would have succeeded under a reformed law, or indeed whether more prosecutions would have been brought if it had been thought they would have stood a greater chance of success.

The Rt Hon Jeremy Thorpe

Earlier in this chapter I quoted John Mortimer, QC as saying that 'high above the great British contributions to world civilisation . . . must rank our considerable achievement in having produced the best murder trials in the long history of crime'. The trial of the former leader of the Liberal Party on charges of conspiracy to murder and incitement to murder was clearly one such trial. Few who have read reports of the evidence will ever forget it; even now it is hard to believe that such a popular and respected figure as Jeremy Thorpe could ever have faced charges of this nature. The jury found Mr Thorpe not guilty and so the case amounts to one of Sir Thomas Hetherington's most spectacular failures, but — despite what Jeremy Thorpe must have hoped — the former MP's acquittal did not lead to his return to public life.

The decision to charge Jeremy Thorpe, a Member of Parliament and Privy Counsellor, cannot have been an easy one. The Director of Public Prosecutions operates under the 'superintendence' of the Attorney General, a relationship I will be explaining in Chapter 10. The Attorney at the time was Mr Sam Silkin, now Lord Silkin of Dulwich, a member of a Labour government which had just ended a formal 'pact' with the Liberals. Before the prosecution of Thorpe was announced, Silkin had been accused of a cover-up designed to promote harmony with the Liberals in order to defeat the Conservatives at the forthcoming election. Following the charges, the rumours changed: now Silkin was said to be trying to destroy the Liberals' electoral chances. In fact, Mr Silkin made it clear that he had had nothing to do with authorizing the prosecution of his parliamentary colleague, or its timing: that job had been left to the Director of Public Prosecutions, Sir Thomas Hetherington, who had acted independently of the Attorney General.

Hetherington reminded me that although some statutes — such as the Official Secrets Act — provide that no prosecution can be brought without the Attorney General's consent, the charges against Thorpe did not require his approval.

> But of course he was a public figure, and it was right that I should keep the Attorney General in touch. And I did keep him in touch. But because of the political background to the case it was decided that it would be much better for the decision to be taken by a non-politician, which was me, and that I should not seek the guidance — as I might otherwise have done — of the Attorney General on whether or not to proceed.

It was said at the time that Sir Thomas Hetherington had acted independently of the Attorney General in reaching the decision to prosecute Mr Thorpe — although I imagine it must have been very hard for Mr Silkin to avoid giving the Director any inkling of his views. But much less well known is the involvement of the previous Attorney General, Sir Peter Rawlinson, now Lord Rawlinson of Ewell.

As you may remember from the Crippen case, it is quite normal for the

Director of Public Prosecutions to seek the advice of counsel in sensitive cases before deciding whether to proceed. What's more, the barrister chosen might well expect a brief to appear for the Director in court if there is to be a prosecution. By convention at that time, the Attorney General nominated counsel to lead for the Crown, and accordingly Sam Silkin selected the barrister who was to advise the Director on allegations in which Mr Thorpe's name had been mentioned. It could be seen as a tribute to Mr Silkin's independence of mind that he chose a political opponent. He was also somebody who knew Jeremy Thorpe well as a fellow member of the House of Commons, a fellow member of the Privy Council and leader of the Bar Circuit to which Mr Thorpe belonged — Sir Peter Rawlinson, QC.

It is essential to understand the sequence of events. At the time Rawlinson was asked to advise the Attorney General, Jeremy Thorpe was not a potential defendant or even directly involved in the case — although it was suspected that he might have been connected indirectly. The initial enquiries related to the shooting of a dog, a Great Dane called Rinka, on the Devon moors near Porlock in October 1975. The dog belonged to a man called Norman Scott, who had previously claimed to have had a homosexual relationship with Mr Thorpe. The man facing a charge of possessing a firearm with intent to endanger life was a former airline pilot called Andrew Gino Newton, who had driven Norman Scott and Rinka to the remote cliff top area where the dog had been shot.

In view of the importance of this case (mainly because of Mr Thorpe's indirect connection) Sam Silkin asked Peter Rawlinson, as leader of the Western Circuit, whether he would be willing to conduct the prosecution case. For what Lord Silkin later told me were 'entirely proper reasons', Lord Rawlinson preferred to be relieved of that duty'. Sam Silkin agreed, and the case for the Crown was taken over by another senior member of the circuit. In March 1976 Newton was duly convicted and sentenced to two years in prison.

Newton served just over a year of his sentence before being released on parole in April 1977. He approached the London *Evening News* in the hope of selling his story and various tape recordings he had made. The newspaper duly tipped off the Director of Public Prosecutions, who asked the police to make fresh enquiries. In October 1977, while police enquiries were continuing, the *Evening News* published a story under the headline I WAS HIRED TO KILL SCOTT.

Unlike the previous proceedings, these allegations seemed to involve Mr Thorpe directly. Sir Thomas Hetherington discussed the case with the Attorney General. Lord Silkin told me what he did next:

> It became necessary for me to nominate counsel to advise and, if a prosecution followed, to prosecute. In view of Lord Rawlinson's preference not to be involved in the dog case, which indirectly concerned Mr Thorpe, I though it very likely that he would prefer not to participate in the case which directly affected Mr Thorpe. Having regard, however, to the importance of the case and to Lord Rawlinson's position and experience, I

nonetheless thought it right to ask him whether he would be willing to take the leading brief for the prosecution. I would not have been surprised if he had at once declined.

But Lord Rawlinson did not decline the brief at once. He told me that on 10 February 1978 he saw the Attorney General in his room at the House of Commons. Mr Thorpe was, in Lord Rawlinson's view, 'not a potential defendant' at that stage. On 15 February Lord Rawlinson had a consultation with the Director of Public Prosecutions, and on 23 February a further consultation attended by junior counsel (Mr John Bull) and the police officers in charge of the enquiry. Lord Rawlinson advised the police to make further enquiries. On 27 February he saw the Director again and during early March Lord Rawlinson considered the result of those further enquiries. Once there was what Lord Rawlinson considered to be clear evidence against Mr Thorpe, he withdrew from the case. On 14 March he returned his instructions to the Director, and recommended that the Attorney General should brief the leader of another circuit instead. Peter Rawlinson suggested Peter Taylor, QC (now Mr Justice Taylor) and Sam Silkin agreed.

Some months later, in July 1978, the police enquiries were completed. The following month, Thorpe was arrested with a friend, David Holmes, and two other people. They were charged at Minehead police station in Somerset with conspiracy to murder Norman Scott. Thorpe was also charged with inciting Holmes to murder Scott. All the defendants were eventually acquitted.

Many questions are raised by the way the case was handled in the period before Peter Taylor became involved. Should Sam Silkin have asked a leading member of the parliamentary Opposition to take on a prosecution involving Mr Thorpe? Should not Peter Rawlinson have declined immediately? Did Sam Silkin brief Peter Rawlinson in the expectation that the brief would have been declined immediately? If Sam Silkin had expected or even intended Peter Rawlinson to decline the brief, could not his actions have been misunderstood by Rawlinson?

As you saw, Lord Silkin valued Lord Rawlinson's experience. He had been Solicitor General from 1962 to 1964 and Attorney General from 1970 to 1974. In 1975 he became Chairman of the Bar and in accordance with custom he conducted the major prosecutions on the Western Circuit as Leader. So clearly he was one of the most experienced leading counsel in the country. But should not his prominence in the main parliamentary Opposition party have made it more difficult for him to give advice which would ultimately be passed to his political opponent? Lord Rawlinson denies the suggestion that he was at that time a 'leading member' of the Opposition. In 1974 he had left the Front Bench. In 1977 he had said he would not be standing for Parliament again. In March 1978 he resigned his seat and became a Conservative life peer. His principal occupation at that time was the Bar (he had a very heavy practice) and he told me he understood that the Attorney General wanted the benefit of his experience at the preliminary stages of a particularly difficult and delicate investigation.

For his part, Lord Silkin sees no way in which his actions could have been misunderstood. He told me that both he and Rawlinson both realized that if it came to a prosecution of Jeremy Thorpe, Peter Rawlinson would not handle the case against a professional and Parliamentary colleague. And Lord Silkin says it was quite proper for Lord Rawlinson to have declined the brief once he had studied the papers.

When Jeremy Thorpe and his fellow defendants went on trial at the Old Bailey in May 1979, Peter Taylor, QC outlined the prosecution case against them:

> In 1959, Mr Jeremy Thorpe was elected MP for North Devon. During the early 1960s he had a homosexual relationship with Norman Scott. From then on, Mr Scott was a continuing danger to his reputation and career . . . The higher [Mr Thorpe] climbed on the political ladder, the greater was the threat to his ambition from Scott . . . Early in 1969 at his room in the House of Commons he incited his close friend, David Holmes, to kill Norman Scott. Peter Bessell, a fellow Liberal MP, was present. Holmes and Bessell tried, over a period of time, to dissuade Mr Thorpe from this plan . . .

> Shortly before the first of the two General Elections in 1974, Scott went to live in Mr Thorpe's constituency. He had been talking openly about his relationship with Jeremy Thorpe, and he was seeking to publish a book about it. The accused, David Holmes, eventually became convinced that, as Mr Thorpe had repeatedly urged, the only way to stop this threat both to Mr Thorpe and to the Liberal Party effectively was to kill Scott.

> Mr Holmes . . . knew the accused John Le Mesurier, a carpet dealer. Through him he met the accused George Deakin, a dealer in fruit machines, and a plot was hatched to find someone who would kill Scott for reward. Mr Deakin recruited Andrew Newton, an airline pilot, as the hired assassin . . . Eventually in October 1975 Mr Newton met [Scott] in Devon, gained his confidence, and drove him out to the moors. There Newton produced a gun. Scott had brought a dog with him. Newton shot the dog but failed to shoot Mr Scott. Mr Newton was arrested, charged, and convicted in March 1976 . . . On his release in 1977 he was paid £5,000, half the contract price . . . by Le Mesurier. The money to pay for this contract was procured by Jeremy Thorpe.

Thorpe, Le Mesurier and Holmes called no evidence at their trial: they exercised their options not to go into the witness box. So the case turned on the prosecution witnesses, of whom the most important was Peter Bessell, the former MP. Unusually, the Director of Public Prosecutions had given Bessell immunity from prosecution in order to persuade him to return to Britain from his home in California. Bessell had been offered £50,000 by the *Sunday Telegraph* for his account of the story, a figure that would be reduced to £25,000 if the newspaper was unable to print the story because of an acquittal. Much was made of the fact that Mr Bessell stood to gain financially from a conviction. According to the *New Statesman*, at least one of the jurors thought this 'half-price acquittal' deal destroyed Bessell's credibility; interviews with jurors were subsequently outlawed as a result of this case.

The *New Statesman* article also suggested that the jury would have convicted the defendants if the Director of Public Prosecutions had chosen to charge them with conspiracy to assault Norman Scott. What's more, one defendant, George Deakin, had said in court that, at any rate in the beginning, it had been a conspiracy to frighten Scott, rather than a conspiracy to kill him. Conspiracy to frighten is a criminal conspiracy, and counsel for David Holmes said after his client had been acquitted that Mr Holmes had been prepared to admit the lesser charge of conspiracy to frighten. (Mr Holmes' counsel was in fact John Mathew, QC, son of the former DPP.)

But why then was Thorpe accused of such serious charges? If there had been a better chance of getting convictions against Thorpe and the others for conspiracy to frighten, should not Sir Thomas Hetherington have brought that charge instead?

> My answer to that was, and still remains, that on the evidence before me, if the witnesses were believed, there could only have been one charge. The 'conspiracy to frighten' theory was just not borne out by the evidence.

'Mind you,' added Sir Thomas in a clear reference to Peter Bessell and Norman Scott, 'I had some pretty funny old witnesses there.' So the Director was not surprised by the jury's verdict. He pointed out that the jury had been out for an extremely long time — 52 hours in fact. 'If the jury have that much difficulty in making up their minds,' he told me, 'I feel that the prosecution is justified.' And on another occasion he said that the result of this case would be stored away as evidence to guide his instinct when similar facts presented themselves for his assessment. Perhaps not surprisingly, there was nothing remotely similar while Sir Thomas Hetherington remained DPP.

If Hetherington had thought the witnesses were not going to be believed (in the absence of any corroboration) he would not have brought lesser charges: he would simply have said there was insufficient evidence to bring *any* prosecution. But, on the assumption that there was enough evidence, he was sure he had been right to decide that a prosecution would be in the public interest.

Dr Arthur and the Down's Baby

One of Sir Thomas Hetherington's most difficult cases involved a consultant paediatrician called Dr Leonard Arthur. The doctor had admitted taking steps to hasten the death of a baby suffering from Down's syndrome, and the child survived for just 69 hours. It had been rejected by its parents, and Dr Arthur ordered nursing care only, while prescribing a drug to relieve distress. That drug, dihydrocodeine, also has the effect of suppressing appetite.

In 1981, Dr Arthur was accused of murder. When the case came to court, it emerged that there was no evidence to show that the baby's death resulted from Dr Arthur's treatment. The murder charge was withdrawn from the jury, although the prosecution continued on the remaining charge of attempted murder because the Director thought there was still evidence to show that, even if the baby had not died as a result of the treatment, that was what Dr Arthur had intended. But, in due course, the jury acquitted Dr Arthur of attempted murder as well.

Speaking some months after the case, Hetherington said that if he had known in advance of the expert medical evidence to be produced by the defence, he might not have charged Dr Arthur with murder. But if there was clear evidence that a doctor had deliberately ended the life of a baby, the Director said he would certainly have to consider whether a prosecution would be in the public interest.

Reflecting on the Arthur case five years later, Sir Thomas Hetherington told me that it showed how important it was to check and re-check the medical evidence in support of a charge like this. And experience showed it was always difficult to get a conviction where there were a lot of emotive issues. He then gave me another example of a case which became very emotive and where the jury had reacted by acquitting the defendant. It is the case of Clive Ponting, which I shall turn to next.

Clive Ponting and the Interests of the State

It is with these words that Clive Ponting begins his book *The Right to Know*:

> On 28 January 1985 I stood in the dock of No 2 Court at the Old Bailey charged under section 2 of the Official Secrets Act. I was accused of disclosing 'official information' without authority to an unauthorised person. The 'official information' was two documents about events in the South Atlantic and the sinking of the Argentinian cruiser *General Belgrano* in May 1982. The government had already admitted, during the committal proceedings at Bow Street magistrates' court, that national security was not involved. The documents had been sent to a Member of Parliament and passed to a select committee of the House of Commons where they had played an essential part in its enquiries into the sinking.
>
> I found it difficult to believe this could be happening to me.

The MP Clive Ponting sent the papers to was Tam Dalyell. He passed them to Sir Anthony Kershaw, MP, Chairman of the Defence Select Committee, and Kershaw in turn passed them to Michael Heseltine, MP, who was then Secretary of State. He called in the Ministry of Defence police who had no trouble in tracing their source as Ponting, a fact he freely admitted. Ponting resigned from the civil service.

What happened next, according to a 'leak' Ponting records in his book, was that the Second Permanent Secretary at the Ministry of Defence visited Michael Heseltine at his home (this was the middle of August) and told him the Chief Constable of the Ministry of Defence police did not recommend prosecution. 'Heseltine said he personally favoured a prosecution, but would leave a final decision to the Attorney General.' Ponting says he was told the next day that ministers had insisted that (wait for it) the papers should be sent to the Director of Public Prosecutions. His union lobbied inside Whitehall against a prosecution. But, says Ponting, it was too late:

The papers reached Sir Thomas Hetherington late on Thursday 16 August. He spoke to Hughes and Broome [the two Ministry of Defence policemen] about their report. The next day the DPP spoke to the Solicitor General, Sir Patrick Mayhew. There was then a brief discussion over the telephone with the Attorney General, Sir Michael Havers, who was on holiday in France. They had few papers in front of them. Havers decided on a prosecution.

Ponting says that in October 'Sir Michael Havers decided to intervene in my case again'. He quotes a radio interview the Attorney General gave me in which he stressed the decision to prosecute had been his alone, adding:

> If you recall all the comments and criticism that have happened since, it may be that the decision to prosecute is one that if considered by the cabinet or by certain cabinet ministers, they would like to advise me another way.

Ponting must have seemed an open and shut case to the Director of Public Prosecutions. The defendant had, after all, freely confessed. But at his trial he came up with a novel defence. The Official Secrets Act says it is not an offence for a person to communicate a document if it is his duty to do so 'in the interest of the State'. Ponting argued that it was in the interest of the State for Parliament to be told it was being misled by the government. The judge, Mr Justice McCowan, after being persuaded not to give the jury a direction to convict Ponting, nevertheless directed the jury that 'the interest of the State' meant, in effect, the interests of the government. (The judge had, of course, spoken to counsel about his proposed direction to the jury while they were out of the court: he was mortified to find his remarks immediately reported in *The Observer* which knew — better than he did — that to have prevented the report appearing the judge should have made an order under the Contempt of Court Act 1981.) Despite the judge's summing up, Ponting was found not guilty.

Could the acquittal have been predicted? Probably not. But what is beyond doubt is that juries can no longer be relied on to convict a defendant under the Official Secrets Act who is seen to have acted in the public interest. And by that I mean what the jury sees as the public interest, not what the lawyers may say the law allows.

It is a lesson which has been learned by the Director of Public Prosecutions. The case has become a precedent to guide him for the future: if similar facts were to arise again he says he would be more cautious about authorizing a prosecution. Indeed, David Hooper, in his book *Official Secrets*, says the Attorney General's decision in March 1985 to withdraw secrets charges against Alan Lowther, an accountant in the Home Office Prisons Department, was influenced by Clive Ponting's unexpected acquittal: Mr Lowther, who was awarded his costs, had been accused of showing a business colleague documents discussing plans for prisoners to manufacture toy typewriters. So 1985 had not been a good year for the Official Secrets Act. But there was worse to follow.

The Cyprus Servicemen

You may be disappointed but the Attorney General will be relieved to learn that the Director of Public Prosecutions gave no secrets away when he discussed the case of the Cyprus servicemen with me. What follows then is mainly what was made public at the time. A great deal was not: this was the longest-ever spy trial, lasting 119 days, but only five hours of it was held in open court.

Seven young servicemen were charged under section 1 of the Official Secrets Act with passing 'secrets by the bagful' to Russian agents. They were said to have been blackmailed into spying after being lured into a web of homosexual orgies, but these allegations seemed inconsistent with what was known about the men.

All of them were attached to 9 Signals Regiment and worked in secret communications-monitoring bases at Ayios Nikolaos in Cyprus. The prosecution relied on detailed confessions said to have been made to the RAF police, the Provost and Security Service. But the defendants said that they had been brainwashed by being interrogated over long periods of time and had been forced to make their statements by oppression and threats. The jury appear to have accepted this claim. In October 1985, all seven defendants were found not guilty of the 28 charges they faced.

It was only the second time that defendants facing charges under section 1 of the 1911 Act had been acquitted. The previous occasion was a year earlier when, in similar circumstances, another airman from Cyprus named Paul Davies was cleared of passing secrets to a 'Mata Hari' figure — who surprised everyone by turning up at the Old Bailey to give evidence on his behalf. Again, Davies's confession was said to have been forced out of him.

Prosecutions in secrets cases need the consent of the Attorney General: there are around 40 statutes which impose this requirement. Some, like the Official Secrets Act itself, carry severe penalties: the Genocide Act 1969, the Hijacking Act 1971, the Biological Weapons Act 1974. Other statutes have created less serious offences which it was thought should not be used at the whim of a private prosecutor or even the police: they include publishing newspapers without the printer's name and address, uttering defaced coins, reporting committal proceedings and trespass at foreign embassies.

In all these 'consent' cases the papers go to the DPP so that he can advise the Attorney whether to go ahead. And Sir Thomas Hetherington told me he had advised a prosecution in the case of the Cyprus Servicemen because he thought, on the evidence, that there was a realistic chance of a conviction. He knew, of course, that the admissions made by the defendants could be challenged because of the length of time they had been under interrogation before statements were taken. The confessions were indeed challenged by the defence, and one of the original eight defendants was cleared by the judge as a result. But Mr Justice Stocker found the statements made by the remaining seven were admissible and he let them go to the jury. 'That was all we could hope for,' said Hetherington, 'but to what extent the jury was influenced by the way in which the statements were taken I don't know.'

David Hooper says in *Official Secrets* that one piece of evidence at the secret trial more than any undermined the prosecution case:

> The prosecution claimed that official secrets were passed in return for favours received from Josie, a Filipino dancer, and a lady called Carmelita de Mesa, known on stage as Ning-Ning. To the dismay of the prosecution she appeared at the trial as a witness for the defence and proved to be far from the scarlet lady depicted. She was by then married to an English engineer, who was asked by defence counsel whether his wife had been a virgin when he married her. 'No,' he replied, but seeing the dismay on counsel's face he quickly added 'but she was when I first met her.'

It is easy to criticize Sir Thomas Hetherington's decision to advise prosecution, particularly when one can never know the full facts. On the one hand the Director could reasonably have expected an acquittal: he had a precedent, in the Davies case, for a jury not believing an alleged confession obtained in similar circumstances by the same two RAF policemen. On the other hand, when the case came to trial it was not thrown out by the judge on a defence submission of 'no case to answer': it went to the jury which took more than six days to reach verdicts on all the defendants. So it was clearly touch and go, at least for some of the accused. And it would have taken a bold Director to have said the evidence was not good enough, and thus to have taken it on himself to decide, for example, that a man who faced up to 98 years imprisonment if he had been found guilty of the seven counts he had been charged with should not even have gone to trial.

But the Director of Public Prosecutions is there precisely because somebody is needed to take bold decisions. The fact that men had been arrested was presumably enough to have made the authorities tighten up what appeared to have been woefully inadequate security. And if the Director had decided to advise the Attorney General not to proceed, it would have saved seven men a courtroom ordeal perhaps nearly as frightening as the interrogation they received in Cyprus. It would also have saved the government the political embarrassment of having to order an enquiry under David Calcutt, QC into military interrogation techniques — which found that the servicemen's custody was for part of the time unlawful and that even after they had been lawfully arrested their continued custody was at least improper. And it would have saved the country a trial which the newspapers said had cost £5 million.

The Second Campbell Incident

The first Campbell Incident, you will remember from earlier in this chapter, all started when a man called Campbell wrote an article in a left-wing weekly paper and the Attorney General authorized the police to raid it. So did the second.

This time the publication was the *New Statesman* and the journalist was Duncan Campbell. And of course there were other differences: in 1924 the Attorney General had given way to political pressure which the Prime Minister had tried to hide by lying to the House of Commons.

The second Campbell Incident was all about a military satellite project named Zircon. Details of the project, but not its name, were first published in the space industry newsletter *Interspace* in 1984. (One of its regular subscribers, according to Duncan Campbell, is the *Intersputnik* satellite organization based in Moscow, USSR.)

By the start of 1986, Campbell was aware that Project Zircon was a spy satellite designed to obtain signals intelligence from the Soviet Union. We are told that satellites like these can intercept conversations on car telephones, and even listen in to secretly planted bugs. Not surprisingly, Campbell does not say how he became aware of the project's name, but he points out that Zircon is linked geologically with Rhyolite, the name given to the first American spy satellite aimed at Russia. (Both code-names breach security by having identifiable links with the two projects.) In the past, much of Campbell's supposedly secret information has come from published sources. But on this occasion Whitehall suspected that a 'mole' was disclosing secret information to him.

Despite the fact that Campbell told the Ministry of Defence Press Office in March 1986 that he wanted to know more about Zircon, no action was taken against him. Campbell then suggested to BBC television that Zircon should be the subject of one programme in a series called *Secret Society* that he was making for them.

By July 1986 Campbell had interviewed two former senior Ministry of Defence officials about Zircon. Both had reported back to the Ministry on what Campbell knew. Still no action was taken against him.

In January 1987 the BBC's Director General, Alasdair Milne, said he had been advised that transmitting the Zircon programme would be against national security. Accordingly, the Zircon programme would be dropped. (A few days later, Milne himself was dropped.)

Then events moved fast. *The Observer* revealed that the Zircon programme was to be shown to an audience of MPs later in the week. The next day, the Defence Secretary George Younger, the Foreign Secretary Sir Geoffrey Howe, and the Attorney General Sir Michael Havers met as a Cabinet committee. I had an appointment to see the Attorney later that morning, and when he arrived, a little late, he looked pretty fed up. This was understandable. Havers took care not to tell me anything of what had happened at the meeting, but even though he had taken a copy of the Official Secrets Act to the meeting in his red ministerial box, it emerged later that his colleagues had refused to let the Attorney throw the book at Duncan Campbell.

At that stage, only civil proceedings against Campbell himself seemed in prospect. Havers maintained that he had no grounds for seeking an injunction against the *New Statesman*: although Campbell had contractual links with the paper, and despite the fact that the MPs' screening had been fixed for the *Statesman*'s publication day, the government insisted that there was no hard evidence that the *Statesman* intended to publish anything about Zircon.

This was either incompetence or an excuse. In the past, the Treasury Solicitor has written to newspapers thought to have been on the point of publishing secrets. Failure to give the government's lawyer an undertaking not to publish specified material has resulted in an immediate application by the Attorney General for an injunction.

It was not, in fact, until the following day, Tuesday 20 January, that Havers got ministerial approval to apply for an injunction against Campbell. Another day passed while the head of Government Communications Headquarters at Cheltenham, Sir Peter Marychurch, saw the programme and swore an affidavit in support of the application. So it was Wednesday evening before an injunction was granted to stop Duncan Campbell talking about Zircon, too late to stop the story appearing in Thursday's *New Statesman*.

It was only then that criminal proceedings became a possibility. The Attorney General spoke to the Director of Public Prosecutions and as a result the Director called in the Special Branch. Police officers then raided the magazine and Campbell's home in their search for evidence of the supposed mole. Clearly a prosecution under the Official Secrets Act was in prospect, although the Director would be well aware, following the Ponting case, of the difficulty in getting a conviction against somebody like Campbell who considered he was disclosing information in the public interest. But by May 1987, when the General Election campaign started, there had still been no word of a prosecution.

There were only muted protests when the London Special Branch went in: much louder was the outcry when the BBC's offices in Glasgow were raided a week later and all the programmes in the *Secret Society* series seized, together with a large quantity of additional material which the police took many weeks to sift through. Sir Thomas Hetherington stressed — with some relief — that the BBC raid was nothing to do with him: I will be discussing the political aspects of the case in Chapter 10.

FOUR

The Crown Prosecution Service

It was in the year 1824 that Lord Denman, who was later to become Chief Justice of the Court of King's Bench, identified what he called 'a strange anomaly in the English criminal system — the entire want of a responsible public prosecutor.' His evidence to the Criminal Law Commissioners twenty years later led them to conclude that too often prosecutions were being conducted 'in a loose and an unsatisfactory manner'; they recommended in 1845 that 'the direct and obvious course for remedying such defects would consist in the appointment of public prosecutors'.

Never anxious to make decisions in a hurry, Parliament took 140 years to put these recommendations into effect. In the meantime the newly created police forces had taken on the private citizen's role of bringing prosecutions, and of course from 1880 the Director himself had begun to handle the most difficult cases (as we saw in Chapter 2). But one can only marvel at the fact that until 1986 nobody had succeeded in taking the power to prosecute out of the hands of the police.

Public Prosecutions: Historical Origins

It was not for want of trying. In 1855 the Attorney General, Sir Alexander Cockburn, told a Parliamentary select committee that

> the great want, the great desideratum, is the having of an officer whose business it shall be to prepare cases for trial, to see that when brought into court they are . . . in a state in which the final decision can be taken on them satisfactorily to all parties concerned, or who, upon the other hand, conscious of the infirmity of the case, and that it is one in which the party should not be put upon his trial, either from justice to him, or from expediency to the public, shall have the duty of communicating the circumstance to the Attorney General.

But for the language, Sir Alexander could have been moving the Second Reading of the Prosecution of Offences Bill 1984. That bill, however, was still more than a century off; and three Royal Commissions would be needed before a mainly English Parliament could be persuaded to accept what all Scotsmen took to be self-evident.

In 1929, for example, the Royal Commission on Police Powers and Procedure was told by Sir Archibald Bodkin, then Director of Public Prosecutions, that it was important to keep distinct 'on the one hand, the duty which lies on the police of preventing and detecting crime, and, on the other, the duty of bringing to justice people who have broken the law'. The Royal Commission agreed that the Director's job should continue to be prosecution of criminals rather than investigation of crimes, and thought there was 'much to be said for the view that all criminal prosecutions should be undertaken by officials specially appointed for that purpose, as is the case in Scotland'; it concluded however that such a radical proposal was outside its terms of reference.

In 1962 another Royal Commission on the Police said it was generally undesirable for police officers to appear as prosecutors except in minor cases. 'In particular,' said the commissioners, 'we deplore the regular employment of the same police officers as advocates for the prosecution'. The Commission went on to recommend that every police force should have its own prosecuting solicitor's department.

Most forces, but by no means all, implemented that recommendation. Those that did not were Bedfordshire, Hertfordshire, Surrey, Leicestershire, Staffordshire, and North Yorkshire. In those counties, right up to the establishment of the Crown Prosecution Service nearly 25 years after the Royal Commission had reported in 1962, the police instructed local firms of solicitors to advise them whether to prosecute. Since those solicitors ran the risk of losing their most valuable clients if they offered unpalatable advice, there must have been occasions when they would have been reluctant to tell a chief constable who might have been set on a particular prosecution that it was bound to end in an acquittal. Prosecuting solicitors' departments — though they varied in size and effectiveness — were in a slightly better position: they generally commanded the respect of their chief constables and, as a result, the more enlightened police forces tended not to bring prosecutions if they had been advised not to by their lawyers — always supposing they had bothered to ask the lawyers for advice in the first place. But the crucial point was that the police always had the last word: if they instructed their solicitors to go ahead with a prosecution those instructions had to be obeyed.

London was a special case, and far from perfect. There, the Metropolitan Police had its own solicitors' department (which still exists to handle civil and other non-prosecution work). Since the lawyers were actually employed by the police rather than by local authorities they were seen as even less independent of their clients than prosecuting solicitors were outside London. They also had only a minor role in the prosecution process. The police themselves handled nearly all cases dealt with by the magistrates — the vast bulk of all prosecutions. Apart from the absence of any independent review, this practice provided greater opportunities for police corruption. If the arresting officer was the man who handled the prosecution in court, nothing would have been easier than for the officer to bring a charge which failed to reflect the seriousness of the offence, or to 'forget' the accused's previous convictions, in exchange for an appropriate consideration in used notes. There were cases of corruption outside London of course, but not so many after the prosecuting solicitors' departments — none of which was controlled by the police — got going in the major cities outside London by the early seventies.

Of course, cases dealt with in the Crown Court required the services of a barrister, and so these papers were sent to the Metropolitan Police Solicitor's Department to instruct counsel after the magistrates' court had committed the case for trial by jury. Even then, about half the files — known as 'soup cases' apparently because they were bread-and-butter work — were sent straight on to counsel without any serious consideration by the solicitors, a 'sausage machine' system which had gone out in the provinces by the mid-1960s.

Professor L.H. Leigh mentions what he calls 'a most striking assertion of [police] independence under the old arrangements' in his book on *Police Powers*. It was 'the decision of the Chief Constable of Mid-Anglia to prosecute rioting students on charges of unlawful assembly and riotous assembly, charges virtually unused since the 1930s. The decision to lay particular charges was that of the Chief Constable alone, although advice from the Director of Public Prosecutions was sought'. This was the famous *Garden House Hotel* case of 1970, although Professor Leigh's implied criticism of the chief constable's decision to prosecute must be balanced against the fact that the students were convicted by a jury, and had prison sentences upheld by the Court of Appeal.

Rather better examples of what could go wrong when Chief Constables had the ultimate discretion to prosecute arose when charges of riot and other public order offences were brought against miners involved in the strike of 1984/85. The charges rebounded on the prosecution: of nearly a hundred miners arrested after violent scenes outside the Orgreave coking plant near Sheffield in May 1984, the prosecution failed to win a single conviction for riot or unlawful assembly. In August 1985 the prosecution dropped riot charges against 39 of the men who were due to stand trial; uppermost in the prosecution's mind was the fact that a month earlier they had decided to abandon the trial on the 48th day of 14 other men charged with rioting at Orgreave. In another case 18 miners were charged with riot and affray following disturbances at the end of a union rally in Nottinghamshire. All pleaded not guilty, and all were acquitted after (or, in some cases, during) a trial lasting three months. Charges against other men were then dropped.

So the police solicitor, like a constitutional monarch, had the power to advise and the power to warn; he did not have the power to veto his client's instructions. And that was what changed when the Crown Prosecution Service started work in 1986.

The Philips Royal Commission

But first the government wanted the advice of just one more Royal Commission. Not content to rely on the recommendation in 1970 from the organization 'Justice' (the British section of the International Commission of Jurists) that there should be in England and Wales 'a system of public prosecution broadly following the lines of the Scottish system,' in 1978 the Labour Home Secretary Merlyn Rees appointed Sir Cyril Philips, Professor of Oriental History in the University of London and a former Vice-Chancellor of the university, to chair a Royal Commission on Criminal Procedure. The Philips Commission was required to consider what the Prime Minister of the day had called a 'fundamental balance' between (in the words of its terms of reference) the 'interests of the community in bringing offenders to justice and the rights and liberties of persons suspected or accused of crime.' So it was not surprising that the Commission's report in 1981 led to two pieces of legislation which themselves were seen as attempting to strike that fundamental balance: the Police and Criminal Evidence Act 1984 — which gave new powers to the police — and the Prosecution of Offences Act 1985 — which took old powers away from them.

Much of the credit for this balanced approach must go to Lord Silkin, who — as Sam Silkin — was Attorney General in the Labour government of 1974 to 1979. It was he who urged his colleagues in government not to confine the Philips Commission to an examination of the police; it was the structure he wanted for the Crown Prosecution Service which the subsequent Conservative government eventually adopted.

The Philips Commission found that 43 per cent of all defendants who were acquitted in the Crown Court in 1978 were found not guilty without even a jury having to look at the evidence. In that year, 19 per cent of all acquittals in the Crown Court had been ordered by the judge after the prosecution had offered no evidence, and in a further 24 per cent the judge had directed the jury to acquit because he thought the prosecution had not made out its case. By 1985 the figure for acquittals ordered or directed by the judge had risen to 47 per cent — a 'frighteningly high figure,' in Sir Thomas Hetherington's opinion. Philips thought that in at least some of those cases (probably about a fifth) there were doubts about the evidence at the time the decision to prosecute was made. It is true that some cases will always collapse because the witnesses fail to come up to scratch, which is not something for which the prosecution can be blamed. But what Philips was saying was that there were some cases where an acquittal could have been predicted if a good lawyer had looked at the papers in advance. And if those acquittals could have been predicted they could have been avoided, with considerable savings in public money, to say nothing of private anxiety.

Why, then, were these hopeless cases coming to court? There were two reasons. First, some prosecutors had lower standards than others. Not everyone who is alleged to have committed a criminal offence is prosecuted. There has to be enough evidence to satisfy a court. But some local prosecutors considered that there was enough evidence if they could make out what is called a prima facie case, which Philips defined as 'evidence on the basis of which, *if it were accepted,* a reasonable jury or magistrates' court would be justified in convicting the accused of the offence alleged'.

The words I have stressed are crucial. What is the point of prosecuting somebody if you think the evidence may not be accepted? To let the court decide? But then the chances are that the court may throw the case out, at great cost to all concerned. Are you in fact going ahead in the hope that the accused will suddenly confess, or that he will be convicted despite the lack of evidence? Is that justice?

The Director of Public Prosecutions had a higher standard. There certainly had to be at least a prima facie case in the prosecutions he handled. But there had to be more: a reasonable prospect of conviction. His cases would only go ahead if a conviction seemed more likely than an acquittal. This was the famous 'fifty per cent rule', which you can read about in Chapter 6. The Royal Commission wisely thought it should be extended to all prosecutions.

There was another reason why hopeless cases were coming to court. The Commission had been told of instances where weak cases had been continued by the police officer in charge 'despite and sometimes in the face of contrary advice from the lawyer who has conduct of the prosecution'. Clearly the answer was to separate the investigator's function from that of the lawyer. And this approach, said Philips, was supported by another line of reasoning:

> A police officer who carries out an investigation, inevitably and properly, forms a view as to the guilt of the suspect. Having done so, without any kind of improper motive, he may be inclined to shut his mind to other evidence telling against the guilt of the suspect or to overestimate the strength of the evidence he has assembled.

So Philips recommended a statutorily based prosecution service. The Crown Prosecutor 'would have conduct of all criminal cases once the decision to prosecute had been taken by the police'; he would also provide legal advice to the police on prosecution matters and provide advocates to appear in court. By a majority, the Commission thought the Crown Prosecutor should have complete discretion to alter or drop charges after those charges had been brought by the police.

As you will see, that was just the way it turned out. In the autumn of 1986 Sir Thomas Hetherington was able to tell a conference room full of journalists at his headquarters in Queen Anne's Gate that the main objectives of the Crown Prosecution Service, as recommended by Philips, had been accepted by all parties in Parliament and by the public as a whole. Those fundamental changes were the independent review of each case, after the police had charged or summonsed a defendant, to decide whether it should go ahead or not; and the replacement of police officers by lawyers as prosecutors in the magistrates' courts. But before we get to 1986 it is worth going back eight years to see what Sir Thomas Hetherington though of the idea then.

The Director's View

In his evidence to the Royal Commission, the Director of Public Prosecutions said there were 'disadvantages and difficulties' in creating a national prosecuting agency controlled by him or by his successor. 'In my view,' said Sir Thomas in December 1978, 'if the value of the office of the Director of Public Prosecutions is to be maintained, it is important to restrict 'Director's cases', both in the advisory and the prosecuting roles, to cases of real importance or difficulty with national significance. Other cases, which are essentially of a local nature because they affect the local community rather than the community as a whole,' Sir Thomas thought, 'should continue to be dealt with by local prosecutors (whether they be prosecuting solicitors or police officers).'

In reaching that conclusion Hetherington considered the proposal from 'Justice' I mentioned earlier in this chapter. 'Justice' had recommended (with remarkable foresight) that there should be a Department of Public Prosecutions to be responsible both for the decisions to prosecute and for the conduct of the prosecutions. In addition to having a strong central organization headed by a Director (but under the Attorney General) the department would have regional and local offices staffed by barristers and solicitors. Sir Thomas said, however, that 'it would be an extremely difficult, lengthy and expensive task to graft on to our own system of jurisprudence a system like Scotland's'. Quoting from the 1929 Royal Commission, Sir Thomas said 'it 'would involve a fundamental change in English law'; and there would be great practical problems' in ensuring effective supervision over the much larger number of local prosecutors there would have to be in England than were needed in Scotland.

Turning to the proposal that the police should not be responsible for the decision to prosecute, which he acknowledged was 'not a novel proposition', Sir Thomas Hetherington said it appeared to him that the dangers in the police taking the decision to prosecute had been 'overestimated'. He quoted 'Justice' as saying it had not received 'evidence of systematic abuse or widespread criticism. Generally, the integrity and competence of those concerned with prosecuting . . . is high'. The Director thought instead that the existing prosecuting solicitors' departments should be strengthened and extended to all police forces. He went on:

> For well over a century, the responsibility for bringing the majority of criminal proceedings in England and Wales has rested with the police, and in my view such a radical change as that suggested by the Prosecuting Solicitors' Society [under which the prosecuting solicitor would take the decision to prosecute in certain cases] could only be justified by evidence of general public disquiet with the existing arrangements . . . I am aware of no such evidence, and am therefore unable to support the proposition.

It would not be surprising to find that the Attorney General of the day had agreed with the Director he 'superintended'. In fact, Sir Thomas Hetherington submitted his written evidence before Sir Michael Havers became Attorney General in 1979, but when Sir Michael gave oral evidence to the Royal Commision in 1980 it turned out that he supported what Sir Thomas had already said. 'I am not,' said the Attorney, 'in favour of a comprehensive public prosecution service responsible for all criminal proceedings . . . A fully developed prosecuting solicitor service,' he said, 'will provide a fully adequate service, probably at lower cost, with a smaller administrative tail and, above all, one attuned and conscious to local needs. A local prosecuting solicitors' department is also more likely to be aware of, and respond to, local criminal trends — which may mean that an offence which causes little concern nationally is of local importance and calls for a stricter prosecution policy inconsistent with overall national requirements.' As Professor Edwards says, 'it may be thought the Attorney General was according an exaggerated interpretation to the concepts of 'consistency' and 'uniformity' in relation to a nationally organized prosecution service'.

Second Thoughts

As you have seen, the Royal Commission fundamentally disagreed with Sir Michael Havers and Sir Thomas Hetherington. Even worse, Sir Thomas was the man who had to put into effect recommendations he thought had these 'disadvantages and difficulties'. Speaking some eight years after he had given evidence to the Royal Commission, Sir Thomas Hetherington told me he stood by what he had said on the information he had at that time. 'I wasn't aware at that stage that there was any general public disquiet,' he said. 'It seemed to me that the system worked pretty well, and that it would be difficult to change it. In practice it has proved difficult to change, and it was only by getting the right people working for us that we've been able to resolve those problems.'

Sir Thomas said the Royal Commission's finding that there was a need for change had come after it had taken evidence: he was now persuaded that they were right. He had also been afraid that the proposed prosecution service would become a 'massive bureacracy' and he thought there was still a risk that the Crown Prosecution Service Headquarters would be issuing 'too much bumf' — although by giving local staff a great deal of delegated authority, and even their own budgets, some of this risk could be avoided. But all that comes later in this story.

The Government's Response

In 1981, the Royal Commission had recommended that there should be a new prosecution service covering the whole of England and Wales. It was an idea that was to appeal to the Conservative government even though, as I have said, the Attorney General had some reservations at first. But the Commission's proposals also contained what the government saw as a fatal flaw. Though the new prosecution service would be accountable to a government minister for standards of performance and national staffing levels, it would be funded partly by local authorities and — most important of all — it was to be accountable to a newly expanded police authority for decisions involving management or resources (though not for decisions in individual cases).

Police authorities outside London draw two-thirds of their membership from county councillors and the remainder from local magistrates. It follows that in some areas of the country — Manchester is a current example — police authorities are effectively under Labour control; and a prosecution service answerable to a Labour-controlled police and prosecutions authority in places like Manchester was not something which appealed to the Conservative government at Westminster.

A police authority is obliged to ensure the maintenance of an adequate and efficient police force for its area. It has power to require information from the chief constable, who alone is responsible for operational matters (though he is accountable to the authority for the general conduct of his force). In practice there is not much a police authority opposed to the policy of its chief constable can do, apart from making life awkward for him. But it is an irritation the government saw no need to foist on to Crown Prosecutors.

One official tried to persuade me that the government's reason for not wanting to expand police committees into police and prosecution authorities was certainly not based on political considerations: ministers were simply worried that the ancient structure of these authorities would start to crumble as soon as the government began to interfere with them. Another official explained that since the new service was to be centrally financed it needed to be centrally controlled. The Solicitor General, Sir Patrick Mayhew, gave his explanation in a speech delivered to the Magistrates Associaiton at Southampton in April 1985:

> There is, I suggest, no area of public service — except perhaps the judiciary itself — where outside pressure can be so improper or have such an untoward effect on the working of our system of criminal justice. No-one has been able to devise a locally administered system which contains adequate safeguards against such pressure and, at the same time, secures clearly defined and integrated accountability for policy and resources. This would not have been secured under any scheme that left control over resources at the local level but reserved to the Director and the Attorney General guidance on prosecution policy.

The difficulty facing the government was that Philips had rejected the idea of making the national prosecution service accountable to one individual as too bureaucratic, leading to slow and remote decision making: his report said it would be 'hazardous to argue from the experience of other jurisdictions that a national prosecution service would be workable in England and Wales'. It is intriguing to observe how the government set about legitimizing its decision to overturn the Royal Commission on this small but important point.

When the Commission's report was debated in Parliament the Home Office Minister Lord Elton said he had reservations about the proposal that Crown Prosecutors should be appointed locally by a new police and prosecutions authority; the government had therefore decided to explore alternative systems 'which would avoid the dangers both of over-centralization and of the kind of local accountability which the Commission proposed'. So to quote from a subsequent White Paper, 'ministers asked an interdepartmental Working Party to advise them on what would be the best model for the organisation of such a service'. Lo and behold, the officials duly advised their ministers that local accountability would not be a good thing. As the government's White Paper *An Independent Prosecution Service for England and Wales* said in 1983:

> When the Royal Commission's report was debated in the House of Commons in November 1981, strong reservations were expressed about whether [local accountability] would be workable, or consistent with the service's independence. Further consultation and analysis by the Working Party has confirmed these doubts. The government does not believe that it would be a proper or efficient arrangement to make the Crown Prosecutor accountable in any respect to a local body. It would not be appropriate for local authorities to have control over the conduct of prosecutions under the general criminal law . . . The government therefore proposes that there should be a single line of accountability, both for decision on cases and the management of resources, to the Director of Public Prosecutions.

Despite the firm tone of this White Paper, the government said it would 'be ready to consider comments before final decisions are taken'. But the Home Office was able to say later in an internal guide to the Act that the fifty or so responses received 'revealed no new overt support for the local form of organisation; nor any new arguments which suggested the government's preference for a national system was misdirected'. So the government announced in March 1984 that its plans would go ahead unchanged.

Sure enough, when the Prosecution of Offences Bill was published later that year it proposed that the new service should be run by the DPP; journalists were reminded unattributably by a source not a million miles away from the Home Office that the Royal Commission's suggestion for a locally based service 'was criticised on the grounds that it did nothing to remedy the division of responsibility for funding and prosecution policy; and in addition did not sufficiently secure the desired degree of independence of the new service from the police'. Perhaps to create the impression that the service was nevertheless to be as 'local' as the Royal Commission had wanted, ministers went out of their way to stress how many prosecution decisions would be taken locally in future, even in cases which, under the old system, had been referred to the Director in London. In the government's catchy phrase, making it sound a bit like a daily newspaper, the new service was to be nationally accountable but locally delivered. Leon Brittan, Home Secretary at the time the Act was passed, explained that the new service was

> nationally accountable to parliament through the Attorney General, under whose superintendence the Director of Public Prosecutions will act; locally delivered because the vast bulk of cases will be dealt with by the Crown Prosecutors working close to the police, who investigate, and to the courts, who hear the cases.

Who is to Decide?

While the Prosecution of Offences Bill was going through Parliament the Attorney General, Sir Michael Havers, published a White Paper on 'the proposed distribution of functions between the headquarters and local offices of the service'. As I have just said, the plan was that 'decisions on prosecution in the great majority of cases will be taken in local offices . . . The objective will be maximum delegation consistent with proper accountability'. The White Paper included a list of offences which would generally be handled at local level. These include:

- Murder (but not attempted murder).
- Grievous bodily harm and other assaults.
- Rape, indecent assault, and gross indecency.
- Kidnapping.
- Neglecting a child.
- Drugs offences (except conspiracies).
- Robbery, burglary, blackmail, and theft.
- Criminal damage, including arson.
- Public order offences.
- Immigration offences, except large-scale conspiracies.
- Road traffic offences, including causing death by dangerous driving.
- All offences dealt with in the magistrates' court.

On the other hand, there are a number of cases which have to be referred to the Crown Prosecution Service headquarters in London:

- Attempted murder (cases are generally considered at Headquarters before being prosecuted locally).
- Homicides not included in the previous list.
- Offences of abortion.
- Conspiracy to manufacture controlled drugs and large scale conspiracy to supply them.
- Causing grievous bodily harm by explosives.
- Extradition cases.
- Cases involving European Law.

More than 60 statutes create offences for which prosecutions can only be brought with the consent of the DPP, either in his own right or in place of a Law Officer (the Attorney General or the Solicitor General). The aim of these provisions is to prevent a private prosecutor, or even the police, bringing a prosecution in an inappropriate case. As we shall see, the Director's consent can now be given by the lowliest Crown Prosecutor. In fact, some of these 'consent' cases are still dealt with at Headquarters: Official Secrets cases for example. But others, which the White Paper said produced the great bulk of referrals, are now handled locally; they include

> allegations of buggery and gross indecency between men, one of them being under 21; making false reports causing the wasteful employment of the police; incest; theft of or criminal damage to property belonging to the offender's spouse; assisting an offender to avoid apprehension or

prosecution; sexual intercourse with or ill-treatment of mental patients; and taking, distributing, or having indecent photographs of children.

The White Paper said that other cases would continue to be dealt with at headquarters — and it is these that I shall be dealing with in the next chapter. They include 'large and complex fraud cases'; obscene publications ('it will be necessary to maintain centralised records of material which has been the subject of such proceedings'); allegations against police officers ('to avoid any suggestion that decisions might be influenced by the working relationship between the police and the local Crown Prosecutor'); cases involving MPs, councillors, magistrates, judges, senior officials, members of the Crown Prosecution Service itself and other people in similar situations 'where it might otherwise appear that prosecution decisions have been affected by local influence'; and other cases 'likely to give rise to particular difficulties or likely to attract exceptional public concern'. The White Paper said the Director would continue to handle a number of particularly rare types of case at headquarters; these relate to election petitions, criminal bankruptcies, extradition to or from the United Kingdom, contempt of court, and acquittals referred by the Attorney General to the Court of Appeal for a ruling on a point of law. Appeals to the House of Lords are handled by Headquarters; appeals to the Court of Appeal, the Divisional Court and to the Crown Court against conviction or sentence by the magistrates are handled locally.

As Head of Legal Services, John Wood took the view that he should not keep all the best cases for his staff at the Headquarters of the Crown Prosecution Service: it would not be good for morale locally. Since the service started work there has already been a tendency to allow more cases to be handled locally. John Wood stressed the need for consistency: 'one doesn't want the same book, for example, being prosecuted in one part of the country, the booksellers warned in another part of the country, and in a third area the Crown Prosecutor saying there was nothing wrong with the book and handing it back'. Consistency was also very important in race relations cases, he said.

In its initial White Paper on the proposed independent prosecution service published in 1983, the government said that if the Attorney General answered for decisions taken in every individual case, the result would be excessive centralization. Accordingly, in July 1986 the Attorney told MPs he would remain answerable in Parliament for his own decisions or those taken by Headquarters staff, as well as for the policy of the service generally. But Sir Michael Havers thought it was not appropriate 'to answer in parliament for the intrinsic merits of particular decisions taken by local prosecutors unless the Director's staff have been involved in the case'. And even then he would continue to confine answers to 'the basis of the decision in the particular case, without giving details of the evidence or other considerations which have led to a particular decision'. However, if MPs wanted to know more about decisions taken by prosecutors locally, they were welcome to write to the Director, who would make enquiries. Sir Thomas Hetherington told me this demonstrated his independence from the Attorney General: he was in a different position from a Permanent Secretary who, by convention, has to leave to his minister the task of signing replies to questions from MPs.

The Prosecution of Offences Act 1985

The Crown Prosecution Service became a reality when Parliament gave its final approval to the Prosecution of Offences Act 1985, in May of that year. Leon Brittan MP, who was then Home Secretary, greeted it as a 'timely and beneficial reform of the criminal justice system'. He said he wanted to pay tribute to members of all parties 'for the constructive spirit in which discussions took place on the Bill. This,' said Mr Brittan, 'has made the Bill's remarkably quick progress through parliament possible. It is most unusual for so major a reform to reach the statute book before the end of May.'

An understanding of the 1985 Act is essential to any study of the Crown Prosecution Service; the Act also lays down, in many cases for the first time, some of the rules governing the Director of Public Prosecutions. Lawyers will have to look at the Act itself, but even they might find the following discussion useful; and non-lawyers should find it a little more readable than the statute. I shall take it section by section.

Section 1 establishes the Crown Prosecution Service, headed by the Director of Public Prosecutions. Crown Prosecutors in the new service have to be solicitors or barristers: they work to a Chief Crown Prosecutor for each area. 'Every Crown Prosecutor shall have all the powers of the Director as to the institution and conduct of proceedings but shall exercise those powers under the direction of the Director.' And if a statute says (as about 60 do) that no prosecution can be brought without the consent of the DPP, it is now sufficient for a Crown Prosecutor to give his consent.

Section 2 says that the DPP is to be appointed by the Attorney General: in the past the appointment was the Home Secretary's responsibility. The Director must be a barrister or solicitor of not less than ten years' standing; no other qualities (patience, tact, understanding . . .) are prescribed by statute.

Section 3 confirms that the Director acts under the 'superintendence of the Attorney General'. No attempt is made to explain this phrase (which I shall be discussing in Chapter 10). As head of the Crown Prosecution Service, the Director is given a number of duties: to take over proceedings instituted on behalf of a 'police force'; to institute criminal proceedings where he thinks it is appropriate (because the case is important or difficult, or for any other reason); to take over certain other proceedings; to advise police forces on 'all matters relating to criminal offences'; to appear for the prosecution as the respondent in certain appeals; and to do anything else the Attorney General asks him to.

The definition of 'police force' is important: it includes the 43 ordinary 'county' police forces in England and Wales together with 14 of the major specialized forces named in regulations — the British Transport police; the Dover Harbour Board police; the docks police at Falmouth, Felixstowe, Manchester and Milford; the Mersey Tunnel law enforcement officers; the Ministry of Defence police; the Port Police at Bristol, Liverpool, London and Tees and Hartlepool; the Royal Parks Constabulary; and the UK Atomic Energy Authority Constabulary. (Curiously, the two London forces are also included in the regulations after someone, we may presume, woke up in a cold sweat one night and realized that the 'Met' and the City police might not have been covered by the definition of 'police force' in the statute.) However, some of the smaller and more picturesque — not to say bizarre — police forces do not have to have their cases 'taken over' by the Crown Prosecution Service: they include the Brighton Parks Police, the Yeoman Warders at the Tower of London, the Oxford and Cambridge University constables, the Epping Forest Rangers, the London Borough of Barnet Dog Handling Section (I kid you not), and the men whose job it is to stop you picking the flowers at Kew Gardens.

A rather more important exception relates to public bodies like the Inland Revenue and HM Customs and Excise: since they are not police forces they can in theory ignore the Act and prosecute people in circumstances where a similar police prosecution would be thrown out by the Crown Prosecutor. They are, however, expected to follow the Director's Code (explained in Chapter 7), and the Director — or indeed your friendly local Crown Prosecutor — can take over the proceedings at any time and stop them (see Section 6). The Director does not have to 'take over' cases specified in regulations made by the Attorney General: these are mainly minor traffic offences where the accused is allowed to plead guilty by post.

Section 4 gives a Crown Prosecutor the same right to appear in court as a practising solicitor. At the moment that means the Crown Prosecutor can appear in the magistrates' courts but not the Crown Court. Even if the Crown Prosecutor has been called to the Bar he is not allowed to speak in the Crown Court; as an employed barrister he is not allowed to represent his employer in court.

Section 5 allows the Director to appoint solicitors as agents; also eligible are barristers employed by a public authority. The section gives these lawyers the powers of a Crown Prosecutor, but adds that they must exercise their powers subject to any instructions given by a full-time Crown Prosecutor. This section therefore allows the Crown Prosecution Service to use free-lancers to cover, for example, during temporary staff shortages or in outlying rural courts which do not sit very often. But it also enabled the Service to keep going in areas like London where recruitment of enough experienced full-time prosecutors was impossible, at least on the rates of pay offered to begin with. Another purpose was explained in the unpublished police briefing guide: 'the section,' it said, 'will help to avoid duplication in those areas where a public authority or agency such as HM Customs and Excise and the police are both involved in prosecuting an offender at the same time for separate but related offences. In that situation, it may be sensible for the new service to conduct the prosecution; or for the Customs and Excise solicitor to do so. But it would not make sense for both bodies to have to be involved. This section enables them to make whatever arrangement seems best in the circumstances'.

Section 6 preserves the right to bring private prosecutions. As we have seen, the Director only has to take over police prosecutions: private individuals and public bodies like the Customs and Excise can still prosecute people if they want to. But there is a catch, and a big one: the Director can take over any proceedings at any time. He can carry on with the prosecution or he can offer no evidence. So you still have the right to prosecute me if you want to, but the Director — or of course any Crown Prosecutor — has the power to stop you if he does not think you should. (I shall be discussing private prosecutions in Chapter 9.)

Section 7 will only be used in very exceptional circumstances. Normally, in cases sent by magistrates for trial by jury, the papers are sent by the magistrates' court direct to the Crown Court. This section enables the Crown Prosecutor to intercept the papers before they get there. That might happen if the Crown Prosecutor wanted to see the papers in a private prosecution before it got to the Crown Court. If, however, a private prosecution which was started in the magistrates' court is withdrawn or not proceeded with reasonably quickly — and there appears to be no satisfactory reason — the clerk must let the Crown Prosecutor know. This gives the Crown Prosecutor the chance to take over an abandoned private prosecution if he thinks it is in the public interest to proceed.

Section 8 allows the Attorney General to make regulations instructing police forces to tell the Crown Prosecution Service about crimes of certain types in their areas where there is an arguable case for starting proceedings. The police will, of course, send the papers to the Crown Prosecutor in every case where they think there should be a prosecution. What this section will do — if and when Regulations are made — is to oblige the police to send details to the Crown Prosecutor of cases even if they have not instituted proceedings. The police might take the view that they do not have enough evidence for there to be a realistic prospect that the defendant will be convicted. But if they nevertheless still think there is an arguable case ('prima facie' is the phrase used in the statute) then under the Regulations they would have to send the papers to the Crown Prosecutor for an independent review of the police decision *not* to prosecute. The section is really only intended for serious cases where the police are unsure about going ahead, but in practice the police will normally take the Crown Prosecutor's advice in such a case without the need for a rule telling them to.

Section 9 orders the Director to make an annual report to Parliament. The first one covers the year ending 4 April 1987. The Director's annual reports are to be published, thus resuming a practice which operated from 1886 to 1915. The Home Office expects the Director's annual report to be debated in Parliament 'in the early years'.

Section 10 orders the Director to publish a Code for Crown Prosecutors.

The Code guides Crown Prosecutors on the general principles they must apply in deciding whether proceedings for an offence should be started; or, where proceedings are already under way, in deciding whether they should be discontinued. These guidelines and any subsequent changes are published in the Director's annual report to Parliament. The Code for Crown Prosecutors is discussed in Chapter 7, and the full text is printed at the end of this book.

Section 11 deals with transfer of staff from the old prosecuting solicitors' departments to the Crown Prosecution Service.

Section 12 creates a Staff Commission to safeguard the interests of the Director's new employees.

Section 13 allows the new service to use for up to ten years (and pay for) accommodation previously used by prosecuting solicitors' departments. The long-term plan is that the Crown Prosecutor and his staff should not be in the same building as the local police, in order to emphasize their independence.

Section 14 allows the Attorney General to make regulations setting fees for barristers briefed to appear for the Crown Prosecution Service.

Section 15 is an interpretation clause.

Sections 16 to 21 make up Part II of the Act, and deal with costs in criminal cases. The main innovation is that the Crown Prosecution Service is no longer awarded the costs of a successful prosecution from central funds, because the service is paid for by Parliament anyway. Other public authorities cannot claim costs from central funds either, but private prosecutors can get a reasonable amount to compensate them for the expenses they properly incur. The courts have ruled that this does not include reimbursement for time spent preparing a case.

For the first time awards of costs are available, at the court's discretion, to people acquitted of summary offences by the magistrates: the power to award costs from central funds was previously confined to people acquitted in the magistrates' courts of charges which they were entitled to have tried by a jury. The Crown Court may award costs to an acquitted defendant, and the higher courts may award costs on a successful appeal. These costs are payable out of central funds.

To give the courts more control over the conduct of the proceedings, the Act introduces new powers to make either a prosecutor or a defendant who is responsible for 'an unnecessary or improper act or omission' pay costs incurred by the other side. If there is an award of costs against a Crown Prosecutor — which he will have to pay from his own budget — it is bound to be seen as a public criticism of the service. Convicted defendants, in addition to any other penalty imposed on them, may be ordered to pay the Crown Prosecution Service such costs as the court considers 'just and reasonable.' Like other government departments, the prosecution service is clearly expected to extract what money it can from its victims, distasteful though it may sometimes be. After all, convicted defendants do not have to pay the costs of the police officers who arrested them or the prisons which will incarcerate them. But the instructions from Queen Anne's Gate tell Crown Prosecutors to ask for costs 'at every reasonable opportunity' — which means they need a good reason not to. One wonders if a Crown Prosecutor who was awarded costs against a brothel-keeper could be accused of living off immoral earnings. Probably not, because local prosecutors have to send the money they recover straight to headquarters: they can't set it off against local expenses.

Section 22 deals with the separate (though very important) subject of time limits in criminal proceedings. The long-term aim is for binding time limits to concentrate the minds of prosecutors by restricting the length of time defendants can be held in prison awaiting trial. Time limits have already been introduced in some areas.

Section 23 gives the Crown Prosecutor a new power to discontinue proceedings without the permission of a magistrates' court, though he has to tell the court his reasons for deciding to drop the case. He can discontinue cases which are heard in the magistrates' court before the court starts to hear prosecution evidence and he can discontinue cases to be heard in the Crown Court before the accused is sent for trial.

Although the prosecutor has to give his reasons to the court, he does not have to give any reasons to the accused person. But what he must do is to tell the accused of his right to have the proceedings continued. You may wonder why a person should object to his case being dropped. The reason is that a discontinuance is not an acquittal: a case can be reopened afterwards, if, for example, fresh evidence comes to light. On the other hand, if a case the prosecution wants to discontinue comes before the court, the Crown Prosecutor will normally offer no evidence, which will lead to an automatic verdict of not guilty and rule out any further proceedings in respect of the same offence. If the original arrest or charge attracted publicity, a defendant might also be keen to get a public acquittal in court rather than a notice of discontinuance in the post. So if he wants the case to continue he can tell the court (rather than the prosecutor) and the effect will be the same as if no notice of discontinuance had been issued.

The Crown Prosecutor's unfettered power to discontinue cases is fundamental to an independent prosecution service. Before this Act was passed, a prosecutor was able to withdraw a charge or summons, but for this he needed the permission of the court (which would not be granted unless the court was satisfied with the prosecutor's reasons for wanting to withdraw the case). The prosecutor also had the power to offer no evidence, which would produce a verdict of not guilty. Both these powers remain available, but need the prosecutor's attendance at a court hearing. The new notice of discontinuance does not, and can therefore be used at any time. By avoiding unnecessary court appearance a notice of discontinuance can save both sides money.

Section 24 enables the courts to stop people deemed to be 'vexatious litigants' from bringing criminal prosecutions without the permission of

Right Sir Theobald Mathew, DPP 1944-1964.

Below Sir Norman Skelhorn, DPP 1964-1977.

Below right Sir Thomas Hetherington, DPP 1977-1987.

Left John Wood, Director-Designate, Serious Fraud Office.

Below left David Gandy, Deputy Director of Public Prosecutions.

Below Sir Michael Havers at work in the Law Courts shortly before the end of his eight-year office as Attorney General. (*The Times.*)

Right Sir Thomas Hetherington presenting the British Empire Medal to Mickey Moore, Senior Security Officer at Queen Anne's Gate, 1987.

Below right Sir Thomas Hetherington caught in an unguarded moment by *The Times* photographer, surrounded by the mounting piles of paper which pass through the DPP's office.

Above Geoff Kenton, the Director's Press Officer.

Below Sir Thomas Hetherington with senior Headquarters staff and all Chief Crown Prosecutors, June 1986.

Crown Prosecution Service Headquarters, 4-12 Queen Anne's Gate.

Crown Prosecution Service Headquarters, rear view.

Above Headquarters nameplates: the old . . .

Above right . . . and the new.

Below Conference Room, Queen Anne's Gate.

Right Plaque showing the DPP Sports and Social Club emblem, presented to Sir Thomas Hetherington in January 1980 to mark the centenary of his department.

CENTRAL CRIMINAL COURT   1st October   SESSION 1910

Accused	Offence	Police Officer	County	Prisoner committed case there	County Allowance	Result

the High Court. This extends to criminal cases the existing restrictions on civil proceedings.

Section 25 confirms that any requirement for the Director or a Law Officer (the Attorney General or Solicitor General) to consent to a prosecution does not prevent the arrest of a person for that offence.

Section 26 allows documents signed by Crown Prosecutors to be used in evidence without further proof.

Section 27 requires the consent of the Crown Prosecution Service to any care proceedings where it is alleged that a child or young person has committed a criminal offence.

Section 28 removes the power of a judge to order a prosecution for perjury, although he can still send the papers to the DPP.

Sections 29 to 31 deal with regulations made under the Act; the cost of the Crown Prosecution Service (which, for the first time, is the Attorney General's responsibility); and the usual nuts and bolts required to bring the Act into effect.

Schedule 1 and regulations made under the Act mean that the Crown Prosecution Service does not need to send somebody to court just to read out a statement of facts when the accused is pleading guilty by post. That is now done by the magistrates' clerk, who also reads out any plea in mitigation. Nor is there any need now, as there once was, for a prosecutor to attend court where a defendant who has pleaded guilty by post turns up in court to watch the proceedings.

Building an Independent Prosecution Service

Acts of Parliament hardly ever come into effect immediately they are passed. Civil servants usually need time to tell people of their responsibilities under the new legislation, and to make sure there are enough people in the right places to do whatever it is Parliament has decided. It seems strange that officials appear unable to make their plans while the legislation is passing through Parliament, but they presumably take the view that you can never be sure what our uncontrollable legislators will do with the nicely measured clauses put before them by all-knowing civil servants. And why go to too much trouble when a Parliamentary defeat or even a general election can save you the bother?

So in May 1985, the Director of Public Prosecutions was faced with a major new Act which the government wanted to bring into effect in October of the following year. To be fair to Sir Thomas Hetherington, he had already been making his plans — particularly for the senior staff he wanted to recruit — even though he had no extra money available before the Act was passed and no statutory powers to spend any at that stage. But when the legislation was through he had only some 16 months before the Act was to come into effect — which did not seem very long to find 1,500 lawyers and all the support staff they needed. Some, of course, would move from the existing prosecuting solicitors' departments, but creating new civil servants out of old local government staff was also a fairly daunting prospect.

Worse still, the government wanted the Crown Prosecution Service up and running in some areas of England less than 11 months later. Those were the places where there were Metropolitan councils: they were being abolished from April 1986 and it would have been administratively awkward to find someone else to run the prosecuting solicitors' departments in the six months leading up to October 1986, when the Crown Prosecution Service was to be introduced throughout the country. In fact, because of the strong base of existing prosecuting solicitors, it proved relatively easy to get going on 1 April 1986 in Durham and Northumbria, Greater Manchester, Merseyside, South Yorkshire, the West Midlands and West Yorkshire. London was a different story though.

Planning the new service in 1985 and 1986 was the responsibility of a small team of officials within the DPP's office, some of whom worked remarkably long hours at the task. One of them told me afterwards that he in turn wanted to pay tribute to the Home Office officials who steered the Bill through Parliament and helped to plan the Crown Prosecution Service: Joan MacNaughton, who had been an Assistant Secretary to the Philips Royal Commission, and Bill Bohan, an Under Secretary at the Home Office, who chaired the inter-departmental Working Party which — as I mentioned earlier in this chapter — devised the final structure of the new service. In the early days there had been some reluctance in the Director's office to accept the expansion of a small, comfortable London office into a national prosecution service. At that time, I was told, the very strong commitment coming from the Home Office — coupled with the determination of Sir Thomas Hetherington and a few of his senior staff — was largely responsible for pushing the new service through.

The Crown Prosecution Service: Structure

Just before the Prosecution of Offences Act was passed, the government published a rather unusual document. It was a period when no self-respecting government department or lawyers' professional body was prepared to take policy decisions without the protection of a management consultants' survey. The Home Office was no exception: it had commissioned a firm called Arthur Andersen & Co to produce a bulky report offering advice on the structure, staffing and working methods of the new service (though not about staff numbers or pay). Full of terms like *quantitative relationships, project management, action research, methodology, flexibility of resource usage, case accountability, timeliness indicators, information technology, lawyer scheduling systems*, and even *multiple liaison*, it proved that lawyers are not the only people who cannot write plain English. The report was well received, and most of its recommendations were put into effect: nobody seemed too worried by the rather charmless language. So it is Arthur Andersen we have to thank for recommending that there should be a *Head of Field Management*. And what was he to do? Easy: 'the Field Management function will be responsible for the central resource management of the field'. But in implementing Andersen's recommendations the Director of Public Prosecutions managed to scrap the only clear, simple title which survived Andersen's attempt never to use one word where two would do. The term 'Team Leader' was felt to smack too much of social workers and playgroup organizers: at a very late stage it was replaced by the more impressive-sounding (though much more long-winded) title of Assistant Branch Crown Prosecutor.

I now want to tell you who's who in the Crown Prosecution Service, starting at the top of the pyramid. (There is also a chart at the end of this chapter to help you trace the family tree.) To make things easier, I will leave out the details of 'support services': secretarial, training, personnel, costs and management (which itself includes audits, computer systems, office equipment, design of forms, records and so on). These non-legal departments are, of course, essential to the work of the Crown Prosecution Service, but they can also be found in other areas of government (and indeed, that is where most of the staff came from). So I plan to concentrate on those jobs which are peculiar to the service itself.

The Director of Public Prosecutions is, of course, the top man in the Crown Prosecution Service, although naturally he is only concerned personally with a minute proportion of the cases with which it deals. Beneath him originally was a Head of Legal Services to deal with 'Headquarters cases' (which I shall be describing in the next chapter), a Head of Support Services who is also Principal Finance and Establishment Officer, and . . .

The Deputy Director, David Gandy. When I completed this book Mr Gandy was Head of Field Management, responsible for central management of staff outside Headquarters. His new title had not been confirmed, but he was shortly to take on the enlarged responsibilities I shall be explaining at the end of this chapter together with a team of Regional Directors. As Head of Field Management he had two Assistant Heads, Richard Williamson and Colin Hoad. All three men were Chief Prosecuting Solicitors in different parts of the country before joining the DPP's staff to set up and run the new service. They divided England and Wales into 31 areas (Andersen had called them 'districts') based on the 43 existing police force areas. There are fewer Crown Prosecution Service areas because some prosecution areas combine two of the police areas. This was done to ensure that the Crown Prosecution Service areas each deal with roughly the same amount of work. It was a difficult decision to take because it meant that in some areas the Director was going to have to decide which of the two existing chief prosecuting solicitors was to become the Chief Crown Prosecutor. London, on the other hand, has enough work by itself for three complete areas: Inner London, Outer London (North), and Outer London (South). Each of the 31 areas is headed by a . . .

Chief Crown Prosecutor, who is based centrally in his area. Andersen decided that he would liaise with police, court authorities and private lawyers: he also monitors local changes within the criminal justice system and uses his influence to make changes where desirable. For cases of appropriate difficulty or sensitivity, Andersen said the Chief Crown Prosecutor would decide personally whether or not to continue proceedings; he conducts key cases in the magistrates' court and refers certain cases up to Crown Prosecution Service Headquarters in London. He is also allowed the grave responsibility of talking to journalists. Each Chief Crown Prosecutor has responsibility for between two and five branches, which are generally located near the major Crown Court centres. And, not surprisingly, each branch is headed by a . . .

Branch Crown Prosecutor, who is generally responsible for prosecutions at his local Crown Court (and the magistrates' courts which feed cases into it). Andersen said the Branch Crown Prosecutor would undertake 'quality assurance reviews' of his prosecutors' decisions (in other words, he checks their work). In addition to attending court as an advocate and reviewing the more complex cases, Andersen decided that the Branch Crown Prosecutor would be responsible for taking on freelance lawyers to cover staff shortages. Branches are where the real work of the service is done, and the 86 Branch Crown Prosecutors have a crucial role. Beneath them may be two or more . . .

Assistant Branch Crown Prosecutors who, you will remember, were called 'Team Leaders' in the Arthur Andersen report. Assistant Branch Crown Prosecutors exist mainly in the bigger urban areas where there were formerly metropolitan councils: they carry a level of responsibility (and pay) equivalent to that of some rural Branch Crown Prosecutors. Andersen decided that Assistant Branch Crown Prosecutors would be responsible for supervising a team of prosecutors within a big branch, advising them on the more difficult cases (though not the very complex matters which are handled at a higher level). Whereas each Branch Crown Prosecutor in London is generally responsible for his own Crown Court, each Assistant Branch Crown Prosecutor is responsible for one or two magistrates' courts. Below each Assistant Branch Crown Prosecutor (or working direct to the Branch Crown Prosecutor in Branches without staff at Assistant level) are . . .

Senior Crown Prosecutors, each of whom has beneath him two or more . . .

Crown Prosecutors, who — despite being the lowest grade of legally qualified staff — have all the powers which until 1986 could only be exercised by the Director of Public Prosecutions and his Assistant Directors. That, at least, is the theory: the whole point of this elaborate structure is that the more difficult or important the decision, the higher up the ladder it will be taken. Andersen decided that the Crown Prosecutor would be responsible for reviewing all but the most complex cases to decide whether proceedings were appropriate, organizing the paperwork and strategy of the case, and presenting it in the magistrates' court. He liaises with the police officers on the case and the defence as appropriate. He presents an entire list of cases before the magistrates and drafts briefs to counsel. Andersen said the Crown Prosecutor, who has to be qualified as a barrister or a solicitor, should show an aptitude for advocacy, an ability to think quickly under pressure, sound legal judgment, and an ability to consider cases in terms of the public interest as well as in purely legal terms. Working with the legally qualified staff is a team of . . .

Law Clerks and other support staff who are involved in preparing cases and may attend court as part of the prosecution team. Andersen devised a scheme ranging from Chief Law Clerk (doing, under supervision, virtually all the work of a Crown Prosecutor); Assistant Chief Law Clerk (who prepares briefs to counsel in all but the most complex cases); Senior Law Clerk (with similar responsibilities in smaller offices); and Law Clerks (who also do paperwork, but generally under the supervision of senior clerks). Law Clerks, in Andersen's words, require no formal training or experience, though they must be 'bright, willing to learn, show sound judgment, and be capable of representing the prosecution interests with minimal supervision'. And supporting the entire structure I have just described are staff headed by a . . .

Chief Administration Officer, who is appointed in each of the 31 areas to support the work of the Chief Crown Prosecutor and his staff. Andersen said the Chief Administration Officer would be responsible for the area's finances: he is also in charge of personnel and training, accommodation and security, staffing and supplies. Andersen said he would 'be responsible for co-ordinating the branch performance indicators into [area] level summaries,' which presumably means he has to keep an eye on how well the staff are doing. He has no need of legal qualifications, but it is a measure of the crucial role played by the Chief Administration Officer that he reports direct to the Chief Crown Prosecutor.

Take-off

At the end of September 1986 the Crown Prosecution Service issued a press release which some of the more pessimistic staff in the DPP's office had never expected to see. *All of the 31 areas of the Crown Prosecution Service will be operational from next week*, it declared with pride. *The CPS will be operating in the 90 Crown Courts and the 620 magistrates' courts throughout England and Wales*, it proclaimed with satisfaction. Then, rather more cautiously, it added: *Encouraging progress has been made in the recruitment of staff: nearly 3,000 are now in post and more appointments are expected shortly.*

A year earlier, some of the people who had been planning the new service had viewed with 'trepidation and reserve' the question of whether 'London could be delivered at all as an entity'. The problem was not too bad outside London: many prosecuting solicitors formerly employed by local authorities or working in private practice took the plunge and became civil servants working for the Crown Prosecution Service. But in the capital there was nothing to build on: the Metropolitan Police Solicitor's Department, you will remember from the *Historical Origins* section at the beginning of this chapter, was not as independent of the police as the prosecuting solicitors' departments in some other major cities had been: the vast bulk of prosecuting in London was being done by the police themselves. David Gandy described this as an archaic system which had been abolished in the major metropolitan areas by the early 1970s.

So during 1986 an enormous amount of effort was put into finding accommodation for the Crown Prosecution Service in London, and staff to run it. The effort was only partially successful. When the service officially started on 1 October 1986, just 46 per cent of the lawyers' jobs in London had been filled: 147 out of 318. The figures for England and Wales as a whole were rather better: 1,187 lawyers had been appointed out of a complement of 1,591, about 75 per cent of the figure set by the Treasury. But even among the non-legal staff there were still more than 250 vacancies: by 1 October, 85 per cent of the non-legal complement had been appointed in England and Wales. Totting these figures up you get a complement of 3,724 jobs: but on 1 October only 2,993 — or 80 per cent — had been filled. Sir Thomas Hetherington acknowledged that this was not the 'de luxe' service he would have wished for.

There were a number of reasons, beginning of course with pay. When the civil service began recruiting staff in 1986 the starting salary for a Crown Prosecutor began at £10,500, though recruits could join the pay scale at varying points up to a maximum of £15,000. The pay was increased later in 1986 to a scale running from £11,130 to £15,900. Senior Crown Prosecutors originally got between £13,505 and £18,360: their pay was increased to between £14,318 and £19,465. Assistant Branch Crown Prosecutors could get up to £24,000. In addition, staff working in the capital received a London weighting of up to £1,365 a year — a negligible advantage compared with the massive extra costs involved in finding somewhere to live in the south-east. The Solicitor General, Sir Patrick Mayhew, told the civil service trade unions in November 1985 that, although everyone agreed that the aim was to attract and retain people of the necessary high quality, he wanted to avoid a 'pay bonanza' at the taxpayer's expense with people being recruited from prosecuting solicitors' departments to do the same work for more pay. Sir Patrick was convinced that — while some lawyers could earn much more money elsewhere — the Crown Prosecution Service was paying enough to get good enough staff. Others said privately that more money would have attracted better people, particularly in London where the problem was at its worst.

More important than pay were career prospects: though a Crown Prosecutor had a good chance of being promoted to Senior Crown Prosecutor (at least a 50 per cent chance, a very good chance really, because there are two Crown Prosecutors to every Senior Prosecutor), prospects of promotion to the higher grades were not so attractive.

Recruitment turned out to be a problem of quality rather than numbers: many of the qualified people who applied simply were not up to the job. Advertisements said 'young lawyers of the highest calibre' were needed to join the Crown Prosecution Service: would-be prosecutors were told that few legal careers could offer a 'broader or more challenging caseload, combining unique advocacy experience with the opportunity to shape what is effectively a whole new service'. The phrase 'young lawyers' was used advisedly: many of the new recruits were still in training or had only just qualified.

What sort of people was the Crown Prosecution Service looking for? 'You're looking for a sound academic lawyer,' said the Head of Field Management, David Gandy. 'But that isn't the be-all and end-all. You're looking for people with common sense, you're looking for people who have courtroom presence, people who gain respect in court by showing they know when to ask a question and when not to ask a question. And we are looking for prosecutors not persecutors,' he stressed: a prosecutor, he said, was 'someone who was fair minded'.

Michael Chance, Assistant Head of Legal Services, told me the Crown Prosecution Service had not been looking for people with particularly good academic results:

> The cynical person might say that's because people with good academic backgrounds don't apply to join the Crown Prosecution Service — not true. I personally find myself totally unmoved by a first class degree at one end of the scale, or a third at the other — not being a graduate at all myself, which I've never found a handicap in the prosecution business. I think you can tell in a 45-minute interview remarkably well whether a person has got what it takes, and I think you can tell whether a person is genuinely articulate — which is plainly important — by asking a few 'what would you do in this situation?' questions: you can get a good impression of whether the intuitive judgment is there and you can certainly get an impression of whether somebody thinks quickly. In an odd sort of way, a good academic brain and quick thinking don't necessarily go together. You've got to conduct a case with one eye on the Bench to make sure the magistrates are following every point that's made, so you don't want to conduct the thing on a high intellectual plane. You've got to think on your feet: you can't plan the way you're going to cross-examine a defendant in advance, because the chances are you don't know what his story is going to be in advance. So you've got to spot the weak spots as the thing proceeds, and we look for somebody who's nimble on his feet.

With the staff shortages I have mentioned, the Crown Prosecution Service relied heavily on 'agents' — freelance lawyers paid by the day. They were not meant to decide whether or not a case was to go ahead, although in practice they sometimes took the more straightforward decisions themselves. Generally, though, they were engaged to do the day's 'list' of cases in the magistrates' court and, not surprisingly, they expected to be paid as much as they would be getting for doing defence work in the same courts. The maximum a solicitor could get for a day's work was £250, but I was told this would only be paid to a senior profit-sharing partner: the normal solicitor's fee ranged between £175 and £240. Barristers were getting rather less, because they have lower overheads.

Although it was always intended that agents should be used to deal with temporary staff shortages or to cover occasional busy periods there is no doubt that over-reliance on agents is bad for the Crown Prosecution Service. They cost more than staff, of course, but the problem goes deeper: if Crown Prosecutors have to spend all their time in the office doing paperwork while somebody else does the advocacy they will not end up as very good prosecutors; worse still, the Crown Prosecution Service will eventually lose control over the prosecution process.

Another, more controversial, solution to the problems of staff shortages was to move Crown Prosecutors on secondment for a month at a time into areas where they were needed most, such as London. David Gandy told me that 'cross-fertilisation' in this way benefited the service by giving country prosecutors experience of work in urban areas (just as the use of agents brought a broader range of experience into the service). But the prosecutors' trade union, the Association of First Division Civil Servants, said the system of secondment was over-stretching the resources of the areas which provided the staff, which then meant they in turn had to rely on agents. It also cost the service £52 a night in allowances for every lawyer brought to London. Reports in *The Times* claimed that Crown Prosecutors were being 'press-ganged' into going South. These allegations were firmly denied: everyone who had come to London was a volunteer, I was assured. But there were persistent rumours that going to London for a month would improve a Crown Prosecutor's chances of promotion, while refusal could count against him.

Staff shortages also meant that some lawyers had to work long hours. In December 1986 the Association of First Division Civil Servants — the trade union representing around 600 lawyers in the Crown Prosecution Service — announced that some of its members had 'become so angry about the excessive hours they are being asked to work' that the union was asking prosecutors in nine areas to vote on a plan to ban compulsory Saturday working. In January 1987 the union announced that its members in those areas had given overwhelming support to a proposed strike on Saturdays, but at the last moment the Crown Prosecution Service improved its offer of £1,000 a year to staff for being available one Saturday in two, and the strike was called off.

Meanwhile, Sir Thomas Hetherington had been trying to persuade magistrates and their clerks to reduce the number of cases heard on a Saturday. Clearly some courts will always have to sit on Saturdays to deal with overnight arrests, but the Director was against the policy of some clerks who deliberately listed cases for hearing at the weekend even though they could have been heard during the week.

In general, David Gandy took a long-term view of recruitment problems: rather than engage anyone who came along, he preferred to recruit lawyers with the potential to do the job well, even if that meant accepting younger and less-experienced people, and even though the fruits of this policy might not be seen for three to five years. It had taken more than a hundred years to get a national prosecution service, and he felt they deserved a year or two to get the new system right. What he was careful not to say was that some of the lawyers who had been working in prosecuting solicitors' departments until 1986, and who therefore had the right to transfer into the Crown Prosecution Service, would not necessarily have met the stringent criteria Mr Gandy had set for new recruits to prosecution work.

Should the Crown Prosecution Service launch have been delayed for six months or more, if only in London? Some senior figures in the service said this would have made all the difference. But David Gandy thought not: it would have been a blow to morale and would not have achieved anything. The Solicitor General, Sir Patrick Mayhew, agreed: he had put a great deal of personal effort into getting the Crown Prosecution Service off the ground and he had not been prepared to listen to people who told him the service could not be delivered in the relatively short period of time available.

The Police View

In the Spring of 1986, Maurice Buck, the Chief Constable of Northamptonshire who was also speaking for the Association of Chief Police Officers as Chairman of its Crime Committee, told me he welcomed the new division of responsibility between the police and the prosecution: 'My own personal view — it varies of course between chief constables — but my own personal view is that it is a very sound principle.'

Mr Buck agreed that some police officers had been worried about losing the power to decide on prosecutions. In the early stages there had been quite considerable concern over the proposal, he told me. But he had not shared this concern, and he saw advantages for the police in being able to shift the responsibility of decision making on to someone else's shoulders. In the past, there had been a great deal of criticism directed at the quality of police prosecution decisions — often unfairly, he said — and he thought that some of this might now be deflected on to the Crown Prosecution Service.

Chief Inspector John Symington, the Crime Manager at Bow Street police station in London, was probably the first senior police officer in the country to see how the Crown Prosecution Service would work in practice. A pilot scheme began operating at Bow Street and the adjoining magistrates' court in October 1985. Before then, when he came to work in the morning, Chief Inspector Symington would probably have found he had five or six CID officers on duty. But the first thing he had to do, before allocating the crime load or dealing with overnight arrests, was to find out which officers would have to attend court. Probably three or four, or possibly all five or six, might have to be at the magistrates' court that morning to object to bail or for some other reason. Once the Crown Prosecution Service started work, all his officers were freed to take up their work load for the day, which he said amounted to an enormous saving in police time.

Launching the new service in the autumn of 1986, Sir Thomas Hetherington said that the police, 'having had initial misgivings about the whole of the Crown Prosecution Service, have been extremely co-operative. They've helped us with our pilot schemes, they've arranged liaison all over the country which has proved extremely valuable'.

A few months later, I happened to be speaking to a senior officer in the Metropolitan Police — in the presence of the Branch Crown Prosecutor responsible for prosecutions in his area. Relations between the two men

— the policeman much older than the prosecutor — seemed genuinely cordial: the police officer was keen to discuss certain problems with the prosecutor, but in private and over lunch.

Yes, said the officer, the Crown Prosecution Service had freed some of his constables from attending court, but there was now more paperwork to be done and it was true that some police officers took less trouble over the prosecution documents than before as they no longer had any personal interest in getting a conviction: it was not 'their' case any more.

And attempts to do away with police officers in court had backfired in some areas. One advantage of arranging for lawyers to appear in court, rather than policemen, was that there would be fewer navy blue uniforms around the court buildings: the police would not look as if they ran the place and the old title for the justices' bench of 'Police Court' might finally disappear. But, in some areas of London at least, this had led to problems of security. In the old days, there were generally enough burly men around to stop a defendant jumping over the dock and making a run for it: now, police officers have to be brought in specially to keep the peace — and the defendants.

The police officer to whom I spoke conceded that some of his staff were resentful when their cases were dropped by prosecutors. But he said that this had been happening since 1983, when the Attorney General's guidelines were first issued to the police. 'We always followed the advice of the Metropolitan Police Solicitor's Department,' he said, while acknowledging that the solicitors only saw the papers in a small minority of cases. And, as more and more new officers were recruited, there would soon be a nucleus of young constables who could remember nothing from before the Crown Prosecution Service was introduced.

At this point a lively young detective from the Heathrow Airline Ticket Fraud Squad came up to introduce himself to the Branch Crown Prosecutor. The two men had spoken on the telephone a few days earlier when the officer wanted advice on whether he should fly to Los Angeles to interview a prospective witness: the prosecution service had told him to go ahead and the officer now wanted to thank the prosecutor for advice which, not unnaturally, the CID man was pleased to receive. It was the first time this officer had needed to ask for advice; in the past, he would have spoken to somebody at the police solicitors' department. He was reassured by the approach taken by the Crown Prosecution Service. The officer then suggested tentatively that the Branch Prosecutor might care to designate one or two of his staff to deal with all cases of airline fraud: those prosecutors could then be initiated into the mysteries of ticketing. The Branch Prosecutor thought this was a good idea; indeed, he was just beginning to reach the staffing levels where such arrangement would become possible.

Six months after the Crown Prosecution Service started full operation in London I went to see Deputy Assistant Commissioner Michael Huins of the Metropolitan Police. He works in Specialist Operations at Scotland Yard, and was the police liaison officer with the Home Office when the Crown Prosecution Service was being set up; he continued this role once the service was under way. He confirmed that initially some policemen found it a little difficult to accept that a job they thought they had been doing very well had been taken away from them. Some enjoyed advocacy, and thought they were good at it:

> But I'm sure that they now understand fully what the Crown Prosecution Service is all about and they've come to terms with it: I think it's working better and better. There were some cases in the early days where the liaison between the Crown Prosecution Service and ourselves was a little bit lacking, and maybe the officer in the case did not know why the case didn't go to court, or why if it did go to court it didn't result in a conviction. We've therefore worked hard at improving the lines of communication, so that we do understand the line the Crown Prosecution Service are adopting.

Mr Huins said that to begin with not all policemen had fully understood that if the Crown Prosecution Service, exercising the procedures that were laid down for it, decided that a certain type of case was better dealt with in a way other than by going to court, then the police had to accept that. He added that in due course this would influence the way in which the police reached a decision on whether or not to send a case forward to the Crown Prosecution Service.

It was interesting to find that the police are beginning to anticipate decisions of the Crown Prosecution Service. Even before the service started operation in London, the police were increasingly issuing cautions rather than prosecuting. And as the police learned what types of case were not likely to get past the Crown Prosecutor, either because of insufficient evidence or because a prosecution was not thought to be in the public interest, they were adapting their cautioning policy to the Code for Crown Prosecutors. Clearly, there is no point in sending a case on to the prosecutor if it is going to be dropped; better, say the police, not to send it to the prosecutor at all. Of course, this could mean that some cases which the Crown Prosecution Service would have taken on are not getting to them, but the police discretion to drop cases, which they have always had, is unaffected by removal of their power to prosecute.

How had the shortage of Crown Prosecutors, particularly bad in London affected the police? Mr Huins agreed that the service was not working as well as it might be if it had more of its own staff, and if it did not have to rely so heavily on agents:

> But the difficulties that were occasionally apparent, particularly in the early days, were caused by little problems of understanding and liaison; these have been identified and largely eliminated, and I think really the system is working a lot better than maybe some people are saying. A number of cases have been highlighted where it's alleged that things have gone wrong, and many of those have appeared only in the last month or two [this was the end of March 1987]. But I think that in almost every case, the instances on which they were based dated back to the early days last year when the service was starting up, and therefore the comments were not a true reflection of what was happening at the time they were being published.

I am confident that a few early problems have been eliminated, and the system is really working reasonably well.

This support, though slightly qualified, must come as music to the Crown Prosecutor's ears. But, as Mr Huins made clear, the Crown Prosecution Service had a somewhat uncertain take-off.

Signs of Turbulence

Once the Crown Prosecution Service had cleared the runway, its supporters watched anxiously to see if it could stay in the air. From time to time there were signs of turbulence, such as the November 1986 issue of *Legal Action*, a magazine read more by defence lawyers and legal aid firms than by prosecutors, which carried a report of the difficulties some defence solicitors were facing in the London magistrates' courts:

> The familiar tale . . . is of a Crown Prosecutor arriving at 10.25 a.m. for a 10.30 court, weighed down by a mass of case files which he or she has, in many cases, not had a chance to read. The prosecutor is responsible for all cases listed to be heard in a particular court in a morning or afternoon. Once the court is in session, therefore, defence lawyers complain that they have very little chance of speaking with the prosecutors. Under the old system, a police Court Presentation Officer would often deal with more than one case, but he or she was not solely responsible for an entire court list. The Court Presentation Officers would be familiar with their cases and accessible for discussions with the defence over issues like bind-overs and bail. This is no longer possible because the prosecutors are tied up in court all the time. Instead there is a rather furtive system of passing notes to the prosecutor in the hope that he or she will snatch a moment to read them.

The result of this was that magistrates kept having to grant brief adjournments. But one stipendiary magistrate told me this was no worse than what had happened under the old system when the appropriate Court Presentation Officer was often tied up in another court at the crucial time.

Another sign of turbulence was a half-page spread at the beginning of December in the *Daily Telegraph*, a paper not hitherto known for its criticism of the government's law and order policy, under the headline *Serious concern on under-staffing, under-funding, and damaging administrative bungling*. The feature said the Crown Prosecution Service had been greeted with a chorus of criticism from police, lawyers and magistrates, and it repeated complaints about the way cases had been handled by prosecutors in court.

Sir Thomas Hetherington strongly disputed the charges of incompetence levelled at the service: he said there had been a tendency, especially on the part of those who had opposed its creation, to blame it for any hiccup or delay in court proceedings. And this was confirmed by Sir Patrick Mayhew: during the course of the visits he made to Crown Prosecution Service areas up and down the country, he was told by one magistrate that there had been no prosecutor in court on one occasion. He investigated the complaint, and told me the explanation was simple: the magistrates had finished sitting at a juvenile court earlier than expected and wanted to use their remaining time on cases they had not been expected to hear.

The *Telegraph* article also quoted complaints from the police: 'the lack of resources and consequent under-staffing had led to a series of blunders, some of them causing prosecutions to be dropped or jeopardised,' it said; and gave examples. On the other hand, it was not unknown for files which the police accused the prosecutors of having lost to turn up in police stations. The Solicitor General, Sir Patrick Mayhew, suspected that behind some police criticism was a complaint that the service was doing its job too well: the police were never going to be happy if a man they had arrested was set free by the prosecutor, but that was precisely why an independent prosecution service had been created in the first place. And it was perhaps not surprising that the criticisms in the *Telegraph* article all came from the London area: as I have said, it had the worst staffing problems, but it was also an area where the police had been doing their own prosecutions up until two months earlier, and the shock of the new system was bound to be more pronounced.

Sir Patrick Mayhew was, however, genuinely concerned about complaints that papers were going astray, and he persuaded the Treasury to provide more money for administrative staff so that lawyers would not have to worry so much about the paperwork. It was announced that in the year 1987/88 the complement of non-lawyers would be increased by around 550, with the largest number going to Inner London. Sir Thomas Hetherington said that when the posts were filled it would be a welcome relief for Crown Prosecutors who would then be able to devolve some of their administrative burden. This would give them more time to get on with the job they were employed to do — casework. The Director added that in some areas of England and Wales the increased complement could go some way towards cutting down on the use of outside agents to stand in for Crown Prosecutors.

The complement of lawyers was also increased for 1987/88 from about 1,520 to about 1,730. This would also help in some areas, particularly if it meant lawyers could be recruited in those parts of the country where it was not too difficult to find staff and then seconded to places like London for a while. Areas like Avon and Somerset, Devon and Cornwall, Cumbria and Lancashire, South Yorkshire, Cleveland and North Yorkshire, Norfolk and Suffolk, and Cheshire had managed to recruit all the lawyers they were entitled to. But in another sense, increasing the complement made the problem appear worse, as the proportion of unfilled jobs would rise, at least to begin with. It came as no surprise to see that Inner London was the one place in England and Wales where there was to be no increase in the lawyers' complement. In March 1987 half the jobs were still unfilled — there were 75 in post out of a complement of 152 — and increasing the theoretical complement must have seemed pretty pointless. But Sir Thomas Hetherington denied the suggestion that this was because the existing vacancies in Inner London were unlikely to be filled in the months and perhaps even years ahead. It was simply that the complement originally agreed for London was thought to have been right.

There were 1,237 lawyers working for the Crown Prosecution Service in February 1987. Of these, 922 were solicitors and 315 were barristers.

Yet another sign of turbulence at the beginning of 1987 was a half-hour edition of *The London Programme* about the Crown Prosecution Service on London Weekend Television. The programme raised some interesting issues — in particular, whether the service would be more efficient, and more acceptable to the police, if the prosecutor rather than the policeman was responsible for bringing the initial charge. The point is that it is easier not to charge a defendant in the first place than to drop a charge which has already been brought; and when charges are dropped by the prosecution there is inevitably an implicit criticism of the police decision to bring the original charge. Against that, for the Crown Prosecution Service to bring the charge you would either need an experienced prosecutor in every police station 24 hours a day, or you would have to keep prisoners in custody for much longer to await being charged.

After the programme had been transmitted, Sir Thomas Hetherington wrote to London Weekend Television accusing the programme of 'lack of balance, misrepresentation, selectivity, and inconsistency'. Barry Cox, Controller of Features and Current Affairs at the television station, rejected the charge of unbalanced and distorted reporting. But he said he believed the programme should not have dropped two of the answers Hetherington had given to questions about the underlying problems facing the Crown Prosecution Service. Cox told Hetherington:

> This would have given the programme a more considered finish, and not left viewers wondering what your views on these issues were. I am sorry that this error of judgment was made; I do not however consider it justifies the very strong criticism you made of the over-all tenor of the report.

In all this turbulence there was some comfort for the new service in an article by Ronald Bartle, a London stipendiary magistrate. He told his fellow justices that he thought the benefits of the new system fully justified its introduction. Writing in *The Magistrate*, Mr Bartle said that if the Crown Prosecutor was competent, cases were generally heard more quickly.

> Secondly, the principle that the police should not be advocates in their own cause must be a sound one. Thirdly, it liberates the police from attending court in minor cases and enables them to devote more of their time to their proper duties — policing. Finally, and very importantly, in contested cases the prosecution are always represented by a trained advocate.

Mr Bartle did see some dangers, in particular that too close a rapport might develop between the prosecution and the Bench. But he thought the difficulties could all be solved, and that magistrates 'should avoid excessive criticism' of the new service.

In the early months of the Crown Prosecution Service, no major disasters were reported. But this was hardly surprising: the type of cases which make headlines in the national newspapers are dealt with by experienced staff at headquarters rather than by newly recruited staff in local offices. The problems which beset the new service in its early months were more low-key — though still just as worrying to the individuals concerned. Take this example, told to me by a London solicitor who was doing agency work for the Branch Crown Prosecutor in his area:

A restaurant owner had left some valuables for some weeks in an unlocked safe. They went missing and he named a waiter who he said must have taken them. The waiter had by then returned to his native country, but he was arrested when, in due course, he returned to Britain. He denied the theft, but because he had no settled address here he was remanded in custody for 2½ months awaiting trial.

When the solicitor I spoke to saw the papers on the morning of the trial he immediately realized there was no evidence to support the restaurateur's claim: there was nothing to distinguish this waiter from all the others who might have taken the valuables. The solicitor telephoned the Branch Crown Prosecutor who said his staff had been too busy to read the case properly. The Crown Prosecutor immediately accepted the solicitor's advice and authorized him to offer no evidence. The defendant was acquitted, but was not entitled to any compensation for the time he had spent in custody — even though this was directly attributable to the prosecutor's failure to review the case earlier.

Writing in the barristers' journal *Counsel* at the beginning of 1987, Sir Thomas Hetherington said the new system of prosecutions had disturbed old well-established relationships which had developed for over a century.

Inevitably it takes time for the various bodies and individuals who are affected by the change to adapt to the new relationships. I have in mind in particular the relationship between the Crown Prosecution Service on the one hand, and the police and courts on the other . . . In a few instances, they may have resented the effect of the changes on their former responsibilities and *modi operandi*. Generally though, the challenge of adapting to new circumstances has been accepted in a most commendable spirit.

In the same journal the Attorney General, Sir Michael Havers, said it was important to think positively and not lose sight of how much had been achieved. He conceded that the Crown Prosecution Service was still 'substantially below its complement for legal staff': indeed at that time just 57 per cent of the lawyers' jobs in London as a whole had been filled (with Inner London even worse), and the figure for England and Wales was only about three per cent up on the October figure, at 78 per cent. But Havers thought the greatest danger at that time was of the Crown Prosecution Service being talked into being a second-rate service:

Although the Crown Prosecution Service has had to rely on private practitioners in a few areas to a greater extent than it would have wished, the fact is that it has achieved what was required of it . . . Early statistics suggest that a significant number of cases are being weeded out . . . and there is anecdotal evidence from some areas indicating helpful relief of the congestion in Crown Court lists. Ironically, it is the discontinuing of cases — one of the things the Crown Prosecution Service is meant to do — which has given rise to more complaints than any other single cause.

And Sir Michael Havers took the opportunity to respond to some of them:

We cannot complain when genuine shortcomings, which there are, are exposed. The irritation comes when the outpourings of a disgruntled junior police officer or intemperate but off-the-cuff remarks from the Bench — forensic shooting from the hip is not unknown — are translated for the benefit of the Great British Public into a story of impending collapse. Usually the Director gets no advance warning and is unable to provide an effective rebuttal at the time. Subsequent investigations reveal that the degree of truth in the story is inversely proportional to the size of the headlines.

No Clouds on the Horizon?

Speaking to me at the end of March 1987, Sir Thomas Hetherington acknowledged that the Crown Prosecution Service was still not yet a 'de luxe' service, simply because he had not been given the resources to create a service of that sort. 'It's been a pretty effective service, surprisingly effective,' he said, 'and it has in fact proved much better than I feared it would be.' But he accepted that over-reliance on agents in London and some other urban areas was expensive and inefficient: it also made it more difficult for the Crown Prosecution Service to solve problems which arose at court and for which, sometimes unfairly, the service was blamed. 'We conduct, now, rather more than a million cases a year, and there are always going to be a few that appear to go wrong,' he said, 'but the criticism of those cases has been blown up out of all proportion.'

At the end of March 1987 Sir Thomas Hetherington told his senior staff that he was proposing a major restructuring of his senior management. Difficulties had arisen because all 31 areas had to report to the Director through a narrow channel: the Head of Field Management and his Assistants. So the two Assistant Heads in London would be replaced by four Regional Directors. Not surprisingly, two of the new regional posts went to the existing Assistant Heads of Field Management: Richard Williamson took the Midlands post while Colin Hoad was to be Regional Director for the South West and Wales. Then Brian Crebbin was moved from Chief Crown Prosecutor, Greater Manchester, to Regional Director, North. And Robert Gwilliam moved from being the Inner London Chief Crown Prosecutor to the new job of Regional Director for London and the South East.

Sir Thomas Hetherington made it clear that Regional Directors would not do any casework themselves, but they would be responsible for the overall casework quality within their region. Chief Crown Prosecutors, on the other hand, 'need no longer be distracted by wider policy considerations' and so could be a grade lower than Regional Directors.

Under the new structure the four Regional Directors report to David Gandy. In that sense he retains his responsibility for Field Management. But he also takes on overall command of what used to be called Legal Services — in other words headquarters work — apart from the cases to be dealt with by the Serious Fraud Office. So Mr Gandy has a fifth person reporting to him, the Director of Headquarters Casework.

That post is to go to Marisa Phillips, who as a Principal Assistant Director and then an Assistant Head of Legal Services was initially only responsible for part of the Headquarters casework.

Michael Chance, who had only just become the other Assistant Head of Legal Services, was earmarked to become John Wood's deputy at the Serious Fraud office.

There's a chart at the end of this chapter to show you how it all works.

At the same time as announcing these staff changes Sir Thomas Hetherington revealed new plans for the Crown Prosecution Service itself. In the past he had been concentrating on finding staff and places for them to work. But now he was beginning to look a bit further forward. He announced that the Crown Prosecution Service had asked a firm of management consultants called Hay MSL to work out a 'strategic plan'. He issued a document to senior staff full of words that management consultants enjoy so much: 'action plans', 'strategic objectives', and of course 'goals'. There would be an 'annual planning cycle' consisting of the 'autumn strategic planning and resource review', and 'Spring bilaterals'. It all seemed to boil down to seeing how much money the Crown Prosecution Service could get out of the Treasury each year.

Meanwhile the 'initial strategy statement' was being prepared. There would, of course, be goals — four of them in fact. The Director summarized them for me (in plain English):

- Effectiveness was to be the first priority, coming before the other objectives of economy and efficiency.
- Attempts should be made to improve the standing and reputation of the Crown Prosecution Service by projecting a positive image of progress and achievement: the aims of the service were not always understood by people. The service would put the emphasis on initiatives rather than on responding to bad publicity — which in itself might help recruitment.
- Relationships with other institutions in the criminal justice system would be created and built on, taking full advantage of the uniformity and consistency which could result from the assistance of a nationally controlled service.
- As a long-term aim, the Crown Prosecution Service would seek to use its influence to improve the operation of the criminal justice system as a whole. Examples would be possible improvements in the committal process, or perhaps the system of court listing.

At first sight these proposals seem admirable. Certainly the Crown Prosecution Service is nothing if it is not effective. Certainly people should know how it works: that is the justification for this book. And certainly the

Crown Prosecution Service should try to achieve improvements in the criminal justice system: we are all in favour of making things better.

There is, however, more than a tinge of the public relations hype about all this. While every journalist is in favour of open government, it seems sad that public servants should have to sell their services by 'projecting a positive image of progress and achievement', especially if this means trying to brush proper criticism under the carpet: 'damage limitation responses' was a suggested strategic response. It is sadder still if an essential link in our system of justice can only get the resources it really needs by manufacturing a 'positive image of progress and achievement'.

And while we all know how much the criminal justice system needs improving, is it really the job of the Crown Prosecution Service to decide what improvements should be made? Perhaps the next Director of Public Prosecutions might think a prisoner's life could be made more pleasant provided all remand and committal hearings were abolished: if prison officers no longer had to spend so much time accompanying prisoners to court, warders would be able to spend more time supervizing free association in prisons. The government, on the other hand, might think prisoners would be at risk of being beaten up if they no longer had to appear in public while on remand. What right would the Crown Prosecution Service then have to lobby against government policies? And while it is hard to think of a system of court listing which would be much worse than the present chaotic arrangements, let us just suppose the Crown Prosecution Service — or their tame management consultants — came up with a system which suited the prosecution's needs while making life very awkward for defence lawyers: why should its voice be heard just because it can shout the loudest?

The Crown Prosecution Service should concentrate its resources on ensuring only the right cases come to court. It should take no notice of public relations experts, management consultants or — I have to add — journalists who write books.

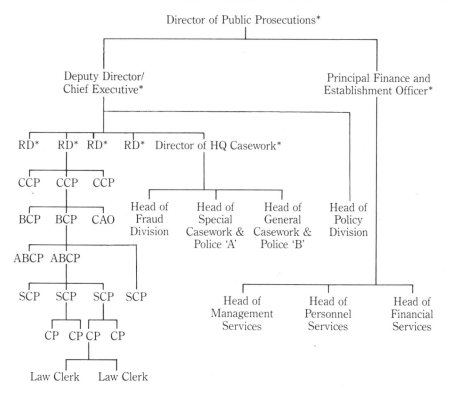

Notes:

*Members of the Board of Management.

RD = Regional Director. They are designated RD (North), RD (Midlands), RD London and the South East, and RD (South West and Wales). Each is responsible for an average of eight CCPs.

CCP = Chief Crown Prosecutor.

CAO = Chief Administration Officer.

BCP = Branch Crown Prosecutor.

ABCP = Assistant Branch Crown Prosecutor (some areas only).

SCP = Senior Crown Prosecutor.

CP = Crown Prosecutor.

This chart has been simplified by omitting most of the Headquarters staff and support staff.

Below the level of Regional Field Manager not all holders of each grade are shown.

Fraud Division is intended to deal with cases which are too difficult to be handled locally but not serious or important enough to go to the Serious Fraud Office.

Police work was divided geographically into two sections ('A' and 'B') but reorganization was expected, with a separate Head of Police Division.

FIVE

The Papers Have Been Sent . . .

As you will have seen in the last chapter, all police prosecutions since 1986 have been taken over by lawyers working for the Director of Public Prosecutions. Since the vast majority of cases are now handled by staff working in branch offices, you should now be seeing phrases like 'the papers have been sent to the Branch Crown Prosecutor'. But somehow that does not have quite the same ring to it. And as I shall be explaining in this chapter, the most important and difficult cases are still handled by a small staff working at the Director's London headquarters: most are based at Queen Anne's Gate and nearby offices in Westminster, and others are in offices off Holborn. So it is still correct to say that some papers, at least, are 'sent to the Director of Public Prosecutions.' But most of them never get as far as the Director himself. What then happens when the papers really *are* sent to the Director of Public Prosecutions?

CPS HQ

All correspondence addressed to the Director is delivered to the Registry, a large, open plan office which looks remarkably spacious in a building full of rather poky little rooms. A card index of all files is kept in three ancient contraptions known, because of their similarity in size and shape to the vats of boiling oil used in the more traditional fast food establishments, as 'fish fryers'. In due course they will be replaced by microfiches and even computers, but not quite yet.

Take the example of a police investigation into an IRA conspiracy. When the police have completed their enquiries they will send the DPP a summary of the case with their comments on the witnesses, as well as copies of the witnesses' statements, and copies of any documentary exhibits. When the papers arrive in the Registry a clerk will make out a card and send the file to the appropriate division, which in this example is the one called Special Casework. A different division handles General Casework which is too difficult, obscure, or important to be dealt with at branch level; and there are other divisions to deal with fraud, criminal allegations against the police, and departmental policy. I shall be looking at all of them in this chapter.

Each of these divisions is headed by a lawyer who would have been graded as an Assistant Director before the start of the Crown Prosecution Service to give him or her the statutory powers of the Director of Public Prosecutions — an arrangement that is no longer needed now that all Crown Prosecutors can exercise the Director's powers. The Heads of each division (formerly Assistant Directors) report in turn to the Head of Headquarters Casework, Marisa Phillips, who in turn is responsible to the Director's deputy, David Gandy. Formerly these divisions reported to the Head of Legal Services, a post which is to lapse when its holder, John Wood, becomes the first Director of the Serious Fraud Office (which I shall be explaining later in this chapter). For the time being Mr Wood remains Head of Legal Services, having been Deputy Director — the DPP's second-in-command — before the Crown Prosecution Service started work.

As Head of Legal Services, just as when he was Deputy Director, John Wood was responsible to the Director for the entire legal staff at Headquarters. But in 1986 the Director acquired another deputy, at the same level as the Head of Legal Services. The second Number Two was the Head of Field Management, responsible — as I explained in the last chapter — for all legal staff outside Headquarters. This division of responsibility was thought to be unsatisfactory, and it was decided in 1987 that in due course the Director would have just one deputy, David Gandy. He would combine Field Management (local offices, explained in the last chapter) with Legal Services (Headquarters work, discussed in this chapter).

I should also mention the Principal Finance and Establishment Officer, John Merchant. Like David Gandy, he reports direct to the Director, although his post is graded one notch lower. John Merchant is a key figure in the support structure; reporting to him are the Heads of Management Services, Personnel Services and Financial Services.

As you will have gathered, the Crown Prosecution Service management structure was undergoing major reorganization just at the time this book was being completed. But at the end of the previous chapter there is a chart which attempts to give you some idea of the structure as I think it will be by late 1987.

Our hypothetical IRA papers will probably be read first by the Head of Special Casework division. He or — as it happens — she will read the most important documents on the file and decide who among the lawyers in the division should deal with the case. Terrorist cases would be handled by experienced staff — barristers or solicitors of ten to fifteen years standing. In some cases the lawyer will take counsel's opinion on the evidence, though this happens more in cases of complicated fraud than in terrorist cases. The lawyer will read the case in detail, have a conference with the police officers in charge of the investigation, and write a note on the case summarizing the facts and any difficulties, together with recommendations on who, if anyone, should be prosecuted, and on what charges. The Head of Special Casework will then consider this note, have another look at the file if she needs to, and in a case of this importance (though not in a more straightforward one) will send the papers up to the Director of Headquarters Casework who will almost certainly read nearly all of the case to check that everything is in order, before she in turn sends it on to the Director's deputy for the final decision. How much *he* reads will depend on the quality of the notes sent up to him.

It surprised me to learn that the Director of Public Prosecutions himself would not take the final decision, even in an important terrorist case. 'I would always tell him about it,' said John Wood — who, as I have explained, was the Director's deputy in this area. 'I would certainly send the Director secrets cases,' said Mr Wood. 'In addition, I would always keep him informed of cases which were likely to hit the headlines, especially if the prospective defendant was a Member of Parliament.'

Sir Thomas Hetherington confirmed that he saw only a few cases himself, especially towards the end of his period in office when he was preoccupied with setting up the Crown Prosecution Service. Indeed, he thought his deputy was really taking over the casework job which had been done by the Director in the days before the Crown Prosecution Service, keeping the Director of Public Prosecutions informed in the same way as Sir Thomas Hetherington used to keep the Attorney General informed of cases which were likely to appear in the newspapers. Hetherington explained that the Official Secrets Act cases were not particularly difficult, but he kept tabs on them because he had a link with the Security Services, and they liked to deal direct with him: the Director has high level security clearance, of course — as indeed does his deputy. Sir Thomas Hetherington also dealt personally with espionage cases, cases involving important people, cases of political significance and national scandals. He would often learn of a case for the first time when he heard on the radio or read in his morning newspaper that the papers 'were being studied' by the Director of Public Prosecutions. This could be amusing — and it could also be very useful because if the case was in the headlines he would ask what it was all about, and get briefed by his staff on something that might not otherwise have reached him.

Many, though not all, of the cases which are most likely to concern the Director himself will have come from the Special Casework Division. Among its responsibilities I have already mentioned terrorist cases; it also deals with Public Order Act prosecutions, espionage and other Official Secrets Act cases, together with a number of cases which may be too rare and obscure to handle locally, such as election offences. And it deals with a subject which is far from obscure these days — the delicate topic of what to do when the criminals we in Britain want, or want to get rid of, travel abroad.

As you may remember from Chapter 4, all extradition cases have to be referred to the Crown Prosecution Service headquarters in London, although staff there hope that eventually some extradition papers will be prepared in local offices and then just sent on to London for approval. The type of case I am talking about at the moment is where somebody who is alleged to have committed an offence in this country has gone abroad: for the prosecutor to bring him before a court here he has first to get him back. But the Director also has an important and very different role when the extradition is to go in the opposite direction: he acts for a number of foreign governments who are trying to get people out of Britain to face trial abroad. Those cases, which are very specialized, are only handled by Headquarters staff in the Special Casework Division. I propose to tell you a little about each type of extradition.

Extradition: Getting them Back

Firstly, the cases where someone who is abroad is wanted here. The Crown Prosecutor will only apply for extradition if he thinks it is in the public interest to seek the return of a fugitive offender: what this means in practice is that the prosecutor will not bother unless the alleged offence is fairly serious. It is hard enough to get people extradited by other countries without wasting time on the trivial cases. Extradition is mainly based on bilateral treaties, but there are fewer than fifty of these in force between the United Kingdom and foreign countries. And as the government's Green Paper on Extradition in 1985 said, 'we have regular extradition traffic with only about a dozen of these'. Although the changes proposed in the Criminal Justice Bill 1987 would not have directly affected extradition from foreign countries to the United Kingdom, the government believed that if we made it easier for foreign countries to get their wanted men out of Britain, they would make it easier for us to get the people we want returned here. (That part of the Bill fell at the General Election in 1987.)

If the alleged offence is covered by a treaty between the United Kingdom and the country where the offender has taken refuge, and if the Director then decides to go ahead with an extradition application, he will usually seek the help of the Ministry of Justice or its equivalent in the foreign country. The Director's staff are in contact with professional colleagues in other countries who will normally handle the appropriate application to their local courts on the Director's behalf. Even though there is a Director of Public Prosecutions in the Irish Republic, he does not assist the English Director in extradition cases: that job is done by the State Solicitor, who in turn will arrange for counsel to represent the British authorities. There is also a Director of Public Prosecutions for Northern Ireland, but he does not handle extraditions for foreign governments either: the job there is done by the Crown Solicitor.

Extradition between Commonwealth countries may be slightly easier: to emphasize the links that exist within the Commonwealth, and the fact that extradition is governed by informal arrangements between Commonwealth countries rather than by treaties, member countries talk about 'rendition' and 'returnable offences' rather than 'extradition' and 'extraditable offences'. One attempt to make extradition between Commonwealth countries even easier was rejected in 1986 by a meeting of Commonwealth Law Ministers in Zimbabwe: the ministers decided not to abolish the so-called prima facie rule, which I shall be explaining later in this section.

Extradition from the Irish Republic should be easier still. It applies to crimes punishable with six months imprisonment or more which are offences in both countries. All that is necessary to start the process in this country is for a magistrate to issue a warrant of arrest in the normal way. His signature is authenticated in another document and the papers are then sent to the Irish authorities who check that they are in the proper form. Next, an assistant commissioner in the Irish police will endorse the warrant and finally the person named in it will be brought before an Irish court which — if all goes well — will order his return to this country.

But of course it doesn't always go well. The Irish court is entitled to investigate whether the warrant is in the proper form. The Director received a great deal of adverse publicity in 1986 when a warrant issued for the arrest of the alleged IRA terrorist Evelyn Glenholmes was rejected — twice in one day — by an Irish court. Officials in the DPP's office were accused of carelessness in preparing the paperwork, but privately they felt that the Irish courts were determined not to send anybody back to the United Kingdom for trial. With the 'political' defence no longer available, it seemed that the Irish courts were finding other means of rejecting extradition requests. Officials did not think the Irish courts would go so far as to invent excuses for refusing extradition: if everything was perfectly in order they would indeed agree to send a defendant back. But they would lean over backwards to find a reason for refusing extradition. Sir Thomas Hetherington said that he could well understand that in Ireland there was a good deal of fear about what terrorists would do if courts agreed to extradition requests. He sympathized with Irish judges who were concerned for their own safety — and the safety of their families.

Hetherington felt the public criticism he had received in the Glenholmes case had been very unfair. There had been a technical error in his office, and even that, he said, did not invalidate the warrants in English law. And the Director rejected the allegation that his staff had spelled Glenholmes' name wrongly: 'in fact,' he said, 'the names on her birth certificate differed from her name on other documents. The names supplied by the Irish authorities were the ones which we put on the papers'. After the Glenholmes incident the Director announced that an internal enquiry would be held to see if anyone was at fault: no action was taken and the whole affair was quietly forgotten.

Extradition: Letting them Go

The Director has a very different role when the boot is on the other foot. He often advises and represents foreign governments which are trying to get alleged offenders out of the United Kingdom. A few foreign countries choose to instruct private firms of solicitors — some for historical reasons, others because they cannot believe that the Director is sufficiently independent of the British establishment to represent their interests fairly. He *is* independent, of course, although he remains a public servant and might decline to act for certain countries if to do so would cause the government political embarrassment.

Assuming, of course, that there is a treaty of some sort between the United Kingdom and the foreign country, the Criminal Justice Bill 1987 proposed ·new conditions under which a person in the United Kingdom who is charged with an 'extradition crime' in that country — or who is alleged to be unlawfully at liberty after being convicted there of such a crime — may be arrested here and returned there. An 'extradition crime' would cover anything which would amount to an offence punishable with a year's imprisonment or more in the United Kingdom *and* in the country seeking extradition. Certain offences committed outside the territory of the requesting country are also included, but the former concept of only allowing extradition for offences on an agreed list formed no part of the Bill's philosophy. Although the Bill was lost, something similar may be introduced in the future.

The procedure for getting somebody handed over by the British authorities is normally long and complicated (although there is now a simplified system to deal with people who consent to being extradited). First, the diplomatic representative here of the foreign country has to supply full details of the case to the Home Secretary. If he is satisfied he will then issue an 'authority to proceed'. This document may be taken to any London stipendiary magistrate, who can issue an arrest warrant. The fugitive is then brought before the magistrate who can grant bail or remand him in custody.

In more urgent cases any magistrate can issue a provisional arrest warrant. The magistrate then has to tell the Home Secretary who can, if he wishes, cancel the provisional warrant — and free the prisoner if there has been an arrest in the meantime. Alternatively, the Home Secretary can issue the authority to proceed and the case will then go ahead in the normal way.

Ultimately, if all the requirements I shall be describing have been met, the stipendiary magistrate may commit the person arrested, either in custody or on bail, 'to await the [Home Secretary's] decision as to his return to the foreign state that made the extradition request'.

A recent example of all this — under the original legislation, passed in 1870 — was the request in 1986 from the Belgian public prosecutor for the extradition of 26 football supporters to stand trial in Belgium on charges of involuntary manslaughter arising out of the Heysel Stadium disaster of 1985, in which 39 people died. The request went via the Belgian Foreign Ministry, the Belgian Embassy in London, and the Foreign Office to the Home Office. After the Home Secretary had issued an order to proceed, the papers then went to the Chief Metropolitan Magistrate at Bow Street court; he considered them and, in due course, decided to issue warrants for the 26 to be arrested and bailed to appear before his court. It was at this stage that the Director of Public Prosecutions became involved, arranging for one of the extradition lawyers from the Special Casework division, Mrs Helen Garlick, to represent the Belgian authorities in proceedings before the court.

The police had no trouble contacting 25 of the 26 defendants, who duly turned up at court: Mrs Garlick asked for the case to be adjourned for two months and the defendants were again given bail; the twenty-sixth man reported to police a few days later and was also bailed. Eventually the Bow Street Magistrate decided that all 26 cases would be heard together at another London courtroom, and seven months after the papers had arrived at the Home Office all the defendants, together with more than forty lawyers and five television monitors, squeezed in.

At the initial hearing an interesting aspect of the case had emerged. Under English law a British citizen accused of committing manslaughter (or murder) abroad may be tried in the English courts. Why then were these young men not being tried here?

The answer came from Michael Sherrard, QC, appearing at the extradition proceedings for the Belgian government:

> The fact is that the unlawful acts of which complaint is made were committed in Belgium and that the deaths which resulted took place in Belgium. The case has no realistic connection with England other than that the accused happen to be British subjects. In the circumstances the natural desire of the Belgian authorities to try these men in Belgium for the acts of wanton violence alleged to have been committed there has been respected. The Home Secretary, having considered the circumstances as a whole, considered that the Belgian government was justified in pursuing its request for extradition.

But if the Belgian government had been told that a prosecution was being mounted in this country it would presumably have been prepared to supply the Crown Prosecutor with the evidence it had collected; indeed some of the evidence had been obtained by the English police in the first place. Naturally, the British authorities would not have wanted to suggest that a defendant might not get a fair trial in an EEC country. But there was no denying the difficulties of an extradition application and the risk that it might not succeed: proceedings here — though very unusual in a case like this — would have been relatively simple.

In the event, the first hurdle was crossed: the Chief Metropolitan Stipendiary Magistrate decided in March 1987 that there was sufficient evidence for the 26 defendants to be extradited to Belgium. Under the old law he had no power to grant them bail, so their counsel went immediately to the High Court where they were given bail to await the next stage in the proceedings — an application for a writ of habeas corpus to challenge the magistrate's decision.

To everyone's surprise, the High Court granted the writ and blocked the extradition. Its reasons were quite technical: the judges decided that the statements made by British police officers who had interviewed the defendants did not become admissible in evidence until the magistrate's hearing, which was held too late to meet the two-month deadline set by the treaty with Belgium. Inevitably, there was a public outcry: the DPP was said to have got it wrong yet again. He denied this: Mrs Garlick had followed the normal practice and the magistrate had raised no objection. But it was an embarrassing defeat, relieved only when the Attorney General Sir Michael Havers, appearing in person on behalf of the Belgian government, persuaded the Law Lords to hear his appeal against the High Court decision in July 1987.

This particular application had the full support of the Home Secretary, though not all do: there could at least in theory be a case where the Director of Public Prosecutions was working hard at one end of Queen Anne's Gate to get somebody extradited from Britain while the Home Secretary — at the other end of the same street — was being advised to exercise the discretion he has to stop the extradition going ahead.

If the magistrate refuses to extradite the arrested person, the Director of Public Prosecutions — or whoever else is representing the foreign country — can appeal on a point of law to the High Court (and ultimately the House of Lords). But the Home Office holds the trump card, because even if the magistrate grants the request for extradition — and the High Court rejects any subsequent application by the fugitive for habeas corpus — the Home Secretary can order the fugitive to be discharged. The Secretary of State has a general discretion not to return a fugitive, but he also has to take specific factors into account: the triviality of the offence, the passage of time and the interests of justice.

The Criminal Justice Bill 1987 would have modified the so-called prima facie rule, which obliges the foreign government to produce an arguable case: as much evidence in fact as would have been needed to justify a defendant being committed for trial by jury if his case was being heard here. But the rule would not have been abolished altogether. Each treaty which makes general extradition arrangements with another country — as opposed to one-off treaties covering particular cases — has to be brought into effect by Order in Council (a rather classy type of delegated legislation). When drafting each Order in Council the Home Secretary would have been able to abolish the prima facie rule for extradition from the United Kingdom to that country. If the Bill had been passed, it would have enabled the United Kingdom to keep the rule for countries whose standards of justice the government was rather unsure about, while removing what the government saw as a 'considerable impediment' to extradition arrangements with many other countries, including those in the European Community, because our legal system in England and Wales is so different from theirs.

When the Criminal Justice Bill was published, the National Council for Civil Liberties said it was opposed to moves to do away with the prima facie rule, which it maintained had not been as formidable an obstacle to successful extradition as had been claimed:

> It is no more than the minimal requirement regularly met in magistrates' courts in committal proceedings in which the magistrates must satisfy themselves that there is some evidence which, if accepted, would entitle a reasonable court to convict. In the same way that an individual should not be committed for trial if this evidence does not exist, neither should

individuals be deprived of their liberty and sent to a foreign country to stand trial if that country has no evidence which, if accepted, would convict . . . Without [the prima facie rule], UK citizens who have returned from a holiday abroad could find themselves extradited back to that country to face charges for which the evidence would not stand up in a British court.

While the prima facie rule remains, the magistrate has to be satisfied that 'the evidence would be sufficient to warrant the trial of the arrested person if the extradition crime had taken place within the jurisdiction of the court'. Under the Bill, all that would have been necessary for most countries would have been for the fugitive to have been accused or convicted of an extradition crime (a term I explained a moment ago).

There were a number of safeguards in the Bill. A person accused or convicted of a political offence or a purely military offence could not be extradited. Extradition would also not be allowed if the request was motivated by an intention to persecute the fugitive; or if he would be prejudiced at his trial, on the grounds of his race, religion, nationality or political opinions. A person cannot be returned to a foreign state if he was convicted there in his absence and it would not be in the interests of justice to return him.

If these changes are reimbursed, the Director's job will be much easier, as he will no longer need to get hold of the sort of evidence he needed in the past. On the other hand, the changes would make him busier, as it was expected that the number of applications by foreign countries for extradition would increase if the main obstacle to success was finally lifted.

Fraud

Lord Roskill's committee of inquiry on Fraud Trials reported early in 1986 that

in recent years the need for a new and more effective body to combine the skills of those involved in the investigation and prosecution of major fraud cases has gradually come to be recognised by the authorities.

The word 'gradually' was not stressed, although it might well have been. The delay in dealing with major fraud hardly compares with the 140 years taken to set up the Crown Prosecution Service which I mentioned at the beginning of Chapter 4, but progress on fighting fraud was still far from fast. Thus in 1978 the Attorney General set up a working party to review the arrangements for investigating and prosecuting fraud. In 1979 the Attorney General appointed a working group to look at the work of the working party. In 1981 a pilot scheme was set up. In 1983 the government reviewed the work of the pilot scheme. In 1984 the government announced the creation of the Fraud Investigation Group. In 1985 the Group started work. In 1986 it was dismissed as inadequate by Lord Roskill's Fraud Trials Committee. In 1987 Parliament created a Serious Fraud Office. And in 1988 the Serious Fraud Office was expected to start work.

Let us start with the Fraud Investigation Group, or FIG as it is generally called. FIG is a rather confusing term: it is more of a concept than a structure. What happens in practice is that from time to time a Fraud Investigation Group is set up to deal with a specific case. The Group is made up of lawyers from the Crown Prosecution Service, who bring in police officers from the fraud squad, and investigators from the Department of Trade and Industry, as required for the case. Occasionally other experts are also brought in to provide specialist help.

In theory the Fraud Investigation Group is headed by a Controller who has the rank of Assistant Head of Legal Services (the grade formerly called Principal Assistant Director). The Controller reports to the Head of Legal Services and through him to the Director. But since Doiran Williams retired from that job at the end of 1986 there has been no Controller as such: instead John Wood, as Head of Legal Services and Director-designate of the Serious Fraud Office (more of which anon), was minding the shop.

The Fraud Investigation Group deals with cases of substance, complexity, and importance. Examples are frauds on government departments and local authorities; cases of fraud involving large scale corruption; and large shipping or currency offences. Other frauds which the police are told to refer to the Group so that the Controller can decide whether or not to take them on include frauds on foreign governments; international frauds; frauds involving nationalized industries or public companies; frauds involving the Stock Exchange or other City institutions such as Lloyds; and frauds involving well-known public figures such as MPs and industrialists.

At the moment, there are three divisions dealing with Fraud at Headquarters. 'Fraud A' — which has five lawyers — deals with the major London Frauds; 'Fraud B' has five lawyers to handle all the substantial frauds from outside London; 'Fraud C' has six lawyers — some at a slightly lower grade — to deal with what are called 'non-FIG fraud cases': frauds which are important enough to be dealt with at headquarters while not requiring the full resources of the Fraud Investigation Group. In addition, each division has as its Head somebody who, in the old days, would have been called an Assistant Director.

At the end of 1986, the Controller's job was vacant and Fraud 'C' was two lawyers short, which means — if you include the three Heads — that there were just 17 lawyers at Headquarters to deal with all serious cases of fraud in England and Wales. The Association of First Division Civil Servants — the lawyers' trade union — pointed out that at the beginning of the year the government had promised to increase the number of lawyers doing fraud work from 15 to 24. In fact, said the union, there had been an embargo on recruiting further lawyers to handle fraud. By the end of 1986 the recruitment ban had been lifted by the Solicitor General, Sir Patrick Mayhew, but only at the expense of prosecutors in other areas of the Crown Prosecution Service.

The Head of 'Fraud A' in 1986 was one of the most approachable lawyers I met in the Crown Prosecution Service. Far from being the stuffy solicitor in a pin-striped suit you might expect to be doing what to many people must seem a rather dry and musty subject, Rosalind Wright is warm, vivacious and open: she even has a well-developed sense of humour, which she would probably say was essential for her job. Mrs Wright struck me as someone who was totally in control of one of the most off-putting jobs in the Crown Prosecution Service — while being remarkably relaxed in the face of frustrations that would give most men ulcers. Did she find the job daunting? Her response was characteristically frank:

> If I was as fraudulent as my cases I'd say I found the whole thing a tremendous challenge. But it is daunting, and the problem is that fraudsmen are terribly, terribly clever. They're probably much cleverer than our police officers, and certainly cleverer than any of us. They know their way round the financial markets with a tremendous expertise that we don't even pretend to have — because we're all lawyers: we came to fraud as prosecutors, having worked on murders, on Official Secrets Act cases. We have no actual experience of the money markets, of the Stock Exchange, and we have to learn it up for each particular case. Our fraudsmen know how to manipulate the system, they know perfectly well which countries we've got no extradition treaties with, which countries we have all the difficulties getting evidence from, which is why they've all got companies in Lichtenstein, and numbered bank accounts in Switzerland. Also they're in countries where you can bribe the local police, and bribe the financial controllers: they know exactly how to play the system.

The most frustrating thing of all, in a division which was constantly under attack for not prosecuting enough people who were assumed by MPs and the public to be guilty of serious fraud, was that Rosalind Wright (and her colleagues in the other fraud divisions) simply did not have enough staff to do the job. Doiran Williams, who was Controller of the Fraud Investigation Group until the end of 1986, wrote in a letter to *The Times* shortly after his retirement that the Group's achievements were obtained 'in the face of chronic and cynical under-resourcing. Given adequate staff and equipment,' said Mr Williams, 'the Fraud Investigation Group could have done even better' — in his view, significantly so.

John Wood, who was directly in charge of fraud before becoming Head of Legal Services, confirmed in the autumn of 1986 that all three fraud divisions were under strength and overworked:

> What people will not recognise is that if somebody who's clever at fraud has taken a number of years to perpetrate a substantial fraud on members of the public, using a variety of bank accounts and playing the system, it takes an awfully long time to investigate it. You can't investigate a fraud in the same way as you can investigate a murder. It needs a particular sort of expertise, it needs very substantial consideration of bank accounts, and — particularly in the large commercial frauds — it needs an input from overseas. It's one thing to get the story, it's another thing to get the story for the purposes of an enquiry where strict proof of documents isn't necessary, but it's quite another thing to be able to get a case in order obeying all the difficult rules of evidence. Where that evidence is overseas, it means we must seek the co-operation of the foreign state before we can get it.

In a case like Lloyds, where we are asking for a terrific amount of evidence
from Switzerland, from Lichtenstein, from Bermuda, the authorities have
got to fit our requests into their ordinary work — and it takes a year.

Let us suppose a major company has just folded. What happens next? The
Department of Trade and Industry would have been involved and may
suspect at an early stage that criminal offences have been committed. It
is at that stage that the Inspector of Companies would get in touch with
the Controller of the Fraud Investigation Group and arrange a meeting. One
of the Group's three in-house accountants would attend, and police officers
from the appropriate fraud squad would also have to be invited. The meeting
might decide that Department of Trade inquiries should continue, or it might
feel the time was right for a police investigation along agreed lines. The
police might need accountancy support, perhaps from an outside firm. If
a stockbroker was involved, advice from the Stock Exchange might be
needed. This would be provided by the Fraud Investigation Group which
would continue to hold meetings with the police at which progress could
be assessed. The procedure is similar if the police think they have a case
worthy of investigation by the Group.

This is a totally different arrangement from the normal system in which
the police investigate and the prosecutor does nothing until all the evidence
has been collected. It is therefore very hard to square with the philosophy
underlining the Crown Prosecution Service — but it is a pragmatic approach
which seems to make sense in the special circumstances of fraud cases.

And, of course, the Crown Prosecution Service still has the last word on
whether to prosecute. Before the Fraud Investigation Group was introduced
this would have been a major task for one of the DPP's staff, who would
have had to sit down and read a massive pile of documents on a case he
or she would have known nothing about. If a vital piece of evidence had
been overlooked the whole police investigation might turn out to have been
a complete waste of time. But now, because the prosecutor will have been
working together with the police and the Department of Trade and Industry
under the umbrella of the Fraud Investigation Group, he or she will have
a good idea even before the investigations are completed of what charges,
if any, would be appropriate.

Rosalind Wright, who was speaking to me as Head of Fraud 'A' Division,
gave me a striking example of how things used to go wrong in the days
before the Fraud Investigation Group was set up:

> I once received papers which the police had to bring in by van, because
> there were so many of them: they were all along the table, about two or
> three feet high. It took me three months to read them, and when I had
> read them I found that the major defendant had died about two months
> before the papers had arrived on my desk. Everybody that was left was
> such a minor character in the plot that you didn't want to be bothered with
> them. Most of the evidence proved offences which were out of time for
> proceedings anyway, and the whole thing was a complete non-starter. One
> policeman, a Detective Constable from a force outside London, had worked

on investigating the case without any assistance from anybody. When he'd gone to his Inspector he'd been told 'just get on with it, lad, and send it to the DPP when you're ready'. It had taken him *three years*. And it took me three months to sort it out, so it was three months of my time wasted and three years of his.

Rosalind Wright recalled other cases where she had had to tell the police to make further enquiries. 'And there'd be another, say, two or three years while the policeman went off to do them. And then he'd be moved from the fraud squad, which was what always happened. So somebody else would have to take over the case from the beginning, and start trying to read it all up to find out what had happened. It was a nightmare. And quite apart from us being understaffed, the police fraud squads are also terribly badly understaffed, and apparently in London they're cutting down on the staff in the fraud squads, which is appalling.'

A report in the *Sunday Times* towards the end of 1986 quoted an unnamed member of the Metropolitan and City of London Police Fraud Squad bemoaning his fate in colourful language:

Too bad we can't get more cases past the DPP. We work our guts out preparing a case and we know we've got the goods on the crook. We take our case to the DPP and then it may or may not get sent to trial. If the case goes to trial and you win then you feel great. If it goes to trial and you lose, well, those are the breaks — as long as you've done your best. But when you go to the DPP and he says 'We won't prosecute,' that's damn frustrating.

This view, though understandable, is depressing. If police officers really see the Director of Public Prosecutions as another hurdle to be overcome, like a witness who is reluctant to give evidence, it shows a vast gulf in their understanding of what our public prosecution service is there for. If the DPP is 'not prosecuting enough of our cases,' as some police officers appear to think, there can only be two legitimate explanations. Either the Fraud Investigation Group has not been given enough staff to do the job, which is hardly their fault. Or cases are being dropped because the prosecutor thinks they should not come to court (for lack of evidence or on public interest grounds) which is exactly what the Director's staff are meant to decide.

Of course, they may get it wrong: and even if the case comes to court success cannot be guaranteed. Take this example, another horror story from Rosalind Wright. A number of bank officials were prosecuted for their part in a major fraud, as a result of which an Indian bank was said to have lost £2 million. In the first trial, the jury failed to agree a verdict on one defendant, while the other was given a conditional discharge. The second trial, of three more defendants, was stopped by a judge at the Inner London Crown Court on the ground that totally false documents were not forged within the meaning of the Forgery Act. 'The three men just walked out,' said Mrs Wright. 'And this was an extremely complicated case, very thoroughly investigated by a very able Detective-Inspector in the Fraud Squad. He was sick as a parrot.'

Even so, the fraud divisions at Crown Prosecution Service headquarters do not seem to be doing too badly. In 1985, the Fraud Investigation Group was responsible for 55 Crown Court trials of which 42 resulted in convictions and 13 in acquittals. In 1986, there were 86 trials, with convictions in 74 of them. Many trials involved several defendants: altogether in 1986, 195 people were prosecuted for frauds involving £171 million. Of these defendants, 173 pleaded guilty or were convicted by the jury and only 22 were acquitted. Now it may be that the DPP's staff, faced with more cases than they can cope with, are choosing only to prosecute the strongest they can find. After all, any prosecutor can get a high conviction rate simply by dropping anything that is not a dead cert. But there is no evidence to suggest that prosecutors dealing with fraud interpret their instructions differently from prosecutors in other areas. And people in the Fraud Investigation Group say there are no certainties in fraud.

As I left Rosalind Wright with her unimaginably vast workload, I wondered how she managed to enjoy her work as much as she did. Wasn't she ever depressed by her inevitable ineffectiveness in the face of so much undiscovered and unpunished crime? 'Well, it's only money,' she said. 'At least in the files I get here, there are no pictures of battered babies.'

Guinness: Not so Good

City scandals are not renowned for capturing the public imagination. Most people have only the haziest idea of how the City of London works, although there is always a suspicion that anybody being paid a huge sum of money for not actually *doing* anything cannot be up to much good.

The Guinness Affair dominated the financial pages in the early months of 1987. It was certainly difficult for most people to fathom out what exactly had been going on, beyond grasping that it was all about the bitterly contested take-over of the Distillers group by Guinness in April 1986. But the fact that everyone is familiar with Guinness gave the story an edge over, for example, the collapse of Johnson Matthey Bankers. 'Guinness is Good for You' is a slogan hard to eradicate from the subconscious: any suggestion that it might not be so good was bound to attract public attention.

The story began in December 1986 when the Department of Trade and Industry appointed two Inspectors, David Donaldson, QC and Ian Watt, FCA, to investigate the company. They made their enquiries quite independently of the Crown Prosecution Service, and reported to the Minister for Corporate Affairs at the Department of Trade; the Secretary of State, Paul Channon, had excluded himself from the affair because of his family connection with Guinness. The Department of Trade and Industry is entitled to supply the Director of Public Prosecutions with information, and in practice the Inspectors kept in fairly close touch with the Crown Prosecution Service headquarters — though not with the police — on the progress they were making.

The police were not making any enquiries at this stage because the Crown Prosecution Service had not asked them to, or perhaps had asked them not to. Theoretically, any complainant can invite the police to investigate an alleged crime, but John Wood told me the police would not respond to a request to look at Guinness without first consulting the prosecution service — 'and we would not want to call the police in until the investigation by the Inspectors is nearly completed'. This was to avoid duplication of work, and because 'witnesses would not be nearly so keen to express themselves freely and honestly to the Inspectors — although they are obliged to — if they knew there was a police enquiry going on which might affect them'.

This seems a bit odd. Nobody who was being questioned by the Guinness Inspectors could have failed to realize that a police investigation was lurking round the corner. Nor would anyone seriously suggest that a QC and a Chartered Accountant would be better at persuading anyone who might be guilty of fraud to 'crack' than the police, not all of whom are men in sharp suits and heavy boots with no financial qualifications beyond 'O'level maths. Why then had the much-praised Fraud Investigation Group concept not been used at the usual early stage, even if only to approve the decision not to involve the police for the time being?

A Labour MP suggested in Parliament that for political reasons the government was 'attempting to duck a full investigation': Dale Campbell-Savours urged ministers to 'let the Fraud Squad go into Guinness to sort it out'. That would have delighted the police: reports in *The Guardian* in February 1987 said they had been angered by a decision from the Director's office to exclude them. The police had made it known that they wanted to start investigations because they thought it possible that serious offences had been committed — and not just under the Companies Act, which is what the two Inspectors were concerned with. But John Wood denied any snub: 'all I know is what I've heard from senior officers, and they don't seem to be terribly concerned. They know that we will play the thing in what we see as the right way of doing it.'

Then suddenly, just before the General Election was announced in May 1987, police officers from the Fraud Squad arrested the former Guinness chairman Ernest Saunders. Saunders had been sacked by the Guinness board in January, and two months later the company started legal proceedings against him to recover £5 million which had been paid to a fellow director for a few weeks' work. However, the criminal charges Mr Saunders faced in May related to various documents. It was alleged that he had destroyed documents and diary entries relevant to the Inspectors' enquiries with intent to pervert the course of justice. He was also alleged to have destroyed and falsified Guinness company records. Mr Saunders was granted bail of £500,000. After his arrest a report appeared in the *Sunday Times* claiming that the Department of Trade and Industry enquiry had been 'thrown into disarray' by the DPP's decision to orders Saunders's arrest.

The Serious Fraud Office

Earlier in this chapter I quoted figures which suggested that the fraud divisions at Crown Prosecution Service Headquarters were not doing too badly. So it seems not too surprising that the government saw no need to try to persuade Parliament to accept Lord Roskill's most controversial proposal: that complex fraud cases should be tried by a judge sitting with two lay people rather than by a judge and jury.

The Roskill committee pointed out that to cope with increasing numbers of fraud cases there was a need for an 'efficient system of detection and trial which will deal with them quickly and act as a deterrent to others'. Their report said this was impeded by the fact that 'the detection of fraud, the consequential enquiries, and the legal processes involved until a verdict is delivered, extend over . . . 43 independent police forces, the Department of Trade and Industry, the Fraud Investigation Group operating under the DPP, the Inland Revenue, and Customs and Excise'. The Fraud Investigation Group only covered two of these organizations — the DPP's department and the Department of Trade — although it also had support from the police. So what Roskill suggested was 'the formation of a single, unified organization responsible for all the functions of detection, investigation and prosecution of serious fraud. The government's response, inevitably, was to set up a committee — chaired by the Chief Secretary to the Treasury.

That, in turn, agreed to the establishment of a Serious Fraud Office, a statutory body which was created by the Criminal Justice Act 1987 to collaborate with the police in both investigating and prosecuting the most serious and complex frauds. The Inland Revenue and Customs and Excise were also to be brought into the new arrangements. In his report, Lord Roskill seemed to have been implying that his 'unified organisation' should exercise control over police officers. That was certainly the impression the police themselves got — and resented: they had no wish to be part of the Serious Fraud Office. The police were not even reassured by the government's decision that although policemen would work in the Serious Fraud Office they would retain their separate identity and chain of command: senior officers remained very wary of being told what to do by civiliam prosecutors, although in effect that was already happening in the Fraud Investigation Group. As the prosecutor had the last word on whether the case would go to court, inevitably he could control the direction of the investigation — while being able to say, perfectly accurately, to members of the public who complained about supposed inactivity that it was not *his* job to investigate crimes.

The government planned that the Serious Fraud Office would start work in the Spring of 1988. It is to be run by a Director who, like the Director of Public Prosecutions, is appointed by the Attorney General and works under the Attorney's 'superintendence', a concept I shall be discussing in Chapter 10. In February 1987 the Attorney General announced that, provided the legislation got through Parliament, he would be appointing John Wood as the first Director of the Serious Fraud Office. This seemed a wise appointment: Mr Wood played a leading part in developing the integrated approach to investigation and prosecution which preceded the Fraud Investigation Group. He was its first Controller before becoming Deputy Director of Public Prosecutions and took on the responsibility for Fraud again after his successor as Controller retired at the end of 1986. It was made clear that Mr Wood would remain Head of Legal Services for some months after being designated Director of the Serious Fraud Office. But if all went according to plan John Wood would be fully occupied with setting up the Serious Fraud Office just at the time the new Director of Public Prosecutions was settling in to his new job. Clearly the Attorney felt it was of great importance to find the right man for the Serious Fraud Office. He would not otherwise have deprived the new Director of Public Prosecutions of a deputy with as much experience of Headquarters work as John Wood had.

The Home Office made it clear that the Director of the Serious Fraud Office would have about 80 staff, 'including experienced lawyers and accountants, from government departments such as the Department of Trade and Industry and the DPP's office and possibly also from the private sector . . . They will work closely with designated officers of the Metropolitan and City Police Company Fraud Department . . . The objective is to bring together the necessary powers and expertise so that major fraud cases can be brought to trial as rapidly and effectively as possible'. The government also confirmed that there would be provision for staff at the new office to exchange information with the Inland Revenue where revenue fraud was suspected.

There were fears, notably from Doiran Williams, the former fraud Controller, that the Serious Fraud Office would be underfunded. 'It will not fulfil public expectation unless adequately resourced,' he said, adding that 'the national determination to deal with fraud is truly to be measured by the provision of resources for all the agencies involved.' It would, perhaps, have been more accurate to have said 'the *government's* determination': at a time, early in 1987, when there was widespread national disquiet about City frauds, the government's improved financial support for the fraud divisions at Crown Prosecution Service Headquarters was conspicious by its absence.

The 1987 Act gives the Director of the Serious Fraud Office power to take over serious or complex fraud cases from the police in much the same way as the Director of Public Prosecutions does. Of course, once the Director of the Serious Fraud Office has conduct of the proceedings the Director of Public Prosecutions is no longer under his normal duty to take over the case. The Director of the Serious Fraud Office is given a staff of lawyers with wider powers than the staff of the Crown Prosecution Service: broadly speaking, they combine the powers of Crown Prosecutors with the long-standing powers available to Inspectors appointed by the Department of Trade and Industry (who, in the past, have been able to use these powers as part of a Fraud Investigation Group enquiry).

The effect of all this is that in cases of serious or complex fraud the Director of the Serious Fraud Office and his staff of lawyers have wide powers to investigate a person's affairs if they think there is 'good reason' to do so. They can require a person under investigation to attend, answer questions and produce documents. Although staff of the Serious Fraud Office do not themselves have police powers of search, arrest and detention, they can obtain search warrants from magistrates authorizing the police to break into specified premises and seize documents. Anyone who knows about an investigation of serious or complex fraud, or suspects one is likely, and falsifies, conceals, or destroys documents which he knows or suspects are relevant to the investigation is liable to imprisonment for up to seven years and an unlimited fine.

One change from the old powers exercised by Department of Trade and Industry Inspectors is that under the new arrangements an admission made in reply to questions from staff of the Serious Fraud Office cannot be used as evidence in court. However, the information obtained can, of course, be used in the course of further enquiries.

The Criminal Justice Act 1987 introduces a new procedure to allow serious or complex fraud cases to be transferred direct to the Crown Court without the need for the normal committal proceedings before the magistrates. For this purpose a 'notice of transfer' must be issued, and among people entitled to issue such a notice are the Director of the Serious Fraud Office, the Director of Public Prosecutions, and their respective staffs. The person issuing the notice must certify that in his opinion there is sufficient evidence for the person to be committed for trial and the evidence reveals a case which is so serious *and* complex that it is appropriate for management of the case to be taken over by the Crown Court without delay. After a case has been transferred to the Crown Court, the defendant may apply to that court at any time before his trial for the charge to be dismissed on grounds of insufficient evidence.

The Act also gives a Crown Court judge power to order a 'preparatory hearing' in a serious and complex case. This hearing can be to identify material issues and areas of agreement between both sides, to help the jury understand the issues, or to speed up the trial. The hearing is part of the trial, but it takes place before the jury is sworn in. At the preparatory hearing the judge has wide powers to order the prosecution and then the defence to supply written summaries of their respective cases. He can rule on points of law and make orders dealing with the evidence. Reporting restrictions apply to preparatory hearings in much the same way as they do to committal proceedings before magistrates. This means the jury will not learn about the defence case at this stage, unless the defence agrees or the judge makes a ruling.

The clauses of the Criminal Justice Bill setting up the Serious Fraud Office were rushed through parliament just before the General Election: one peer pointed out that for all anyone there knew, they might have just voted to repeal Magna Carta. Labour MPs, who had agreed that this part of the Bill should not be lost, were nevertheless worried that the Serious Fraud

Office might be inadequately funded.

The Serious Fraud Office can only deal with serious or complex fraud cases. Who is to say what these are? It seems to be the prosecutors themselves. But where should they draw the line? Indeed, do we still need a separate Fraud Investigation Group once the Serious Fraud Office has got under way? Why not have both categories of fraud dealt with at Headquarters: Serious Fraud on the one hand, and fraud which is not quite so serious or complex but still too difficult to be dealt with in the local areas? Better still, if there is enough money to go round, why not absorb *all* headquarters cases into the Serious Fraud Office? Otherwise the risk is that there will be four different categories of fraud: the simple case of the forged credit card which is handled at local level, the non-FIG Headquarters case, the Fraud Investigation Group case, and the really big case which goes to the Serious Fraud Office. Worse still, a case could go from one department to another as its complexity or seriousness waxed and waned during the police investigation. Perhaps the new Director of the Serious Fraud Office will consider whether a major reorganization is called for?

Complaints Against the Police

The Police and Criminal Evidence Act 1984, known from its initials as PACE, made widespread and far-reaching changes to the powers and duties of the police. Before the Act came into force at the beginning of 1986 all complaints against police officers had to be referred to the Director of Public Prosecutions unless the Chief Constable was satisfied that no criminal offence had been committed. This was a lower standard of evidence than applied to other cases referred to the Director: it meant that the DPP had to cope with a large number of trivial allegations. Before the Crown Prosecution Service was introduced complaints against the police amounted to more than half the number of incoming cases. Many of them were motoring offences; one police officer was reported to the DPP for allegedly failing to buy a dog licence.

In 1978, Sir Thomas Hetherington explained in his evidence to the Philips Royal Commission on Criminal Procedure that almost every Chief Constable was 'extremely anxious to divest himself of responsibility for deciding whether one of his fellow officers should be prosecuted, however trivial the allegation, so there could be no suspicion of improper bias. Hence they normally report all cases involving an officer, even if the evidence is virtually non-existent'. These cases were inconsistent with his general aim of dealing only with major crime, but in view of the anxiety of both the police and public that cases involving police officers should be dealt with by an independent body he could see no alternative to continued referral.

But that alternative turned out to be the Police Complaints Authority, which started work in April 1985. It has two main jobs: hearing disciplinary charges against officers up to the rank of superintendent, and supervising investigations into the conduct of any police officer.

Complaints against police officers are actually investigated by other police officers. Whether or not the investigation of a complaint has been supervised by the Police Complaints Authority, the investigating police officer has to submit a report on it. If it relates to a senior officer, it must be sent to the Director of Public Prosecutions unless it is clear that no offence has been committed. If it relates to a junior officer, the Chief Constable has to decide whether the report indicates that an offence may have been committed by one of his officers and if so whether the 'offence indicated is such that the officer ought to be charged' with it. If he decides that the answer to both these questions is 'yes', he must send a copy of the report to the Director of Public Prosecutions. If the Chief Constable decides that an offence may have been committed but that the officer should not be charged — or if he decides that none of his officers has committed a criminal offence — he must tell the Police Complaints Authority whether he is bringing disciplinary charges instead (and if not, why not). But the Police Complaints Authority can then have the papers sent to the Director of Public Prosecutions if it thinks the officer should be charged with a crime.

The government's hope in putting forward these complicated provisions was that the Director would only have to look at cases which might result in criminal charges, while no longer having to sift through a mass of trivia. But the phrase 'ought to be charged' (in section 90(4) of the 1984 Act) seems to refer to the quality of the offence and not of the evidence. That is certainly how the Police Complaints Authority read it: otherwise, they said, it would give Chief Constables authority to decide whether there was enough evidence for there to be a reasonable prospect of the officer being convicted. And this interpretation is accepted by senior staff in the Director's office. The result of all this is that the Director of Public Prosecutions cannot rely on Chief Constables keeping back the minor matters to be dealt with by disciplinary means (something the Police Federation had fiercely opposed), or indeed cases where there is insufficient evidence to proceed (which is one interpretation of what 'ought to be charged' may mean).

A major criticism made against past Directors was that they prosecuted too few police officers. The stock response was that it was unusually difficult to get a conviction: you may remember from Chapter 2 that Sir Thomas Hetherington was unable to bring prosecutions following a number of unexplained deaths in police custody because there was not enough evidence. But if there is the evidence, are juries still reluctant to convict police officers?

'If you had asked me that question a few years ago,' said the Head of Legal Services, John Wood, 'I would have been able to tell you that it was very much more difficult to get a conviction against a police officer than against an ordinary member of the public. We had a number of cases where there were acquittals simply because the jury didn't like convicting a police officer on the testimony of people with previous convictions.' But Mr Wood said that times had changed. 'It seems to me that juries now are more likely to convict a police officer than they used to be.'

John Wood recalled a number of corruption cases where policemen had been convicted. But cases of violence posed particular difficulties. Very often the victim was struggling: the prosecution sometimes had to decide whether the police were properly restraining somebody who had clearly had too much to drink, or whether 'the knee went into his stomach deliberately'. Mr Wood gave me an example of such a case, then current, which he said was 'clearly a case which the public interest required to be aired'. But he then added that if the police officers were ultimately acquitted, he would not be 'in the slightest bit surprised'.

I found this very interesting. Was Mr Wood *more* likely to prosecute a police officer than a member of the public just to satisfy public opinion? 'I don't think that one would ever seek to prosecute a police officer if the evidence was insufficient,' he said. 'On the other hand, where one has got evidence that something has gone wrong, then I think it is right that one should prosecute . . . even though there may well be a reasonable chance of an acquittal.'

Mr Wood gave as an example the trial in 1987 of Police Inspector Douglas Lovelock on a charge of maliciously wounding Mrs Cherry Groce at her home in Brixton, a shooting which led to major riots there. The police had been looking for her son. Mr Lovelock was acquitted by the jury after a defence submission that there was no case to answer was rejected by the court: whether the judge thought that a verdict, either way, by a jury would be more acceptable to public opinion than a directed acquittal is a matter of pure speculation.

Inspector Lovelock's case was hardly unique. In 1983 Stephen Waldorf was shot and seriously injured by detectives hunting an armed robber: two constables were tried for attempted murder and acquitted, despite what the prosecution thought was a good case. In 1985 five-year-old John Shorthouse was shot dead by a Birmingham police constable who was searching for his father; the officer was later cleared of manslaughter, and promoted.

John Wood admitted that deciding whether to prosecute a police officer in cases like these depended on drawing a 'terribly difficult distinction'. In borderline cases he thought it would not be unreasonable to prosecute so the matter could be aired in public. Unless there was a death, which would normally be followed by an inquest, there would be no other way of establishing the facts in public. Early in the next chapter I shall be quoting a remark made by the Solicitor General, Sir Patrick Mayhew: he said it would be wrong to prosecute simply 'if it was thought useful to clear the air by means of a public trial'. But I do not think John Wood was suggesting that.

Pornography

You may remember reading in Chapter 3 how the law's opinion of what we are allowed to read and watch has changed over the years. The Obscene Publications Act 1959 is still in force, but trials like that of *Lady Chatterley's Lover* and *Oz* seem unlikely to be repeated. Instead the trend is to use forfeiture proceedings.

Pornography is very subjective. It is said to be like an elephant — you cannot define it, but you know it when you see it. John Wood told me of the office 'porn committee', half-a-dozen members of staff, including men and women of different ages (and not all of them lawyers), who look at the films and video tapes referred to Headquarters to decide whether there should be a prosecution. They usually reach agreement, but sometimes there is a split and in such cases John Wood himself would watch the film, perhaps with two senior colleagues. People are neither keen to serve on the porn committee nor reluctant to take it on: 'they just regard it as a job,' said Wood. Nobody stays on long enough to have their senses blunted by seeing too much porn. John Wood, on the other hand, sees very little, which can be a disadvantage: 'when I first came here in 1958,' he said, 'if we had a full frontal still photograph showing pubic hair, magistrates regarded that as obscene. Gradually, throughout the years, standards have been liberalised, and of course one sees these glossy magazines on sale in bookshops now. If something appears subjectively obscene I've got to stand back and ask what the average jury at the Old Bailey is going to make of it. It's far easier to decide whether to prosecute somebody for murder,' Mr Wood said. 'The two really difficult things to decide in this office are porn, and careless driving — which is also subjective.'

John Wood pointed out that the boundaries of obscenity were ever increasingly being pushed further on. 'Straight' heterosexual material is not normally prosecuted; nor is homosexual pornography. 'The convictions tend to come where one's got sadism, masochism, sex with animals, sex with children, group sex,' he said, 'and of course the video nasties.'

These video cassettes emerged early in 1982, when the taste for violence led to a number of horror films which depicted deaths and mutilations with such realism that it was believed some involved real killings, if not of humans then certainly of animals. In August 1982 the infamous *Driller Killer* video nasty was the subject of a forfeiture order, followed by such charming productions as *I Spit on your Grave*. The Director's response to those who said a full-scale prosecution should have been mounted instead was that there had been no deliberate attempt to break the law, and that forfeiture proceedings under section 3 of the Obscene Publications Act 1959 provided a speedy means of removing such films from circulation.

The section 3 procedure effectively allows the prosecution to seize under warrant a stock of obscene material and arrange for the nearest magistrates' court to order its destruction. Any person claiming an interest in the material can contest the forfeiture, but this rarely happens. Robertson and Nicol write in *Media Law* that

> the procedure has little deterrent effect: the case is brought against the material, rather than its publishers, and has no criminal consequence whatsoever. Section 3 seizures occupy a great deal of court and police time, but judgments in these cases do not serve as precedents and the only object of the exercise is to diminish the profits of soft-core pornographers by destroying some part of their stock.

There are prosecutions from time to time over video nasties, but they seem to attract little public attention. Possession of the same film may lead to an acquittal in one court and a conviction in another: the staff at Indecent Publications (as the section is called) fill in score cards, like football pools, in an attempt to keep track of what the courts are doing. The films are carefully, if incongruously, classified in alphabetical order: the mind boggles at what lies behind their deliberately suggestive titles.

Sir Peter Rawlinson, as Solicitor General, gave an undertaking to MPs in 1964 that if a publisher wished to contest a seizure before a jury then proceedings would continue by way of a prosecution under section 2 of the Act instead. In practice this option is likely to be used only by the bravest or most foolhardy of publishers: they risk a prison sentence if convicted of publishing an obscene article.

The general policy nowadays is to raid publishers or distributors rather than booksellers or newsagents; such is the bulk of the material often seized that a jury trial would involve disproportionate effort, and so the forfeiture proceedings are as attractive to the prosecution as they are (relatively) painless to the pornographers. However, retailers who hired out video nasties which had already been the subject of forfeiture proceedings found they, too, were having their stock seized. Video tapes which have been approved by the British Board of Film Censors are less likely to be the subject of forfeiture proceedings, and steps have been taken to ensure that the Board (which is a private organization funded by the film industry) is kept in touch with the DPP's office over just what is considered acceptable for people to watch in the privacy of their homes.

Indecent Publications comes under General Casework at Headquarters. The section is staffed entirely by non-lawyers, who refer cases up the line to legally qualified staff when they think there should be a prosecution.

One porn case which cannot have been too difficult to decide was the prosecution of a leading childen's doctor in 1986 on charges involving child pornography. Professor Oliver Brooke, former head of paediatric medicine at a leading London hospital was given 12 months imprisonment after pleading guilty of taking and supplying indecent photographs of children. There was no suggestion that he had behaved improperly to any of his patients, but in sentencing him Mr Justice McCowan described what Brooke and two other defendants had been involved in as a trade which was disgusting in itself, adding that 'anyone who plays a part in it is contributing to the corruption of children and may well be causing adults to commit serious offences against children'.

It all seems a far cry from the 'saucy' seaside postcards of Donald McGill which used to keep the Director busy right up to the mid-1950s. Some of them seem quite charming now, such as the picture of two rather jolly storks standing on a roof-top. One says 'any business today?' and the other replies 'No real business, but I put the wind up a couple of typists this afternoon'. Orders for destruction of that card were made by magistrates in Portsmouth, Liskeard and Folkestone between 1954 and 1956. Nor could the publishers hide behind a *double entendre*: in 1954 D. Constance Ltd gave an undertaking not to publish a card showing a military type in a hotel bedroom (alone). He asks the porter about the noise downstairs, and is told 'they're holding an Oddfellows' Ball'. 'Well,' says the major, 'if he makes all that row about it, why the devil don't they let him have it back?'

Drugs

Only the most difficult drugs cases are handled at Headquarters, in the General Casework division. They include cases where one of the participants in a conspiracy has tipped off the police, who have then put in an undercover officer to buy the drugs. The informant may be required to give evidence in court, but he will still have to be prosecuted for his part in the conspiracy. Requests from a 'supergrass' for immunity are always refused, but the courts generally co-operate by imposing a reduced sentence. An informant's evidence is by definition tainted: for that reason it will generally need corroboration.

Racial Hatred

The Public Order Act 1986 strengthened the existing offence of incitement to racial hatred. That offence was previously contained in section 5A of the Race Relations Act 1936, although it was not inserted into the 1936 Act until 40 years on when Parliament passed the Race Relations Act 1976. Like the old offence in the 1936 Act, the new offences created by Part III of the Public Order Act require the consent of the Attorney General before a prosecution can be started. In such cases the Attorney seeks the advice of the Director of Public Prosecutions, and so the cases are considered at Headquarters. Successive Attorneys have expressed their reluctance to authorize prosecutions which they think will fail, as they feel that unsuccessful prosecutions will do more harm than good to race relations.

Section 18 of the Public Order Act 1986 makes it an offence for a person to use threatening, abusive or insulting words or behaviour — or to display threatening, abusive or insulting written material — if it is likely to stir up racial hatred and he intends or believes his words or behaviour to be threatening, abusive or insulting; or if he merely intends that the words, behaviour or writing will stir up racial hatred. The addition was thought necessary because racially inflammatory material has in the past been circulated among level-headed people (the Home Office generously included MPs in this category) who were themselves unlikely to be incited to racial hatred. This meant the distributors had escaped prosecution. The provision could also be used against a racist who addressed a crowd of his own supporters; he would not be likely to stir up racial hatred in those who are already racists.

'Racial hatred' is defined as 'hatred against a group of persons in Great Britain defined by reference to colour, race, nationality (including citizenship) or ethnic or national origins.' This does not seem to cover religious hatred as such, but the Commission for Racial Equality says a decision in the House of Lords in the case of *Mandla v. Dowell-Lee* in 1983 'reveals the close connection between religion and ethnicity, and shows that the present Race Relations Act offers considerable assistance where the religion's practice is a cultural norm associated with the ethnic group as in the case of Muslims, Sikhs and Jews'.

The 1986 Act also makes it an offence to publish, distribute or broadcast racially inflammatory material. The offence covers people who put on plays and films (or other recordings). Possessing racially inflammatory material with a view to distribution or publication is now an offence.

The Attorney's aim in such cases has always been consistency: a leaflet stirring up racial hatred may be distributed throughout Britain, and it is important to ensure that the leaflet is not treated differently in different parts of the country. Prosecutions under the old Act were rare, not least because the publisher of an inflammatory leaflet is often hard to find.

Policy

Ken Ashken is Head of the Policy and Information Divison at Queen Anne's Gate. It was his idea to have a separate division unburdened by casework: its three main responsibilities are policy and legislation, information, and legal training.

In addition to keeping abreast of legislative changes in the field of criminal justice, the policy division provides advice to government departments on prosecution policy issues: it provides representation on departmental working parties and outside committees and prepares evidence, on request, to Royal Commissions and the like. It keeps a constant eye on prosecution policy throughout the Crown Prosecution Service, and is responsible for editing the Crown Prosecutor's Policy Manual (discussed in Chapter 7).

The division also has the vital responsibility of holding the Crown Prosecution Service's store of information. Not surprisingly, the whole system is based on what are called precedents: previous prosecution decisions — and their consequences — which can be drawn on when similar circumstances recur. The policy division is responsible for gathering in new precedents from local areas, reviewing and updating the existing precedents, and putting the whole system on to a computer. In addition, the division runs the law library at Headquarters, acts as a clearing house for appeals on points of law to avoid duplication, and writes speeches for the Director of Public Prosecutions on policy issues. At the end of the division's list of duties in the field of information comes its responsibility for 'dealing with enquiries from researchers'. Enquiries from journalists are, however, handled by Press and Public Relations Officers in the Director's Private Office who therefore have direct access to the man at the top.

The Policy and Information Division is also responsible for providing advice on the legal training of lawyers and law clerks: it advises on the content of these training courses, though not on the way in which they are organized. That is done by a separate training branch, which in the early months organized a large number of courses at all levels for staff new to the Crown

Prosecution Service, and continues to organize regular courses on legal, management and other subjects for all staff.

SIX

The Fifty Per Cent Rule

The DPP is used to criticism. Sometimes his critics complain that an unsuccessful prosecution should never have been brought in the first place. On other occasions he is blamed for deciding not to prosecute in a particular case. These criticisms are often misplaced. But they do at least recognize that, in bringing a prosecution, the Director has a discretion.

The Director's Discretion

Sir Thomas Hetherington conceded that the discretion to prosecute could be quite a burden:

> Sometimes it's fairly obvious that a case must go ahead; sometimes it's fairly obvious that a case should not go ahead. There is however a grey area in which difficult decisions have to be taken. But that is part of the job: it's the exercise of discretion which was part of the function of the DPP's office in the past and the Crown Prosecution Service from 1986.

The decision not to prosecute was at the heart of two cases which received widespread news coverage in 1986. One of them concerned an eight-year-old girl from Essex who claimed she had been raped by a doctor. The Essex police were advised by the local county prosecuting solicitor not to prosecute the doctor she had named. The prosecuting solicitor had in turn been advised by counsel that there was not enough evidence to go ahead with a prosecution, and in due course the decision was upheld by Sir Thomas Hetherington when he looked at the papers so that he could reply to a letter from the local MP.

The problem was one of corroboration: a child who is too young to understand the nature of the oath taken by a witness in court must give his or her evidence unsworn, and nobody can be convicted on a child's unsworn evidence unless there is corroboration from an independent source such as another witness. But rape by its very nature is not normally committed in public: it would not count as corroboration for a parent to say the child had complained immediately afterwards, even if she named the man who attacked her. And the Director's legal advice at the time was that a child of eight or nine — who at that age is considered below the age of criminal responsibility — was too young to be allowed to take the oath. What's more, even if there is a sworn evidence from the victim, the judge must still ask the jury to look for corroboration. John Spencer of Selwyn College Cambridge, arguing in *The Times* that the law of corroboration should be simplified, pointed out that cases of alleged child rape were likely to collapse — even if the child gave credible evidence — unless the forensic scientist found evidence on the accused which implicated him in the offence, or an adult saw him committing it, or he was foolish enough to confess to the police.

That did not deter the journalist George Gale, who maintained in the *Daily Express* that the Director of Public Prosecutions should have begun proceedings in the case even if the chances of an acquittal were high. This, said Mr Gale, was 'a case where the public interest requires a prosecution, even if it be thought that the evidence might not yield a conviction'. He even went so far as to assert that 'there are times when the law must be seen to be being applied, even if justice is not necessarily seen to be done at the end of it'. This strikes me as quite absurd. As the Solicitor General, Sir Patrick Mayhew MP, said (of a different case), 'justice must be even handed, and it would be a cause for complaint if the formidable prosecuting power of the State were to be exercised against a citizen where, to take a purely hypothetical example, it was thought useful to clear the air by means of a public trial'. Indeed, as you will see, the idea that people should be prosecuted in the hope — rather than the expectation — of success is totally at odds with a policy which has been followed by successive Directors over the years.

That policy was hardly likely to worry the mother of the little girl George Gale was writing about. Supported morally and financially by *The Sun* newspaper, which had seized the opportunity to make news instead of simply having to report it, the mother began a private prosecution — alleging rape and, as an alternative, the lesser charge of indecent assault. Committal proceedings were heard before a full-time stipendiary magistrate, who surprised lawyers by deciding that the girl was not too young to take the oath after all. After hearing the prosecution evidence the magistrate sent the doctor for trial at the Crown Court, where the girl gave evidence and was cross-examined. However, the vital piece of alleged corroboration had been destroyed: what the girl's mother had claimed was a stained nightdress had been put in the washing machine long before it could be examined by forensic scientists. And the judge told the jury to look for corroboration: 'With a child of this age and a case of this nature,' said Judge Greenwood at Chelmsford Crown Court, 'it is not only good law but good, sound common sense to look for corroboration. Of course you may convict on [the girl's] evidence alone without corroboration, but it would be dangerous.' Having heard this the jury duly acquitted the doctor — much to the relief of those who had supported Sir Thomas Hetherington's decision. (There will be a detailed look at the case in Chapter 9).

In bringing rape charges against the Essex doctor, the mother and her lawyers were no doubt thinking of another case which was making headline news at the time: Gary Austin's conviction for manslaughter only a few weeks earlier, following a private prosecution brought by the mother of the man he killed — the only successful private prosecution for manslaughter so far this century. In that case, too, the Director had decided not to bring proceedings. He had reached his decision after three conferences with the pathologist who had examined the body of 19-year-old John Williams, and advice on two occasions from 'very experienced counsel'. Austin had injected Williams with a drug called Palfium, which is usually given in tablet form to relieve the pain of cancer sufferers. Williams collapsed almost at once and, according to the medical evidence, died soon after. But at first the doctors could not agree on whether that injection had caused his death. Accordingly the Director told Austin that he would not be prosecuted for manslaughter. One can only speculate on whether this influenced Austin a few days later to plead guilty to a charge of possessing the Palfium tablets (for which he received one year's imprisonment, served concurrently with a longer sentence for other offences).

But the dead man's mother, Mrs Pauline Williams, decided to go ahead with her private prosecution of Gary Austin. As I shall be explaining in Chapter 9, the Director then had to decide whether to take over the prosecution and support it, or take over the prosecution and end it, or just let Mrs Williams get on with the case by herself. To begin with he chose the last option: his reasons were explained later by the Solicitor General, Sir Patrick Mayhew, in a letter to Mrs Williams:

> After the most careful consideration, the Director took the view that the conflict between the experts was likely to undermine any prosecution. The Director additionally concluded that there were other factors which he should properly take into account in deciding whether the interests of justice required him to take over your prosecution after it had been instituted and before it was tested by the justices at the committal proceedings.
>
> One was the fact that in March 1983 Austin had been informed that he would not be prosecuted for manslaughter . . . Additionally, the Director bore in mind that nearly three years had elapsed since the death of your son and the institution of the private prosecution . . . This fact, together with the fact that Austin had been sentenced to three years' imprisonment in March 1983, raised doubts as to whether he would receive an immediate custodial sentence if he was convicted of the offence of manslaughter. The cumulative weight of these factors, added to what the Director saw as the evidential weaknesses, were such that the Director was not satisfied that there was a sufficient case.
>
> Once the case, however, had been committed to trial, the Director felt it would be wrong for you to be put to further time, trouble and expense in prosecuting this matter yourself in the Crown Court. Accordingly he was prepared to take the matter over.
>
> Decisions of the kind that the Director was called upon to make . . . are always difficult. It would be simple for him if he were permitted to say in every case in which there was even a chance of conviction 'I will prosecute and let the court decide', but he is not. He has to apply his judgment and

experience to the question of what would be the likely outcome of proceedings.

There, in a nutshell, is the Director's prosecution policy. It can be summed up in two questions. Firstly, is there enough evidence to make a conviction more likely than an acquittal? Secondly, is a prosecution in the public interest?

Enough Evidence?

Sir Thomas Hetherington first explained that policy in the evidence he submitted in 1978 to the Royal Commission on Criminal Procedure. He began by explaining what became known as 'the fifty per cent rule':

> The test normally used in the Department in deciding whether evidence is sufficient to justify proceedings is whether or not there is a reasonable prospect of a conviction; whether, in other words, it seems rather more likely that there will be a conviction than an acquittal.

An even higher standard would be set if an acquittal could have unfortunate consequences — for example, an unsuccessful prosecution of an allegedly obscene book could increase sales. Sir Thomas continued:

> There are some who maintain that it is right to prosecute whenever there is a bare prima facie case as, it is said, to raise the minimum standard above this level is to usurp the proper function of the courts. In my view, however, the universal adoption of a 'bare prima facie case' standard would not only clog up our already over-burdened courts but inevitably result in an undue proportion of innocent men facing criminal charges.

'Fifty per cent rule' is not a phrase used by Sir Thomas Hetherington in his evidence: in a rash moment he agreed with a journalist's suggestion that he would normally allow a case to go ahead if the chances of success were better than fifty-fifty. And so, for a time, the DPP was known as 'Mr 50 Per Cent' — a phrase Hetherington dislikes because it suggests, wrongly, that chances of conviction can be calculated with mathematical precision. (The phrase 'fifty-one per cent rule', which some people think more accurate, is equally misleading.)

In the Public Interest

If the Director, after applying the fifty per cent rule, decided there was enough evidence to make a conviction more likely than an acquittal, he then had to ask himself whether a prosecution was in the public interest. 'Again,' Sir Thomas told the Royal Commission, 'there are some who maintain that if the evidence is sufficient, a prosecution must necessarily follow.' He went on:

> I, however, strongly prefer to adopt the point of view expressed by Lord Shawcross who, when he was Attorney General, said in a House of Commons debate: 'It has never been the rule in this country — I hope it never will be — that suspected criminal offences must automatically be the subject of prosecution. Indeed the very first regulations under which the Director of Public Prosecutions worked provided that he should . . .

prosecute 'wherever it appears that the offence or the circumstances of its commission is or are of such a character that a prosecution in respect thereof is required in the public interest'. That is still the dominant consideration.'

The remarks Sir Thomas quoted were made to MPs by the then Labour Attorney General, Sir Hartley Shawcross, one evening early in 1951. Lord Shawcross went on to say that it was 'not in the public interest to put a man upon trial, whatever the suspicions may be about the matter, when the evidence is insufficient to justify his conviction, or even to call upon him for an explanation'. He added that the prosecution must have regard to 'the effect which a prosecution, successful or unsuccessful as the case may be, would have on public morale and order, and with many other considerations affecting public policy'.

In his evidence to the Royal Commission, Sir Thomas Hetherington then proceeded to list the most common of these considerations, and his attitudes towards them. Here are some examples, which I have summarized and simplified:

Likely Penalty: do not prosecute in the Crown Court if the defendant is not likely to get more than a conditional or absolute discharge;

Staleness: do not prosecute if the trial will not begin until three years after the last offence unless it is likely the defendant will get a long prison sentence;

Youth: do not prosecute a young person if a warning would be sufficient, especially if the offence is unlikely to be repeated;

Old age and infirmity: do not prosecute elderly or infirm people, unless there is a real possibility the offence will be repeated or it was so bad that you cannot overlook it. Do not prosecute someone who is too ill to stand trial: have the defendant medically examined if necessary;

Mental illness or stress: do not prosecute someone whose mental illness will be worsened by the strain of a trial; but do not be taken in by a psychiatrist's report which says that the defendant is depressed simply because he was caught;

Sexual offences: do not prosecute a boy of 17 for having sex with a girl of 15 if she agreed; do not prosecute a man off 22 for having sex with a man of 19 unless, say, the elder man had gone into a public toilet looking for a male prostitute;

Complainant's attitude: do not prosecute, say, a husband for assaulting his wife if she went to the police in the heat of the moment and she has now calmed down.

These guidelines were rewritten and then issued to all police forces by the Attorney General in 1983: in summarizing them I have left out some of the exceptions and qualifications. But Sir Thomas Hetherington's concluding paragraph in 1978 is well worth reading in full:

If, having weighed such of the above factors as may appertain to the case, I am still in doubt as to whether proceedings are called for, I would throw into the scales the good or bad character of the accused, the attitude of the local community and any information about the prevalence of the particular offence in the area or nationally. Should doubt still remain, I consider that the scales should normally be tipped in favour of the prosecution as, if the balance is so even, it could properly be said that the final arbiter must be the court.

Sir Thomas Hetherington was the first Director to publish such a clear summary of his approach to prosecutions. But the policy of his immediate predecessor, though less well known at the time, was broadly similar. Sir Norman Skelhorn, DPP from 1964 to 1977, maintained in the memoirs he published four years after his retirement that 'a prosecuting authority should only prosecute when, at the time when the decision has to be made, in its view the evidence, if it stands up, will establish the guilt of the accused . . . A prosecuting authority,' said Skelhorn, 'should not institute proceedings upon evidence that it believes is insufficient, albeit suspicious, to establish the case. A prosecutor's main duty is to . . . endeavour to see that . . . guilty people are if possible brought to justice. Side by side with this, he has a duty to endeavour to see that no innocent person is convicted, or even charged'.

Reading Sir Norman Skelhorn's book *Public Prosecutor*, one gathers that he was a little sensitive to criticism that certain spectacular acquittals during his time resulted from prosecutions which should not have been brought. It is a phrase he uses twice in this paragraph:

> The enforcement of criminal law would clearly be brought into disrepute if there were an inordinate number of unsuccessful prosecutions, and the public interest would certainly not be served thereby. This does not mean that every prosecution that is brought must succeed, or else that it should not have been brought. Obviously the reliability of the evidence when tested by cross-examination may be eroded, or a different slant put upon it when the evidence for the defence is given, and in the end a court may quite properly say that the prosecution has failed to satisfy it beyond reasonable doubt of the guilt of the accused, and hence acquit. This, however, does not mean that the prosecution should never have been brought.

The introduction in 1986 of a Crown Prosecution Service, with its own prosecution guidelines, marked the end of the old fifty per cent rule, though the change may turn out to be one of form rather than substance. A highly detailed academic study of how the old rule operated can be found in *Director of Public Prosecutions* by Graham Mansfield and Jill Peay. Unfortunately, their book — though completed in July 1985 — was not published until the beginning of 1987. By then, much of the book was sadly out of date — although the authors' views on the fifty per cent rule will remain valuable to those prosecutors who think the new guidelines I am about to explain are simply the old rule by another name. Even so, there is a rather poignant note from Mansfield and Peay added just before their book went to press, in which they stress that no reference is made to the Code for Crown Prosecutors, published in the summer of 1986. 'Such an inclusion at the time of writing,' they say, 'would have required the skills, not of researchers, but of clairvoyants.'

SEVEN

A Code for Prosecutors

At the heart of this book is the Director's discretion. I explained in the last chapter how Sir Thomas Hetherington was the first Director of Public Prosecutions to discuss in any detail how he decided whether to prosecute. This chapter brings the story up to date. The Attorney General's guide-lines of 1983, based on Sir Thomas Hetherington's memorandum of 1978, have now become the Director's code of 1986.

Under the Prosecution of Offences Act 1985, the Director has to issue a Code for Crown Prosecutors, giving guidance on the general principles they must apply in deciding whether proceedings for an offence should be started; or, where proceedings are already under way, in deciding whether they should be discontinued. Section 10 of the Act says the guidance should also cover the principles to be applied by Crown Prosecutors in deciding what charges should be preferred. The Code is an important document: it applies to cases handled at Headquarters as well as those dealt with locally. It is set out in the Director's annual report to Parliament; and the full text, as published in June 1986, is also printed at the end of this book. I shall be analysing the Code in this chapter.

How much Evidence?

Like the Attorney General's guide-lines of 1983, the Code for Crown Prosecutors begins by saying that the first question to be determined is the sufficiency of the evidence: a bare prima facie case is not enough. And then there is a subtle shift in emphasis. The old guide-lines said the Director applied the test of

> whether there is a reasonable prospect of conviction; or, put another way, whether conviction is more likely than an acquittal before an impartial jury properly directed in accordance with the law.

The new Code says the Crown Prosecution Service

> will apply the test of whether there is a *realistic* prospect of a conviction. When reaching this decision the Crown Prosecutor as a first step will wish to satisfy himself that there is no realistic expectation of an ordered acquittal or a successful submission in the magistrates' court of no case to answer.

I have emphasized the word 'realistic', which has now replaced 'reasonable' as a measure of the prospect that a prosecution will succeed. No doubt a learned thesis could be written on the difference in meaning, if indeed there is one, between 'realistic' and 'reasonable'. I suppose the point is that, since juries are not always reasonable creatures, it might be possible for a case to have had a reasonable prospect of success before a jury of reasonable men but no realistic prospect of success before a jury of real people. Perhaps more significant, the test of whether a conviction is more likely than an acquittal — the famous fifty per cent rule — has vanished. The test of whether the case is likely to be thrown out before the defence have had their say is clearly not the same thing: a case might be strong enough to need answering (no 'realistic prospect of an ordered acquittal') but not strong enough to secure a conviction on the balance of probabilities (with 'a conviction more likely than an acquittal'). So does this mean the fifty per cent rule has been weakened, perhaps to, say, twenty-five per cent? I think not, because paragraph 4 of the Code also makes it clear for the first time that

> a prosecution should not be started or continued unless the Crown Prosecutor is satisfied that there is admissible, substantial, and reliable evidence that a criminal offence known to the law has been committed by an identifiable person.

It also stresses that the Crown Prosecutor 'should have regard to any lines of defence which are plainly open to, or have been indicated by, the accused and any other factors which in his view would affect the likelihood or otherwise of a conviction'. So it seems reasonably clear that Crown Prosecutors are not being told to go ahead now in cases which the Director would have dropped; but there is a much firmer emphasis on the realities of the jury system. In certain parts of London juries are thought to be more sympathetic to some types of villainy than in the more law-abiding rural shires. In certain types of case juries are thought to express their disapproval of the prosecution by acquitting in the face of the evidence. Such a verdict is sometimes described as perverse, but no less a judge than Lord Devlin has said that 'if there is a law which the juryman constantly shows by his verdicts that he dislikes, it is worth examining the law to see if there is anything wrong with it, rather than the juryman'.

I put these points to Sir Thomas Hetherington on the Radio 4 programme *Law in Action* shortly after the Code was published. He pointed out that the 'so-called fifty per cent rule was really just a shorthand way of describing the sort of tests we apply in considering whether the evidence is good enough to justify a prosecution'. Sir Thomas did not think the new Code amounted to a change in the rule:

> It is perhaps a change in the terminology with a little more emphasis on taking a realistic view rather than a view which a reasonable jury might accept. There is sometimes a case in which — to put it coldly — the evidence seems good but in which realistically we feel that we would probably not get a conviction. That is what is meant by the change in phraseology.

John Wood, who moved from being Deputy Director of Public Prosecutions to Head of Legal Services in the Crown Prosecution Service, told me had had never liked the word 'reasonable' in the old fifty per cent rule: he thought it was a much more subjective word than 'realistic'. He thought it inevitable that local prosecutors would take into account the likelihood of convictions by juries in their own areas. But Mr Wood said this policy should not be applied unfairly: if an allegedly obscene publication was on sale in London and Truro, and the prosecution thought that a jury would convict in Truro but acquit at the Old Bailey, it would be wrong to prosecute the bookseller in one place and not the other. It would be even better, he said, to prosecute the publisher first: a conviction would then put the bookseller on notice that he was liable to be prosecuted.

Ken Ashken, Head of Policy at Crown Prosecution Service Headquarters, stressed that in changing the test from 'reasonable' to 'realistic', he and his colleagues were not trying to alter the standard which had been applied in recent years — and which they wanted to be applied in the future. But there had been some evidence, particularly from Graham Mansfield and Jill Peay in the research for their book *The Director of Public Prosecutions*, that people did not really understand the old 'reasonable prospects' test. 'It was felt by some of those who'd thought about it,' Ashken told me, 'that 'realistic prospect' better described what we were actually doing and ought to be doing — without it being intended to signal any dramatic change.'

The Academic Approach

I said earlier that a learned thesis could be written on the difference in meaning between 'realistic' and 'reasonable'. Mansfield and Peay's book, though much more learned than this one could ever be, is not such a work, because — though first published in 1987 — it was completed a year before the Code for Crown Prosecutors was first issued. But Ken Ashken had seen a proof copy of that book before finalizing his proposals on the new guidance for prosecutors, and the two Oxford criminologists can take some comfort from seeing a number of their conclusions reflected in the Code.

Their main concern was that, in deciding whether there was, under the old criteria, a reasonable prospect of proving a case beyond reasonable doubt in front of an impartial jury properly directed in accordance with the law, the prosecutor was being asked to predict the unpredictable. Who could forecast how credible or persuasive the witnesses would turn out to be? Don't forget that the prosecutor has only been able to read a pile of statements; he will not have seen the witnesses perform in court. And, said Mansfield and Peay, the other elements in the reasonable prospects test ('beyond reasonable doubt', 'impartial jury', 'properly directed') were equally uncertain. What's more, they said, once the trial had passed the half-way stage and the defence had its turn, the more chance there was of something going wrong and the prosecution failing. Ironically, the more the prosecutor hears of the defence case, and the clearer it becomes to him that he no longer has a reasonable prospect of success, the less chance he has (short of dropping the whole case) of doing anything about it.

So Mansfield and Peay came up with the novel idea of moving the goal-posts. Too difficult to decide whether there is a reasonable prospect of a conviction? No problem: just tell the prosecutor to decide instead whether there is a reasonable prospect of what is called a 'directed acquittal' — the case being thrown out by the judge at half-time.

By asking the prosecutor merely to predict the success or failure of a possible claim by each defendant — after the prosecutor has called all his evidence — that there is 'no case to answer', Mansfield and Peay are making things much easier for the prosecution. None of this bother about worrying whether the defence have got any good witnesses; no problem about trying to guess how a lay jury will make up its mind, or why it has reached a perverse decision in the past. Instead the prosecutor will be able to claim success whenever his case gets as far as the jury, irrespective of the final verdict.

In support of their new test Mansfield and Peay say it would substitute ' "the art of the possible" for a "belief in the impossible"; the prosecutor would have to work with the "here and now" rather than the "hereafter" '. And they reject the obvious criticism that it would increase the number of unsuccessful prosecutions because the prosecutor would no longer need to worry about anything the defence might have to say: 'focusing the prosecutor's attention more closely on the stage of directed acquittals,' they maintain, 'may result in a more thorough assessment of the strengths and weaknesses of the prosecution case. This,' they claim, 'should reduce the actual numbers of directed acquittals. Standards may thus be raised above the routine practice of reasonable prospects. Thus, substitution of an attainable but ostensibly less ambitious 'half-time' prosecution standard should represent a net gain, in terms of avoidable prosecutions, over the attempt to sustain a rigid adherence to the 'full-time' jury standard which, this research shows, may jeopardise consistency'.

It is very reassuring to see that these proposals were not adopted in this form by the Crown Prosecution Service. 'Consistency' may be an aim of academic researchers but by itself it will do little to solve the problem identified by the Philips Royal Commission of too many hopeless cases coming to court. The aim of the Crown Prosecutor must be to predict which cases will — and should — result in convictions. Instructing the prosecutor to ignore what the jury will get up to is the last thing anybody wants.

The then Head of Legal Services, John Wood, gave his view of the 'half time' test in a private lecture to fledgling Branch Crown Prosecutors in the spring of 1986. In his view it was 'a most imperfect test'. He asked what point there was in starting proceedings and knowing that it was likely to get past the judge at half time while equally knowing that the case was likely to end in an acquittal. The example he gave was admittedly an extreme case, but it demonstrates the drawbacks in what Mansfield and Peay were proposing:

You have a perfectly simple murder case where a man has stabbed another. On the facts put badly like that there is no problem about charging and continuing with that charge. But you know that the offender is a perfectly responsible person and he was defending his house against a man who has previous convictions for violence: he was using what in your view was reasonable force to expel the trespasser. Now you can get that case beyond half time without any trouble at all, but there really isn't a great deal of point in doing so in the knowledge that the result is almost certain to be an acquittal.

So much for the half-time test. Why, then, do I suggest Mansfield and Peay can take any comfort in the Code for Crown Prosecutors? The answer can be found in paragraph 4 of the Code: 'the Crown Prosecutor as a first step will wish to satisfy himself that there is no realistic expectation of an ordered acquittal or a successful submission in the magistrates' court of no case to answer'. But that test, which the two researchers would have made the last word on the subject, is only what the Code calls the 'first step'. The Code goes on to say that the Crown Prosecutor 'should have regard to any lines of defence . . .' The Mansfield and Peay test, by itself, is not enough.

The Likelihood of a Conviction

One example of a prosecution where it must be assumed there are what the Code calls 'factors which in [the Crown Prosecutor's] view would affect the likelihood or otherwise of a conviction' is in a case like Clive Ponting's in 1985. We shall never know what went on in the minds of the jurors who acquitted Mr Ponting, the former civil servant who was charged with sending Mr Tam Dalyell, MP documents about the sinking of the *General Belgrano* during the Falklands conflict, because the Contempt of Court Act 1981 makes it an offence for a journalist to ask them what was said in the jury room. However Clive Ponting himself says in his book *The Right to Know* that he had to face a vetted jury, part of the trial in camera and a summing up by the judge that left him with no legal defence. 'Yet despite all of this,' writes Clive Ponting 'I was acquitted, probably because the jury did not like the way in which the judge had interpreted 'the interests of the state' as being the same as 'the political interests of the government'. This,' he says, 'was widely seen as a victory for common sense and a blow for democracy by the jury.' It might also be seen as a warning to the Director — and ultimately the Attorney General, who of course has to authorize prosecutions under the Official Secrets Act — that such prosecutions are, in the current climate of public opinion, difficult to sustain. Sir Thomas Hetherington told me that, at the time the decision was taken to prosecute Ponting, it had been right to proceed. But he agreed that the verdict would affect his judgment in deciding whether there was a realistic prospect of getting a conviction if a similar case arose in the future.

In case the message still is not clear enough, the next paragraph of the Code for Crown Prosecutors lists as one of thirteen questions which the prosecutor should ask himself in evaluating the evidence

are the facts of the case such that the public would consider it oppressive
to proceed against the accused?

It is worth stressing that this still relates to the sufficiency of evidence: we
have not yet got on to the public interest criteria. So it seems clear that the
prosecutor is being asked to consider whether there is enough evidence,
bearing in mind that what would otherwise be an overwhelming quantity
may not be enough if a jury — or a bench of lay magistrates — 'would consider
it oppressive to proceed'. The phrase could almost have been designed to
fit Mr Ponting, or indeed *Lady Chatterley*.

Perhaps that was why the nine airmen accused in the so-called Cyprus
secrets case were acquitted in 1985. Sir Thomas Hetherington told me he
really did not know what the jury had in mind in acquitting them

> The evidence was fairly strong, and once the judge had ruled admissible
> the various statements and interviews [with the military police] I would
> have expected a conviction. Probably what went wrong was that the jury
> didn't like the length of time the defendants had been in custody. In law
> the evidence was admissible and maybe the jury shouldn't have taken the
> length of time into account, but I suspect they did. Given the same case
> again, we'd think hard about the length of time but we'd have to proceed.

Sir Thomas Hetherington pointed out that an enquiry into the case by David
Calcutt, QC had found nothing wrong with the prosecution. The Director
also noted that the jury had been out for a long time, which he thought
supported his initial decision to go ahead with the case.

In some work places, petty theft is regarded by local people as a perk
of the job. David Gandy, Head of Field Management at Crown Prosecution
Service Headquarters, told me that a case which would lead to conviction
in Dorchester would not necessarily result in a conviction in Liverpool, if
the juries were locally recruited. He confirmed that it was hard to get a jury
to convict a police officer if he was neither young, charged with dishonesty,
nor accused of using serious violence. He thought a prosecutor needed a
'sixth sense' to know when a jury would not convict an offender for no obvious
reason. It was something that one could only acquire from experience gained
over many years, and he conceded that new recruits to the service wouldn't
have it. But the system was designed so that cases would be passed up the
line of command to more experienced staff.

Another factor Mr Gandy mentioned was media coverage of a case, which
— despite reporting restrictions — could influence the way a jury dealt with
the case. 'I'm not saying the press behave irresponsibly,' David Gandy told
me. 'It may well be that they act as a test of public opinion. Where there
is sage and sound comment in the press suggesting that a particular
prosecution would not deter others and would not achieve anything except
spending a great amount of money, the prosecutor has to take that into
account because otherwise it could bring the law into disrepute — which
is a matter I consider of very considerable importance.'

I well remember a BBC television *Newsnight* film on Clive Ponting, broadcast while he was awaiting trial and showing him climbing hills and dales rather in the manner of an old menthol cigarette commercial: it even featured an interview with his local vicar. It seems this had not appeared by chance: Mr Ponting says in *The Right to Know* that his solicitor, Brian Raymond, 'showed great flair in handling the huge and continuing interest' shown in the case by the media:

> At our first meeting Brian and I decided that we could certainly use the 'interest of the State' defence. How we would do it we would consider in more detail later. Our first aim was to make public the real nature of the charges I faced. We decided to run an exclusive story with David Leigh in *The Observer* a week after my first appearance in court. *The Observer* wanted a photograph and a statement and so suddenly I had to get used to the attentions of the media and how to handle them.

Incidentally, not all stories about Clive Ponting were planted by him on co-operative journalists. In the course of a radio interview Sir Michael Havers gave me about his work as Attorney General, he said that the Ponting case was 'simply a question of a very senior civil servant disclosing matters which I say he had no right to disclose'. Sir Michael made it clear afterwards that he was simply outlining the case which he, as prosecutor, had to prove: there was, after all, no doubt that Mr Ponting had disclosed the documents to Mr Dalyell, and what the prosecution turned on was whether, as the Attorney asserted, he had no right to do so. But Clive Ponting viewed it as 'comment on questions that had still to be decided'. Far from having set up the interview, Mr Ponting did not even know it was to be broadcast on *Law in Action*. He says it nearly caused a nasty accident:

> As I happened to be driving along the M4 at the time with the radio on such outspoken comments might well have stopped the case there and then as it was difficult to control the car and listen to such surprising remarks at the same time.

One can think of other cases where a prosecutor might think it 'oppressive' to proceed. Some offences under election law are very technical and may hardly merit a prosecution if the result of the election was not affected. In general, the members of a jury might think it 'oppressive to proceed' with a prosecution for minor offences which had come to light many years after they were committed.

Thirteen Questions of Evidence

The 13 questions to be considered by the prosecution in evaluating the evidence are a much-expanded version of a paragraph in the Attorney General's guide-lines of 1983. But some bits have been left out of the new Code. As I have said, the old guide-lines contained the fifty per cent rule (though the phrase itself was never used) and went on to say that 'an even higher of standard is set if an acquittal . . . might produce unfortunate consequences. For example . . . an unsuccessful prosecution of an allegedly obscene book will, if the trial has attracted publicity, lead to a considerable increase in sales.' This is now obsolete for two reasons: firstly, if no standard (such as fifty per cent) is now specified for ordinary cases it is hard to specify a 'higher standard'; and secondly, obscene books are no longer prosecuted by the Director (though obscene visual images sometimes are).

The first of the 13 questions is perhaps the most important. The Crown Prosecutor has to consider whether any of the evidence is likely to be excluded under the Police and Criminal Evidence Act 1984. If the police have broken the rules, perhaps by using 'oppressive behaviour' to get evidence, then the evidence may be excluded by the court. No evidence means no conviction, which in turn means there should be no prosecution. It must be particularly hard for a police officer to accept that his case is likely to collapse in court because he or his colleagues have put too much pressure on the defendant or a witness. If it had still been up to the police to decide whether a case should go to court there would be no doubt still be cases coming to trial where evidence, though crucial, was likely to be excluded under the 1984 Act and its Codes of Practice. In theory at least, a Crown Prosecutor should not find it so difficult to make an impartial decision before the case gets that far. But in practice the prosecutor may have difficulty in spotting a case where the defendant will be able to convince the court he was leaned on by the police: usually the paperwork presented to the prosecutor by the police appears to be perfectly in order and as he has no right to cross-examine the police or their witnesses he is unlikely to stop the case unless there are obvious worries.

The next question for the prosecutor is related to the first: if the defendant has made a confession (normally, of course, to the police), are there any grounds for believing the admissions 'are of doubtful reliability having regard to the age, intelligence, and apparent understanding of the accused'? Although there are other more recent examples, this seems a clear reminder of the Confait case, which goes back to 1972. Three boys were found guilty of arson at a house in South London where the body of a male prostitute, Maxwell Confait, was found; one of the boys was found guilty of murdering Confait and another, Colin Lattimore, was convicted of manslaughter on the ground of diminished responsibility. Some three years later their convictions were quashed by the Court of Appeal, and an enquiry by Sir Henry Fisher found in 1977 that the police questioning of Lattimore — who, though aged 18, was said to have a mental age of eight — was unfair and oppressive to a person of his mental age. Sir Henry Fisher's enquiry into the Confait case and its aftermath were described in more detail in Chapter 3. The Code of Practice under the Police and Criminal Evidence Act to deal with detention, treatment and questioning by the police includes in a 'note for guidance' the warning that juveniles, the mentally ill and the mentally handicapped may sometimes be prone to provide information which is unreliable, misleading or self-incriminating: 'because of the risk of unreliable evidence it is also important to obtain corroboration of any facts admitted wherever possible'.

The remaining questions which a prosecutor has to consider in evaluating the evidence are mostly concerned with witnesses and the impression they are likely to make in court. For example:

- is the witness exaggerating?
- has he a motive for telling less than the whole truth?
- could his credibility be attacked in court?
- will the witness make a good impression?
- do the eye-witnesses disagree?
- do they agree to the extent that they may have made their story up?
- will all the witnesses be available?
- are any child witnesses likely to be able to give sworn evidence?
- how reliable are any witnesses who may have to identify the accused?
- if there are two or more defendants, and separate trials are ordered,

is there enough evidence against each defendant?

If the evidence is not good enough for a prosecution, that may not be the end of the story. The Assistant Head of Legal Services, Michael Chance, says good prosecuting is not just abandoning weak cases: it is a perfectly respectable aim of the Crown Prosecution Service to get less good cases made into good ones. 'People get terribly sensitive about this, as if in some way you're bending the rules. That's rubbish: if you get a weak case which if presented to the court in its existing form would be a loser, it's a very skilled exercise, and an extremely worthwhile one, to spot the holes in it ·and fill them up: often, by getting the police to interview fresh witnesses.'

Michael Chance thought the more this happened, the better. 'We are not in the business of putting criminals out on the streets,' he said. But he stressed the need for the prosecutor to behave ethically. Was there a risk that an over-enthusiastic police officer, keen to fill a gap, might manufacture the missing evidence? 'I reckon that 99 times out of 100,' Mr Chance told me, 'if you can see what's missing you'll also spot the policeman who's trying to fill the hole with dishonest material. And very often, in a case of complexity, the missing material is actually on a piece of paper somewhere — a bank statement, for example.'

Michael Chance summed up the prosecutor's role by saying that although the statutory clout of the Crown Prosecution Service was to abandon weak cases, the clear duty was to think first whether a weak case could properly be made into a strong case.

The Public Interest

Once the Crown Prosecutor is satisfied that there is enough evidence, he must then move on to consider whether a prosecution would be in the public interest. Here the Code mentions the passage from Lord Shawcross I quoted in the last chapter, and then goes on to reproduce many of the factors which first saw the light of day in the evidence Sir Thomas Hetherington gave to the Royal Commission on Criminal Procedure, before it was absorbed into the Attorney General's guide-lines of 1983 (which I also mentioned in Chapter 6).

Two of the factors raise interesting questions. The first tells the Crown

Prosecutor to consider the likely penalty where the circumstances of an offence are not particularly serious. Dr Andrew Ashworth of the Oxford Institute of Criminology, points out that this could be a potentially far-reaching power in the hands of a Crown Prosecution Service determined to decrease the number of people dealt with by the criminal courts and make more use of cautioning powers. Dr Ashworth also draws attention to the factor headed 'complainant's attitude', which tells the Crown Prosecutor he does not always need to prosecute if the complainant changes his or her mind and asks for proceedings to be dropped. Dr Ashworth asks why, in a system of public prosecutions, the complainant's wishes should carry any more weight than those of anyone else. If the victim has a right to stop a case when the prosecutor wants to go ahead, does he or she have a right to insist on a prosecution when the prosecutor has decided not to proceed? The answer is no, unless there is a private prosecution — and indeed the Home Office guide-lines to the police on cautioning offenders (Circular 14/1985) says 'it is desirable to avoid the situation where the police decide to caution and the aggrieved party wishes to institute private proceedings,' though they go on to stress that 'the interests of the victim, although a most important factor which needs to be weighed in deciding whether the public interest points to prosecution or a caution, cannot, however, be paramount'.

There have been some significant additions to the Attorney's guide-lines which I mentioned in the last chapter. The advice that Crown Prosecutors should take account of the ages of people who have taken part in sexual offences now goes on to say that:

> Sexual assaults upon childen should always be regarded seriously as should offences against adults, such as rape, which amount to gross personal violation. In such cases, where the Crown Prosecutor is satisfied as to the sufficiency of the evidence there will seldom be any doubt that the prosecution will be in the public interest.

In this cost-conscious age there is now a new factor to be considered by the Crown Prosecutor where the 'circumstances of the offence are not particularly serious' and the prosecutor is thinking of simply imposing a caution. He should weigh the likely penalty with the likely length — and cost — of a jury trial. There is a firm belief in the Director's office that, with legal costs as high as they are, it is perfectly proper to take them into account. Taken literally, though, this section could allow the Crown Prosecution Service to reserve prosecution for only a small number of the most serious cases, which would revolutionize the criminal justice system.

The public interest criteria in the new Code conclude with a paragraph almost identical to one in the Attorney General's guide-lines of 1983: the only significant change is that the Crown Prosecutor no longer 'throws into the scales the good or bad character of the accused'.

Though there is no mention of it in the Code (and though it may be inconsistent with what the judge said in the Ponting case), Sir Thomas Hetherington has stressed in the past that the public interest is not the same as the interests of the government. After listing — in a speech to the Media Society in 1980 — some of the factors he took into account in weighing up the public interest, the Director said he wanted to make it clear that

> political motivation should never be amongst those points. In my view, the question of what effect a prosecution would have on the fortunes of the government, or any political party for that matter, either locally or nationally, can never be a proper question to ask oneself when deciding whether to prosecute.

Sir Thomas conceded that this was a difficult principle to explain, partly because he was appointed — and supervised — by politicians. The relationship between the Director of Public Prosecutions and the Attorney General is so subtle and important that I shall be devoting Chapter 10 to it.

The remainder of the Code for Crown Prosecutors is brand new. As you saw in Chapter 4, the Crown Prosecutor now has the power under section 23 of the Prosecution of Offences Act 1985 to end criminal proceedings by issuing a notice of discontinuance. This power is in addition to the power a prosecutor has always had to withdraw a case or offer no evidence. Paragraph 10 of the Code reminds prosecutors that, unless they have already given advice to the police at a preliminary stage in the proceedings, the police decision to bring charges 'should never be met with passive acquiescence but must always be the subject of review'. It goes on to remind Crown Prosecutors that they should continue to review cases even when proceedings are under way, 'not least because the emergence of new evidence or information may sometimes cast doubt on the propriety of the original decision to proceed'.

The Code seems to acknowledge that in some cases the initial review may have been a bit scrappy, and in effect says that a decision to discontinue what turns out to be a bad case is better late than never. There must be a number of cases where the prosecutor only gets round to reading the papers properly just before a hearing. In some cases he will have no choice: he may be faced with a pile of overnight charges when he arrives at court early in the morning. (This was a particular problem in certain London courts which at one time insisted — though they had no power to do so — that the police should not grant extended bail. This in turn ensured that all defendants appeared in court within 24 hours or so of being charged. It was a tactic which seemed designed to produce a plea of guilty before the defendant had time to consult a solicitor, although magistrates defended it by arguing that it reduced the number of absconding defendants.)

In other cases the Crown Prosecutor will already have approved the police charges at an earlier stage, and there must be a temptation for him to let the case go ahead and hope for the best, rather than admit publicly that his original decision to proceed was wrong. But the Code tells him to be 'resolute' when faced with new information, and presumably he is expected to be just as resolute if he realizes he was wrong the first time: 'public confidence in the Service can only be maintained if there is no doubting its commitment to taking effective action at whatever stage whenever it is right to do so'. Even so Crown Prosecutors should be tactful: 'It will be the normal practice to consult the police whenever it is proposed to discontinue proceedings instituted by them'.

The Code then deals with the tricky subject of accepting pleas of guilty. It may be, for example, that a defendant charged with burglary is prepared to admit the lesser charge of theft; another defendant might be prepared to admit to one of two alternative charges. The Code says that 'administrative convenience in the form of a rapid guilty plea should not take precedence over the interests of justice, but where the court is able to deal adequately with an offender on the basis of a plea which represents a criminal involvement not inconsistent with the alleged facts, the resource advantages both to the Service and to the courts generally will be an important consideration'. The Code might have added — but does not — that if a prosecutor accepts a plea of guilty he knows for sure the defendant will be convicted: a trial may always lead to an acquittal.

Despite the Code's dismissal of 'administrative convenience', there must be times when a prosecutor finds it tempting to make the defendant an offer he cannot refuse: plead guilty to a lesser charge and get the case over and done with. Some defendants in this position are even prepared to plead guilty to offences they have not committed: after all, if they have no confidence in being acquitted in court of offences they deny committing, they might as well take advantage of the prosecutor's offer to limit the damage. But it can never be in the public interest for a defendant to plead guilty to an offence he did not commit. And just in case a prosecutor may be too keen to twist the defendant's arm, the Code goes on to warn Crown Prosecutors not to increase the number of charges 'to obtain leverage for the offering of a plea of guilty'. In any case, prosecutors are told to keep the number of allegations as low as possible, perhaps by picking specimen charges. And they do not have to throw the book at a defendant:

> The charges laid should adequately reflect the gravity of the defendant's conduct and will normally be the most serious revealed by the evidence. Provided, however, that the offence charged is not inappropriate to the nature of the facts alleged and the court's sentencing powers are adequate, the Crown Prosecutor should take into account matters such as speed of trial, mode of trial, and sufficiency of proof which may properly lead to a decision not to prefer or continue with the gravest possible charge. The Crown Prosecutor should also take into account probable lines of defence when exercising his discretion.

The constant aim of saving time and money appears in the next section of the Code, which deals with offences that can be tried either by the magistrates or before a jury. The Code makes it clear that while the attraction of getting the case over quickly should never be the Crown Prosecutor's only reason for asking to have the case tried by the magistrates, he is entitled to consider the delay and additional cost a jury trial will involve. It would be interesting to discover how many Crown Prosecutors have interpreted this section to mean 'have the case dealt with in the magistrates' court whenever you can get away with it'.

The Code ends with a section on juveniles — people aged under 17. It stresses the importance of using prosecution as a last resort ('a severe step') in dealing with young people and reminds Crown Prosecutors that they can suggest the local social services department should take care proceedings instead. The Code refers to police guide-lines on cautioning juveniles (Home Office Circular 14/1985) which say that 'the prosecution of a juvenile is not a step to be taken without the fullest consideration of whether the public interest (and the interests of the juvenile concerned) may be better served by a course of action which falls short of prosecution'. Even a formal caution is enough to give a juvenile what amounts to a criminal record, and the police are encouraged to consider giving an offender 'an informal word of advice or warning' instead. A caution can only be isued if the evidence is sufficient to justify a prosecution and the juvenile has admitted the offence. A first-time juvenile offender who admits a non-serious offence will generally be cautioned rather than prosecuted.

The Crown Prosecutor's Manuals

Though the Code goes much further in revealing policy than any published document has so far, it is by no means the last word on the subject. The Director has prepared two bulky loose-leaf manuals which are issued to each Crown Prosecutor. They are marked 'restricted', the lowest level of security classification, and prosecutors are warned to look after them and not disclose their contents to people outside the service. One is on policy; the other deals with practice and procedure.

Sir Thomas Hetherington told me that writing the policy manual had been a formidable task, blending matters of principle with practical considerations and the experience of prosecutors from many parts of the country. He stressed that it contained policy, not dogma: the guidance, with very few exceptions, was not rigid. Its purpose was not to tell a Crown Prosecutor how to decide every situation, but rather to help bring about the correct decision on the basis of sound judgment and the sensible exercise of discretion.

In his introduction to the first edition of the policy manual — which deals with general policy matters as well as specific categories of offence — Sir Thomas emphasized the importance of achieving the maximum possible degree of consistency in matters of policy. He said the public were entitled to expect from the Crown Prosecution Service a reasoned and uniform approach to the many vital areas in the prosecution process where discretionary authority lay with the prosecution, and the manual aimed to provide every Crown Prosecutor with guidance on the factors to be taken into consideration when such decisions were made.

The practice and procedure manual was also designed to give guidance in areas where some consistency was thought necessary — bail applications, for example — but it does not attempt to describe detailed working methods or office procedures, which the Crown Prosecution Service believes are better designed locally. There are, however, rules governing the level at which decisions can be taken. Any Crown Prosecutor, however new, has all the legal powers of the Director of Public Prosecutions himself — but in practice Crown Prosecutors have to consult Branch Crown Prosecutors on certain decisions, and there are others where the Chief Crown Prosecutor must take the final decision or even refer the case to Headquarters.

Sir Thomas explained that he could not show me the two manuals because this department had never thought it right to reveal to the public precisely the circumstances in which they would prosecute, or not prosecute. The general principles were in the Code, he said, 'but if, for instance, the manual revealed the principles we apply in deciding whether or not to prosecute someone for incest, it would be a licence to commit incest for anyone who came within that particular category'. (I shall be taking a closer look at this argument in the next chapter.)

The manuals also warn young prosecutors of pitfalls in proving particular offences: alternative offences are suggested where these are just as effective. This again is something which the Crown Prosecution Service does not particularly want defence solicitors to have.

I suggested to Sir Thomas that he should have done more to explain to the public his reasons for not bringing a prosecution on occasions when it was clear a crime had been committed by somebody. 'Sometimes we do explain our reasons,' he said, adding that

> in some of the serious complaints against the police, where it hasn't been possible to identify a particular defendant, I have said so. But generally we confine our reasoning either to 'there was insufficient evidence' or 'it was not in the public interest to proceed'. We get into all sorts of difficulties if we try to give reasons. The reason for not prosecuting might be that we just didn't believe the complainant, or the witnesses, but if we say so it would be very damaging to the potential witness and it would discourage others, in future cases, from coming forward and making statements to the police.

The Attorney General, Sir Michael Havers, told me that if the Director gave his reasons for not bringing a prosecution it could lead to trial by media. It was very unfair on the person who was not to be prosecuted if he was then tried by the press.

In Chapter 3 I speculated on the reasons for prosecution decisions made by past Directors. In the next chapter I shall be going one better, and looking at the specific cases which will undoubtedly arise in the future. But first, a general point: can the Director of Public Prosecutions decide *never* to bring prosecutions for a particular crime?

EIGHT

The Duty to Proceed

In its obituary of Sir Theobald Mathew, Director of Public Prosecutions from 1944 to 1964, *The Times* discussed the difficulty Mathew faced in deciding whether to prosecute a book such as *Lady Chatterley's Lover*. Was it obscene? It is worth quoting again from a passage in the obituary to which I referred in Chapter 2.

> On the one hand the law prohibited the publication of obscene material and it was the Director's duty to act; on the other hand the public and general conception of what was immoral or obscene was in a fluid state and no one could tell the outcome. It may be that Mathew made mistakes in choosing to prosecute some particular work or in choosing some particular form of procedure but it was a measure of his courage that he did not act in such a way that he could be taken to regard the law prohibiting obscene publications as a dead letter. While recognizing that his task was well nigh impossible, Mathew nevertheless sought fairly to enforce the criminal law in the state in which it had been entrusted to him.

What *The Times* seems to be arguing is that it is not up to a mere Director of Public Prosecutions to thwart the will of Parliament by failing to prosecute obscene material, even if he happened to think a conviction was unlikely — in other words that the Director should not use his discretion to stop *all* such prosecutions for a particular offence. The same argument was used in 1985 by the Attorney General, Sir Michael Havers, in a speech he made folowing the acquittal of Clive Ponting on a charge under Section 2 of the Official Secrets Act (quoted in my earlier book *Your Rights and the Law*). It seemed to many people that, following the jury's verdict, the Act could no longer be used with any degree of confidence against civil servants who disclosed confidential information in what they saw as the national interest. So Sir Michael asked himself if he should 'simply sit back and say I won't prosecute anyone'. To this he replied that if he took such a view he would, quite rightly, be accused of a serious derogation of duty:

> I do have a duty to enforce the criminal law. I have no right, nor must I seek to usurp the functions of parliament by effectively repealing legislation myself. Parliament has given me a discretion as to which prosecutions

I should bring but not a discretion to say for all time I will not bring any prosecutions under this section. As I have a discretion, should I then say to myself — well, I will only bring proceedings where there are serious security implications, or only in line with the recommendations in the Franks report [which recommended the replacement of section 2]? Likewise I think it would be a remarkable constitutional innovation for me to proceed automatically as if the law had been amended by the Franks Report. While Section 2 stands I and my successors have to recognise that parliament has given us a discretion and it would be wrong for us to fetter that discretion in any way.

Really? Is there any practical difference between deciding, on each occasion a certain type of crime is committed, that there should be no prosecution in the particular case — and deciding, in principle, that there should never be prosecutions for that type of offence? If the Attorney General and the Director of Public Prosecutions have been given a discretion by Parliament to prosecute if they see fit, why shouldn't they be allowed to exercise that discretion by not prosecuting if they do not see fit? *The Times* speaks of Sir Theobald Mathew's 'courage' in not treating 'the law prohibiting obscene publications as a dead letter'. Surely Mathew's obituarist did not think there should be prosecutions from time to time just to keep this offence alive, and no doubt other offences too. Then how often? And what would be the point if they all resulted in acquittals? Surely to insist on regular prosecutions whatever the circumstances is to fetter the very discretion that Sir Michael Havers and others were so keen to preserve.

Of course, the Director of Public Prosecutions cannot admit publicly that he will never prosecute for particular offences. To do so would lead to a public outcry, as people would suppose that these crimes would then be committed with impunity as a result. But it is well known that in certain circumstances some offences are hardly ever the subject of a criminal prosecution by the Director and those who follow his guide-lines — for example, incest between a brother and sister, or shop-lifting by elderly ladies of hitherto unblemished character (other examples can be inferred from the Code for Crown Prosecutors, discussed in the last chapter, and from John Wood's remarks which I shall be quoting in the next section). That is precisely why we give the Director a discretion to prosecute: what Parliament or the judges may have laid down as the law many years ago may not be what is wanted today. Perhaps in due course Parliament will get round to changing the law. In the meantime judges and juries rightly do their best to ensure that the law reflects the views of society by treating certain criminal behaviour as unworthy of punishment. Better still is to have a prosecution service with a discretion to stop certain types of case coming to court in the first place.

I put these points to Sir Thomas Hetherington. He agreed that a Director of Public Prosecutions could say to himself that in all normal cases of a particular type he would not bring a prosecution. But Sir Thomas said that for two reasons no Director could say that publicly.

First, he did not think it right for any Director to modify the criminal law.

I suggested that if he decided not to prosecute in those cases he would, in effect, be doing just that. He explained that he would not say he would *never* prosecute in, for example, cases of elderly shop-lifters. 'What we would say in a case like this is that we would give a lot of weight to the age of the defendant — which is in the Code. If we're not prosecuting somebody,' said the Director, 'we never give reasons for non-prosecution. We don't say what particular policy we've applied: we say we've decided it's not in the public interest to go ahead. It might be that our reason for not prosecuting is that we didn't believe a word that the principal witness said. But I can't say that: it would be defamatory and it would discourage witnesses from coming forward in the future.'

His second reason for not revealing publicly a policy not to prosecute crimes of a certain type was that it could lead to an increase in those crimes. I am not convinced: the brother and sister who commit incest do so because they think nobody will ever know; the elderly female shop-lifter often does not think rationally at all. Since they are not inhibited by what they assume is the risk of prosecution they will not alter that conduct if they discover that there is no risk after all. Perhaps some not very elderly, not very confused ladies with long criminal records will think they have suddenly been given a licence to steal things — but they would soon find out that the new policy does not apply to them anyway.

Hard Cases

At the beginning of March 1986, just a month before the Crown Prosecution Service started work in the metropolitan areas of England, a group of prosecuting solicitors gathered at a Birmingham hotel for a 'standardization course' designed to turn them into Branch Crown Prosecutors. They heard a talk given by John Wood, then still known as Deputy Director of Public Prosecutions rather than Head of Legal Services — or, indeed, Director-Designate of the Serious Fraud Office. At one stage Mr Wood spoke about 'consent cases' — crimes in which Parliament had said a prosecution could only be brought with the consent of the Director of Public Prosecutions. As you may remember, some of these cases are still dealt with at Crown Prosecution Headquarters: in others, the consent to prosecution is now given at local level. So the prosecutors in Birmingham that weekend were within a month of having to decide whether to proceed with prosecutions in cases which in the past they had always sent to the DPP: the most dramatic example of these was murder. John Wood's lecture was aimed at helping them make these decisions, but it also provides a fascinating insight into how a prosecutor exercises his discretion generally.

Mr Wood began, however, with the offence of wasting police time, which he said Parliament had made a 'DPP's consent' case to lessen the risk that the police would use it to discourage people from making perfectly proper complaints against the force. It followed, he said, that if prosecutors ever came across a case where the purpose of the prosecution was, in fact, to stop a man or woman complaining, they should 'give short shrift to that set of papers'. But the more difficult question was: how many hours had to be wasted to justify a prosecution for wasting police time?

Of course, it all depends. Mr Wood gave two examples:

> A bank phones the police and says it has been told there is a bomb in the strongroom. The police arrive, clear the building, search the vault, and within a quarter of an hour they discover it is a hoax. Several officers are involved: the total time wasted is three hours.

John Wood said that in those circumstances he would prosecute the hoaxer if there was enough evidence because the incident would have disrupted the bank's business, inconvenienced the public and alarmed the bank's customers — as well as the police officers who would have been sent to search for what might have been a bomb.

Mr Wood then gave another example:

> A 17-year-old girl comes into the police station after midnight on a Saturday night and says she has been raped. She's convincing and makes a statement, but does not identify her assailant. Police start making enquiries and some ten or fifteen hours of police time is taken up before she admits she was not raped after all: she was late coming home and the complaint had been a way of mollifying her father who is rather strict.

In those circumstances John Wood said he thought 'a thorough ticking off was the thing to do' rather than a prosecution. He then added a new factor to the case:

> Suppose the girl has now named her alleged assailant. He is brought in at one o'clock in the morning, put in a cell overnight, heavily questioned, and not released until 3 o'clock the following afternoon.

In those circumstances John Wood said he would certainly have advised on bringing a prosecution for wasting police time.

Next, the fledgling Branch Crown Prosecutors moved on to consider cases involving homosexual behaviour:

> Two males are found in a public toilet in the middle of Birmingham engaged in homosexual acts at one o'clock in the afternoon. One is aged 50 with a string of previous convictions and the other is 13 years old.

Clearly, said John Wood, you prosecute the man and not the boy. Once more, he altered the facts:

> Suppose one man is 25 and the other is 18. Again, it is the middle of the day and there are plenty of people going to and fro.

The prosecutors agreed with John Wood that in those circumstances they would prosecute both men unless there were very good reasons for not doing so. The scenario changed again:

> Suppose there are two men of 25 found in a public car park in Birmingham at about 10.30 on a Saturday night. They are engaging in a homosexual act, maybe in a corner of the car park but nevertheless reasonably visible to anybody who happened to go fairly close by.

In those circumstances Mr Wood would have prosecuted. But:

> Suppose you get the same situation in the same car park at two in the morning. The car park was locked at midnight and the two men had climbed over the fence to get in.

This was a bit of a trick question, though everybody spotted it at once. If the car park was not a public place there could be no prosecution: the law allows homosexual acts between consenting adults in private.

In summing up, John Wood suggested that the key to the problem was whether a member of the public was likely to see what was going on and be offended:

> There are, as always with the criminal law, great difficulties in the borderline cases. What do you do in the lavatorial case where there is a brick loose between two cubicles and where the policeman climbs over the top and looks down to see what's happening? Now I don't think that, without knowing the full facts, I can help you on that. If this is a notorious public toilet where this sort of thing is constantly happening, I would prosecute. If it isn't, and if perhaps the brick has only been loose one day and these two were overtaken by the urge, and the two men have no previous convictions, a caution might suffice. But you've really got to exercise your judgment and decide if the public interest requires proceedings in that sort of case.

The discussion then moved on to incest:

> You have a father who has sexual intercourse with his daughter when she is about 14. It is admitted. There are other young girls in the house.

In that situation, John Wood said he would undoubtedly prosecute. Generally speaking, the approach to father/daughter incest was to prosecute unless there were good reasons for not doing so. But if the act of intercourse had only taken place once, and the daughter had been removed to a place of safety so that incest was not likely to happen again, John Wood said he would be looking to see if a caution would suffice.

Mother/son incest, said Mr Wood with relief, was really rather a rarity. He would not normally prosecute unless they were of adult age, living together virtually as husband and wife, and showed no signs of breaking off the relationship.

There was, however, just such a prosecution early in 1987. The *Sunday Mirror* reported the case of a woman imprisoned for incest with her son. It explained that the woman, Sandra, had been just 16 when her son Dale was born. The boy's father, Brian, was away in the army so his sister and her husband adopted Dale. Sixteen years later the boy was told his real father was Brian, the man he had believed was his uncle. A year later Dale was introduced to his mother, Sandra, who had been married three times and by now was living with her new husband, Phil. 'I couldn't believe it,' Dale told the *Mirror*. 'I kept saying to myself that she can't be. She's too young, too attractive.'

After a while, Dale became jealous of Phil. Meanwhile Phil started seeing another woman and, after a row with Dale, left Sandra. Dale moved in with Sandra, and despite the advice of a solicitor who warned them incest was an offence, 'one night it just happened. It seemed the natural thing to do.' But it was not. After pleading guilty Dale was put on probation and Sandra got nine months imprisonment. To complete the story, Dale told the *Mirror* he would wait for her. 'They can't stop us seeing each other or living in the same house. There is no law against us having a loving relationship, only a sexual one'.

Brother/sister incest was a more difficult area, according to Mr Wood:

> Suppose you get a brother of 18 and a sister of 14 living in the same house as part of a 'problem family'.

One of the prosecutors suggested it depended on whether the brother and sister would continue living together. John Wood agreed. 'If you've got a problem family where the father and mother are not taking a great deal of interest in the welfare of the children then you may well have to mount a prosecution, if only to make sure the offence is not repeated. If you've got a good family where they are horrified that this has happened and they immediately send the boy or the girl off to an uncle or aunt, then in those circumstances one would caution them and hope that it would not be repeated. If there was a fairly large difference in age between the brother and the sister — if the brother was 25 and the sister about 14 — one may well prosecute the brother because there has been, in a sense, a breach of trust'.

After that, a word of warning: please do not treat this part of the book as advice on how to waste police time, commit homosexual acts in public, or have incestuous relationships, without being prosecuted. Everything depends on the facts of the individual case. And different prosecutors have different views. But it was interesting to see how the lawyers listening to John Wood's remarks would have exercised their discretion in these difficult cases. It was also salutory to remember that few of the facts in these hypothetical examples would have become public knowledge in real life. One should always be slow to criticise prosecution decisions on the basis of sketchy newspaper reports.

Some Problems for the Future

With the Crown Prosecution Service so newly established its staff have quite enough problems of their own to be getting on with. But Dr Andrew Ashworth, of the Oxford Centre for Criminological Research, raised one or two more in a lecture at the University of Southampton late in 1986.

Firstly, why should the defendant be allowed to decide where a case which can be tried in either the magistrates' court or the Crown Court should be heard? Should not the Crown Prosecutor be allowed to make the decision?

Secondly, should not the Crown Prosecutor be allowed to recommend a sentence to the court once the defendant has been convicted? Is that very different from the proposal in the Criminal Justice Bill 1987 to allow the

Attorney General to refer sentences seen as over-lenient to the Court of Appeal?

These questions point to a much more active role for the Crown Prosecutor. He would no longer be restricted to putting the facts before the court: instead he would virtually become part of the courtroom process. But then to some extent he is already. The court knows that the Crown Prosecutor will only let cases go through if he thinks the defendant is guilty and deserving of punishment. The Crown Prosecutor will have studied the prosecution evidence to the best of his ability; in bringing it before the court he is asking the court to put the seal of approval on his pre-judgment of the case. So in one sense it may be the Crown Prosecutor himself, or at least his judgment, that is on trial. But this approach by the courts could have alarming results.

It courts tend to feel they can safely rubber-stamp the Crown Prosecutor's decisions there will be two possible consequences. Either the prosecutor will become sloppy and over-confident, letting too many cases through because he is sure that anything with his name on will lead to a conviction. Or the prosecutor will feel under as much pressure as a judge or jury to decide the case on what can only be incomplete evidence, and he will only prosecute in cases where he is virtually certain that the defendant will be convicted.

On the other hand, if the Crown Prosecutor thinks his judgment counts for nothing he may tend to feel undermined and demoralized. If a prosecutor finds too many of his cases being thrown out he will either restrict his prosecutions to cases that can hardly fail (which will mean too many people getting off) or he will lose confidence in his own ability to assess a case (which will probably mean yet more weak cases getting to court). Who would be a prosecutor?

NINE

Private Prosecutions

In general, everyone has the right to bring criminal proceedings against anyone else. Before the invention of the Crown Prosecution Service (described in Chapter 4), the police used to do the vast majority of prosecutions, but in theory a police officer was in no better position than any other person to bring a criminal case. The police had no statutory duty to prosecute, and no special powers or immunities in bringing a case. It was for this reason that Sir Theobald Mathew, Director of Public Prosecutions from 1944 to 1964, was able to say — as he often did — that his title was a misnomer because he directed nobody and there were no public prosecutions. The point he was making was that all police prosecutions were really private prosecutions, and the prosecutions he brought as Director were only a tiny proportion of the total number.

There is, however, an important restriction on the right of private prosecution. Around 40 statutes contain offences which can only be prosecuted with the agreement of the Attorney General. There are also more than 60 statutes which require the Director's consent to a prosecution. The Director's consent can now be given by any Crown Prosecutor. But unless a private prosecutor can get the consent Parliament has insisted on, there can be no prosecution.

The aim of these provisions is to stop busybodies blundering in and prosecuting people in circumstances which would not be seen as appropriate. Sir Thomas Hetherington has said these 'consent provisions' are useful in particularly sensitive areas of criminal law such as race relations and film censorship.

The Director also has the power to stop any private prosecution: I will be explaining how it works later in this chapter.

The Right to Prosecute

The right of an ordinary member of the public to bring a private prosecution was described by Lord Diplock as 'a useful constitutional safeguard against capricious, corrupt or biased failure or refusal of [the] prosecuting authorities to prosecute offenders against the criminal law'. Lord Wilberforce said the right 'remains a valuable constitutional safeguard against inertia or partiality on the part of the authority'. (The two judges were giving their decisions in the case brought in 1977 by John Gouriet, who was secretary of a pressure group called the Freedom Association, against the Union of Post Office Workers which had decided to instruct its members not to handle mail in transit between Britain and South Africa. In that case, the House of Lords decided that the Attorney General was not required to bring an action to prevent a breach of the criminal law when requested to by a member of the public, as distinct from somebody materially affected by the breach.)

Nevertheless, the Royal Commission on Criminal Procedure reported in 1981 that private prosecutions for offences other than shop-lifting or common assault were 'very rare indeed', and said they 'scarcely seemed' sufficient to justify the submission that the private prosecution was 'the ultimate safeguard for the citizen against inaction on the part of the authorities'. In any case, the Philips Commission pointed out, in well over a hundred acts of Parliament the right to prosecute was subject to consent from the DPP or the Attorney General. Expense was also a factor in reducing the number of private prosecutions. In the Commission's view, the criminal law was only appropriate where the community's interests were at risk:

> Criminal sanctions are imposed for the benefit of society as a whole, on its behalf and at its expense. We do not think that private citizens should have an unlimited right of access to the criminal process to remedy wrongs for which other measures might be more appropriate. But where criminal proceedings are taken, they should be paid for out of public funds. We therefore recommend that if a private citizen wishes to initiate a prosecution he should apply in the first instance to the Crown Prosecutor. If the latter is satisfied about the case, applying the same criteria as he would for any other prosecution, he should take the case on. If he is not, and the private citizen, after explanation, still wishes to proceed, the latter should be able to make an application for leave to commence proceedings to a magistrates' court . . . Where leave has been given, this should automatically carry with it a right for the prosecutor's reasonable costs to be paid out of central funds.

The Government's View

The Royal Commision's proposals were rejected by the government, though it did accept a related proposal which would give courts power to thwart 'vexatious' prosecutions (now enacted as section 24 of the Prosecution of Offences Act 1985). In its White Paper *An Independent Prosecution Service for England and Wales* published in 1983, the government said it saw 'no sufficient justification' for imposing the restrictions recommended by the Royal Commission. 'Nor would it be justifiable, simply because magistrates had given leave for such a prosecution to be brought,' said the White Paper, 'for the costs thenceforward (irrespective of outcome) to be borne by public funds.'

Private prosecutors are not bound to follow the Code for Crown Prosecutors issued by the Director of Public Prosecutions, although in a Parliamentary written answer the Solicitor General said he proposed to 'invite all other prosecuting authorities . . . to adopt it to the extent that it is applicable to their respective functions'. But the Solicitor General's attempt to extend the Code to other prosecutors seems inconsistent with Paragraph 2 of the Code itself, which says the Crown Prosecution Service's Code is 'designed for and aimed directly at those who prosecute in its name'. In any case, 'prosecuting authorities' presumably covers only public bodies, such as the Inland Revenue or the Customs and Excise — and perhaps private organizations such as the RSPCA, but certainly not the shopkeepers and other private citizens who choose to bring prosecutions. And even if those private prosecutors who consider themselves to be 'prosecuting authorities' choose, when they feel like it, to accept the Solicitor General's 'invitation' to follow the Code, private citizens are unlikely to take much notice of it, especially if the Code has been the reason why the Crown Prosecutor has refused to go ahead with a public prosecution on the same facts.

It seems anomalous that the government should have imposed pretty stringent restrictions on the prosecuting powers of police forces while continuing to allow private prosecutors to do just what they like. The Crown Prosecutor has to take over all police prosecutions and decide whether they should go ahead; he does not have to interfere with private prosecutions, even though some private prosecutors are less likely to know what they are doing than police forces which charge hundreds of people every day. Perhaps the government was trying to save money by rejecting the Royal Commission's recommendation; perhaps it was trying to be fair to private prosecutors whose cases really have slipped through the net. Or maybe it was just trying to spot a political storm on the horizon and sail away from it. But it did keep for itself the trump card.

The Director's Powers

Section 6 of the 1985 Act, which preserves the right of anyone apart from the police to bring a private prosecution, goes on to make it clear that the Director — or indeed any Crown Prosecutor — can take over these proceedings at any stage. Once he has taken over a private prosecution he can discontinue it under section 23 of the Act (see Chapter 4), or withdraw the charge, or offer no evidence. If no evidence is offered the accused person must be acquitted. Withdrawal of a charge requires the court's permission, which will only be granted for good reason; it is also theoretically possible for the charge to be reopened later.

If somebody brings a private prosecution against you (and I do mean a criminal prosecution in the magistrates' court, not a civil action in the county court) then it may be worth your while contacting your local Branch Crown Prosecutor and asking him if he will intervene to stop it. You will not find it easy though. Sir Thomas Hetherington, in his evidence to the Philips Royal Commission in 1978, made it clear that this would only be done in very exceptional cases. The Director told Philips that he and his predecessors had always considered that taking over a private prosecution with a view to offering no evidence would be an improper exercise of his powers, 'save in an exceptional case like Turner's' — which I shall be describing later in this chapter. In Hetherington's view, the protection against unjustified prosecution lay with the courts, as the magistrates had discretion in deciding whether to grant a summons to a private prosecutor. If the justices gave the go-ahead, the Director thought the case should generally go to court.

This view was supported by another senior member of the Crown Prosecution Service to whom I spoke: he said he would only interfere in a private prosecution if it was something approaching an abuse of the courts. 'We've got to feel that the proceedings represent a genuine injustice to the defendant,' he told me, 'because if it is an utterly hopeless case the defendant will have the opportunity in court to establish his innocence'. That, of course, may involve time, expense and anxiety — but the Crown Prosecutor to whom I spoke pointed out that Parliament had chosen, contrary to the Royal Commission's advice, to keep the right of private prosecution and it would be contrary to the spirit of the Act if he and his colleagues habitually used their powers to stop private prosecutions.

There is a further problem. Let us imagine that you have been arrested by a store detective and the shop is prosecuting you for theft. You contact the local Crown Prosecutor and say you can prove you bought the goods somewhere else, but the shop refuses to believe you. The Crown Prosecutor has no way of finding out what evidence the shop has got, and the shop is under no obligation to tell him. Faced with only one side of the story, it would be hard for the Crown Prosecutor to stop the case unless, perhaps, it clearly falls outside the public interest criteria in the Director's Code (discussed in Chapter 7).

The *Nolle Prosequi*

For the past four hundred years and more, the Attorney General has had the common law power to bring any proceedings to a premature end by doing something called 'entering a *nolle prosequi*'. Strictly speaking this only postpones the prosecution indefinitely, though in practice the case is unlikely to be reopened. It is not a power which can be used in the magistrates' court.

Although the Attorney's powers are theoretically very wide, the *nolle prosequi* has generally only been used in recent years where an accused person who had been committed for trial was found to be seriously ill. Exceptionally, Sir Michael Havers entered a *nolle* in 1980 to stop a man named Gleaves, who called himself Bishop of the Medway, from bringing a second private prosecution against the authors of the book *Johnny Go Home* after his first attempt had resulted in their acquittal at a cost to public funds of £50,000.

Another very unusual use of the *nolle* was in the private prosecution brought by Mrs Mary Whitehouse against the director of *Romans in Britain*, a play at the National Theatre which protrayed homosexual rape. At a late stage in the trial, counsel for the prosecutor decided to withdraw. He duly told the defendant, Michael Bogdanov, only to discover that the judge thought there was sufficient evidence to put to the jury. It was too late to 'offer no evidence' and the judge refused to allow the prosecution to withdraw. So Sir Michael Havers entered a *nolle prosequi* as it would have been oppressive for Mr Bogdanov to have been put in jeopardy after he had been told the case would be stopped, and in the absence of the judge's consent this was the only way in which the prosecution's wishes could be put into effect.

It was to avoid the need for any further public display of the Attorney's wide discretionary powers that section 24 of the 1985 Act, dealing with vexatious prosecutions, was introduced. Only the Attorney can enter a *nolle prosequi*: it is not a power that is available to Crown Prosecutors.

The Doctor and *The Sun*

At the beginning of Chapter 6 I mentioned two recent private prosecutions: the trial of an Essex doctor accused of raping an eight-year-old girl (a case funded originally by *The Sun* newspaper), and the private prosecution of Gary Austin on manslaughter charges by Mrs Pauline Williams. In the second of those two cases, I quoted Sir Patrick Mayhew's explanation of Sir Thomas Hetherington's decision: 'Once the case had been committed for trial,' the Solicitor General said, 'the Director felt it would be wrong for [Mrs Williams] to be put to further time, trouble and expense.' It is interesting to note that the Director decided not to take over the prosecution of the Essex doctor after that case had been sent for trial. The reason was simple: in the view of Sir Thomas Hetherington, and everyone in his department who had read the papers, the evidence was just not good enough.

But the magistrate's decision that there *was* an arguable case must surely have given the Director a few anxious moments. And however confident Sir Thomas was that he had got it right, when the jury at the doctor's subsequent trial stayed out for more than three hours there must have been a certain amount of nail-biting in Queen Anne's Gate, as well as in the cells beneath Chelmsford Crown Court. But in the end the Director was vindicated by the jury's verdict: they found the doctor not guilty on the two (alternative) charges of rape and indecent assault. (Incidentally, it was not generally realized that the leading counsel who had been briefed for a prosecution which the DPP had refused to bring was John Mathew, QC, the son of one of Sir Thomas Hetherington's predecessors.)

Despite the failure of its prosecution, *The Sun* took some comfort from a ruling by the trial judge that some of the paper's costs would be met from central funds. This, claimed the newspaper, was 'the clearest possible indication' that it had acted properly in funding the case. *The Sun* believed it was 'a matter of the utmost concern that an eight-year-old girl has been sexually abused and the guilty party, whoever he is, has not been brought to justice.' What *The Sun* failed to explain was how making allegations unsupported by sufficient evidence against someone who was then acquitted was going to help convict the guilty man.

In its editorial column *The Sun* demonstrated how much difficulty it had in understanding the workings of the English legal system. 'The girl was undoubtedly sexually abused by someone,' it maintained. But since the doctor was found not guilty, 'we now have the unique position of an eight-year-old girl being raped but no one who did it'. That *The Sun* finds this 'unique' — or even unusual — is itself staggering. Huge numbers of crimes go unsolved every year, particularly in cases of rape and indecent assault. Sadly, it is by no means unusual for a girl to be sexually abused without the offender ever being prosecuted. The only difference in this case was that the girl gave evidence in court, but it is hardly surprising that — as appears to have been the case — a jury was reluctant to accept the uncorroborated evidence of a child. Surely even *The Sun* must know that we have an imperfect system of justice in this, as in other countries, and that the guilty are not always convicted if only because we do not want to see innocent men behind bars.

The same leader then went on to demonstrate that *The Sun* had learned nothing from the doctor's acquittal. 'It still puzzles us why the Director of Public Prosecutions decided not to finance the trial,' the newspaper maintained, suggesting it might be better 'if *The Sun* represents the judiciary in future and the DPP and his department stick to what they appear best at: pushing pens and keeping their heads down.'

Another twist in the tale led to an equally bizarre editorial in the *Daily Mirror*. After the Director of Public Prosecutions had decided not to start proceedings, the Conservative MP, Mr Geoffrey Dickens, proceeded to run the risk of being seen as judge and jury rolled into one by giving the doctor's full name in a question to the Attorney General. Mr Dickens asked the Attorney if he would now prosecute the doctor he named 'in respect of sexual offences involving an eight-year-old girl in Chelmsford'. That gave *The Sun* the protection of Parliamentary privilege: it was then immune to any libel claim the doctor might otherwise have brought. Taking full advantage of what Mr Dickens had done, the paper reported his question on its front page, printing the doctor's name, address, education, family details and hobbies, together with an impression of his social background. Just to help the story along a little, *The Sun* threw in an allegation that the doctor had once 'groped' a 20-year-old woman on a boating holiday. And it printed a large, if slightly blurred, picture of the doctor against the half-page headline *RAPE CASE DOC!*.

After the doctor's acquittal Mr Dickens attempted to defend his actions. 'I feel what I did was right,' he said. 'A doctor is a person of supreme trust. I thought it was right that this case should come to trial to be tested.' But the *Daily Mirror*, while saying that what Mr Dickens had done in naming the doctor was 'a gross abuse of parliamentary privilege', managed to put the blame on the Director of Public Prosecutions. 'What is certain,' said the *Mirror*, 'is that the DPP's refusal to prosecute led to the doctor being named by Tory MP Geoffrey Dickens . . . If the DPP had brought [the case], the doctor would not have been named . . . Because he was named, the girl can be identified. That couldn't have happened if the DPP had brought the case. We hope he has learned something from the mess.' Presumably what the *Mirror* wants to teach the Director is that he should subject a man to the risk of imprisonment and ruin on the basis of insufficient evidence in the hope that this will discourage MPs from what the *Mirror* itself admits is an abuse of their privileges.

But then the story took off in a new direction. The Attorney General started proceedings alleging that *The Sun* had been guilty of contempt of court in printing the doctor's name after Mr Dickens had referred to him in Parliament. The newspaper was not accused of breaking the law, which at that time said men charged with (or acquitted of) rape could not be named in those proceedings. But the allegation was that the information published about the doctor might prejudice a fair trial, which was then 'imminent' under the old common law rules of contempt. Certainly, at the time of writing its report, *The Sun* knew better than anyone that the doctor was to be prosecuted. It had announced in that morning's newspaper that it was paying for a private prosecution.

The Director Steps In

Sir Thomas Hetherington was sure that the original decision not to prosecute the Essex doctor had been right. Even so, he was not prepared to use his powers to step in and stop a private prosecution. Following the policy I mentioned earlier, he felt it was right to leave the case to the court. But an example from 1978 shows the type of case in which the Director is prepared to intervene and end the proceedings. A man called Turner was convicted of robbery as the result of information given to the police by an accomplice, Saggs. The Director had given Saggs an undertaking that he would not be prosecuted for his part in the crime. Turner then successfully applied to a magistrates' court for a summons to be issued against Saggs. The next day, a letter was sent to Turner's solicitors by a Principal Assistant Director in the DPP's office asserting that it was not in the interests of either justice or the public for the prosecution to continue. Accordingly, the Director had 'decided to assume responsibility for the proceedings with a view to offering no evidence when Saggs appears before the court'. Turner then began civil proceedings against the Director, claiming that his action was unlawful. Mr Justice Mars-Jones disagreed. What the Director was doing, he said, paralleled the action of the Attorney General in entering a *nolle prosequi*, a power with which the courts never interfered. He was acting in the public interest to prevent the prosecution of a witness.

Explaining his decision in evidence to the Philips Royal Commission, Sir Thomas Hetherington said that, having given Saggs an undertaking, the interests of justice required him to implement it. And, said the Director, 'I had to take into consideration the possible effects of allowing such a private prosecution to proceed on current and future criminal investigations and proceedings'. In other words, if the law could not grant 'supergrasses' immunity, there would be no more criminals who were prepared to put their fellow conspirators behind bars.

In the same year there was another example of the Director offering to stop a private prosecution which might be launched against his wishes. The

Rt Hon Jeremy Thorpe, former leader of the Liberal Party, had been charged with conspiracy to murder: the case was outlined in Chapter 3. Sir Thomas Hetherington told solicitors acting for the main prosecution witness, Peter Bessell, not only that he would not be prosecuted by the police or anyone else for any part he might have had in the case, but also 'in the event of the private prosecution of Mr Bessell in respect of any such matter, the Director will assume responsibility for the conduct of those proceedings and offer no evidence against Mr Bessell'. The Director took his decision because Bessell was in the United States, and there was no means of getting him to give evidence unless he was prepared to come back voluntarily.

There was a good example of the Director's approach in taking over a private prosecution at the request of the prosecutor in 1986. It happened just before the Crown Prosecution Service was introduced, and it is unlikely to recur now that the police must refer all cases to the Crown Prosecutor. The private prosecution was brought by the parents of a man who died in a road accident, against the driver of the car in which he was travelling. The Essex police had decided to charge the driver with careless driving and having excess alcohol in his blood. The parents of the dead man, Tony Hewlett, thought the driver should face the more serious charge of causing death by reckless driving. Despite strenuous opposition from the Essex police, Mr and Mrs Hewlett decided to issue their own summons. The Director of Public Prosecutions supported their action and in the event the driver was convicted and sentenced to two years in prison.

We saw in the last chapter that Gary Austin had been told by the Director he would not be prosecuted for manslaughter, only to find the Director then agreed to take over a private prosecution brought by the dead man's mother. When the case was debated in Parliament in April 1986, the Solicitor General Sir Patrick Mayhew said, in effect, that the Director would in future be able to change his mind over a decision not to prosecute a suspect. In the past, Sir Patrick said, the Director had taken the view that once someone had been told he would not be prosecuted 'the decision should not remain open for reappraisal and possible reversal'. In future, but only in exceptional circumstances, 'if on a review of each relevant case, it appears that the public interest would be served by a prosecution in all the circumstances, this policy will be overridden'.

Appeals

In October 1985, the Solicitor General answered a Parliamentary question about the Director's policy in taking over private prosecutions. First, he decides if there is enough evidence. Then he decides if taking on the prosecution would be in the public interest. It went on:

> The Director adopts the same approach when considering a request for intervention made after a conviction has resulted (ie to conduct any appeal) but in such circumstances he takes into account that the public interest requires that ordinarily convictions properly recorded by the criminal courts should not be allowed to be quashed simply for want of prosecution.

This is a fine example of obfuscation. What this tortuously worded sentence seems to be referring to is the case of a defendant who has been convicted as the result of a private prosecution and then appeals against his conviction, only to find that the prosecutor has lost interest in the case and is no longer willing to act as respondent to the appeal. Unless anyone else steps in, the appeal will then automatically succeed and the conviction will be quashed. In such a case, the Director of Public Prosecutions will normally step in to defend the appeal.

Do We Still Need Them?

You will remember from Chapter 4 that prosecutions begun by virtually every police force worthy of the name are now taken over the Crown Prosecution Service. 'Private prosecutions' seems a fair way of describing cases taken to court by anyone else. A case brought by the Inland Revenue, Customs and Excise, the RSPCA, or Marks and Spencer is just as much a private prosecution as one brought by Mrs Mary Whitehouse. So if you ban private prosecutions to stop self-appointed individuals having access to the criminal process, you also stop public bodies and reputable traders from taking cases to court without the assistance of an overburdened Crown Prosecution Service.

Attractive though it might seem to deny the right of private prosecution to people who think they know what is best for the rest of us to see or read, such a restriction would be difficult to introduce. It would either have to withdraw the right to prosecute from many organizations which bring cases perfectly properly at the moment, or involve complicated definitions of the organizations which were considered fit to prosecute. Another possibility, of course, would be to introduce a requirement of permission to prosecute — which the Royal Commission recommended. The government's solution, on the other hand, is to allow anybody to start a prosecution — while preserving for itself the right to stop the case at any time. This seems a pragmatic approach to an awkward problem. But in a perfect world busybodies would be denied the right to treat the criminal law as their private property.

TEN

The Director and the Attorney

The Director of Public Prosecutions and the Attorney General have a close and intimate relationship: they have worked together now for a hundred years and more. They first met in 1879, when the Director's office was created; the Prosecution of Offences Act which was passed in that year said:

> It shall be the duty of the Director of Public Prosecutions, *under the superintendence of the Attorney General*, to institute . . . such criminal proceedings . . . as may be . . . prescribed by regulations . . . or may be directed in a special case by the Attorney General. (s. 2).

The latest Prosecution of Offences Act, passed in 1985, says:

> The Director shall discharge his functions under this or any other enactment *under the superintendence of the Attorney General*. (s. 3(1)).

As you will have noticed from the emphasis I added, the modern Act preserves the original reference to 'superintendence', while not repeating the duty to prosecute when 'directed' by the Attorney General. In the hope of finding out who has the ultimate power to prosecute, I now want to discuss these terms in some detail.

The Power to Direct

The Attorney's power to direct the Director to prosecute 'in a special case' was included in the original Act of 1879. The 1879 Act was repealed just a hundred years later, but the 1979 legislation re-enacted the power in similar terms.

Quite what amounted to a special case is far from clear, but presumably the intention was to give the Attorney the last word in a dispute. If the Director refused to prosecute, the Attorney could apparently have insisted on a prosecution going ahead; if the Director wanted to prosecute, the Attorney could have stopped him. And this is what seems to have happened. Sir Theobald Mathew, Director from 1944 to 1964, did say in a lecture that 'the Attorney General can give me directions to prosecute in a case in which I have announced a decision in the opposite sense'. One of the Attorneys he served under, Sir Hartley Shawcross, said (in the House of Commons on 29 January 1951) that he received advice from the Director of Public Prosecutions and Treasury Counsel. 'I have hardly ever, if ever, refused to prosecute when they have advised prosecution,' he said. 'I have sometimes ordered prosecution when their advice was against it.' This suggests that Lord Shawcross actually used his power to direct a prosecution, but it could simply mean that he stood his ground in the face of unacceptable advice and as a result the Director was forced to change his mind. Some light has been thrown on the subject by a letter Mathew wrote to Shawcross just before he made his statement (which is quoted in a footnote to Professor Edwards' second book). 'As I act under your superintendence and directions,' the Director told the Attorney, 'you are responsible for my decisions but you can and have, albeit politely, overruled decisions of mine. True, so far as the public is concerned, you have allowed me to reconsider my decision in the light of further representations, but you could give me a direction to act contrary to a decision that I had announced, which would not be open to you if it had been your original decision.'

These days, differences of opinion are settled in private by agreement between the two men. Sir Thomas Hetherington told me that if the Attorney General had ever rejected his advice and insisted on a case going ahead, the Director would normally then have prosecuted without the need for a formal direction. The former Attorney General, Lord Silkin, is quoted by Professor Edwards as saying that although he had power to direct the Director to institute or not to institute proceedings, in practice he had never done so. Sir Thomas Hetherington, in his Upjohn Memorial Lecture, confirmed that although the Attorney could give the Director directions in a special case, 'in practice he has never done so in my experience'.

He would have done so at his peril: if normal relations between an Attorney and a Director had ever deteriorated to the point where the Attorney had to rely on his power to insist on a prosecution against the Director's firm wishes, the Director would probably have felt he had no alternative but to resign. However, the question is quite academic: the 1979 Act was repealed in 1985 by a new Prosecution of Offences Act which made no provision for the Attorney General to 'direct' the Director.

For many years there was an additional power to give directions. Regulations made in 1886 said that

> the action of the Director of Public Prosecutions shall in all matters . . .
> be subject to the directions of the Attorney General

That provision remained in force until the end of 1978, but it was not included in new Regulations made that year. Sir Thomas Hetherington said in his evidence to the Philips Royal Commission on Criminal Procedure that the provision was left out of the 1978 Regulations because it was somewhat superfluous: it was already in Section 2 of the 1879 Act. But John Edwards points out in his 1984 book that the wording in the Regulations was much broader than in the statute, which only referred to directions in 'a special case' rather than in 'all matters'. Professor Edwards also detects a whiff of independence among staff in the Director's office who seemed reluctant — at the time the Regulations were being revised — to be 'subject to the directions of the Attorney General'. And now the 1879 Act has itself been repealed.

So there is no longer a formal power to direct the Director. But is he now more independent as a result? While the Director was still obliged to take directions from the Attorney, he could never have maintained he was truly independent: the most he could say was that he was directed by a man who himself was considered to be independent of the government (as I shall be explaining shortly). But abolishing the power to direct a prosecution made no difference at all to the relationship between Sir Michael Havers and Sir Thomas Hetherington; indeed, the change went largely unnoticed in their respective offices. That was because the key link between the two men remained unchanged: by Section 3(1) of the 1985 Act, the Direction of Public Prosecutions must still 'discharge his functions . . . under the superintendence of the Attorney General'. Does this mean the Director can still be directed? In the hope of analysing the elusive concept of 'superintendence' I shall begin with some explanations from recent superintendents, before looking at the relationship from the superintended's point of view.

Superintendence: Views from Above

Lord Silkin of Dulwich, who as Sam Silkin was Attorney General from 1974 to 1979, wrote about the relationship between the Attorney and the Director in the July 1978 issue of *The Parliamentarian*, published by the Commonwealth Parliamentary Association:

> It is a relationship which parliamentary colleagues often find hard to follow. Some seem to think that the Director is a mere creature of the Attorney General. They are mistaken. The Director is essentially an independent, non-political figure. He is not a civil servant, although two of the last three Directors came to that office from the civil service . . . His decisions are his own and not those of the Attorney General. Indeed, prosecutions under many statutes require his consent, which he is entitled to give or withhold without reference to the Attorney General. The vast majority of cases dealt with by the Director or his staff are never seen or heard of by the Law Officers [the Attorney General and the Solicitor General]. However, the powers and responsibilities of the Attorney General, which I have described above, necessarily involve a close and continuous relationship of trust between him and the Director. Each will consult the other, even when no statute obliges them to do so; they could not otherwise perform their respective functions effectively. Yet each is independent of the other.

Lord Silkin then went on to stress the Director's working independence:

> The Attorney General's general responsibility to parliament for the work of the Director's department and his power to direct (a power rarely, if ever, used) do not require him to exercise detailed or day-to-day control over

the Director's work. Nor indeed could he possibly do so — even assuming that this were desirable — without an enormously increased staff. Thus it is vital to a successful relationship that the Director and his staff should be perceptive as to the kind of case about which the Law Officers are likely to be concerned and as to the public interest factors which are likely to concern them. And it is equally vital that so far as practicable the Law Officers should leave the Director to carry out his functions without any greater interference than is necessitated by the duty of 'general superintendence'.

Sam Silkin's successor as Attorney General was Sir Michael Havers. In May 1979, shortly after his appointment, Sir Michael discussed his relationship with the Director of Public Prosecutions in a speech at the Police Staff College:

The Director . . . has no responsibility to ministers collectively or to any individual minister apart from the Attorney General who himself is in the unique position as a minister of the Crown of not being subject to the collective decision of the Cabinet, nor required to obey the orders of the Prime Minister, in relation to those matters in which he exercises his prosecuting role.

That, incidentally, has been true since the Campbell incident of 1924, when the Prime Minister tried to control the Attorney and through him the Director for political purposes: I described the case in Chapter 3.

In his speech Sir Michael Havers went on to say that he had 'general superintendence' over the Director's activities and to that extent he was responsible to Parliament for them:

. . . but I am not responsible for the individual decisions of the DPP or his officers. The DPP, although being an officer under the Crown, is thus completely independent and non-political. He acts for the public, in the public interest, and for no-one else. He will of course discuss particular cases with me and consult me generally; but the decisions taken in the field where he is vested with the discretion to prosecute will be his decisions.

At the end of 1979, Sir Michael Havers explained his working relationship with the Director of Public Prosecutions in a Commons answer:

My responsibility for superintendence of the duties of the Director does not require me to exercise day-to-day control and specific approval of every decision he takes. The Director makes many decisions in the course of his duties which he does not refer to me but nevertheless I am still responsible for his actions in the sense that I am answerable in the House for what he does. Superintendence means that I must have regard to the overall prosecution policy which he pursues. My relationship with him is such that I require to be told in advance of the major, difficult, and, from the public interest point of view, the more important matters so that should the need arise I am in the position to exercise my ultimate power of direction.

Those statements, although made before the Crown Prosecution Service was introduced, are still the basis of the relationship between the Attorney and the Director. However it is worth recording in full the Parliamentary answer I mentioned in Chapter 4. Sir Michael Havers was asked on 14 July 1986 to what extent he intended to answer Parliamentary questions on the Crown Prosecution Service on behalf of the Director of Public Prosecutions. He replied:

> I intend to adopt the proposals set out in the White Paper on *An Independent Prosecution Service for England and Wales*. I shall therefore remain answerable in parliament for decisions or actions that I or the Director of Public Prosecutions and his headquarters staff take on prosecution matters, and for the policy that is applied by the Crown Prosecution Service in the handling of particular cases. For the reasons given in the White Paper, however, I do not think it appropriate to answer in parliament for the intrinsic merits of particular decisions taken by local prosecutors unless the Director's headquarters staff have in fact been involved in the case in question. Insofar as cases in which the Director's headquarters staff have been involved are concerned, I propose to continue my existing practice, as a general rule, of confining answers to the basis of the decision in the particular case, without giving details of the evidence or other considerations which have led to a particular decision. Insofar as cases which are handled locally are concerned, the Director has told me that he is prepared to inquire into the circumstances of particular cases to which his attention is drawn by Hon Members.

Logically, the Attorney General should either be answerable for every decision taken by the Crown Prosecution Service, or for none at all. The division between Headquarters cases, on which the Attorney General is prepared to answer questions, and cases handled locally, on which MPs are told to go straight to the Director, is purely arbitrary. But it does keep the amount of work for the Attorney and his staff within existing limits. It also means that the Attorney General only has to deal with difficult or important cases, which seems reasonable. And, as I pointed out earlier, the fact that the Director can write his own letters to MPs sets him apart from civil servants, whose powers are limited, at least in theory, to 'advising' ministers.

I said at the beginning of this chapter that the Director of Public Prosecutions and the Attorney General have a close and intimate relationship. They speak almost every day and meet regularly. But few holders of those two offices can have worked as closely together as Sir Thomas Hetherington and Sir Michael Havers. Hetherington served Havers for an unbroken period of some eight years — the longest period in peacetime a Director has ever been under the superintendence of one Attorney. And in the early 1970s, when Sir Michael Havers was Solicitor General, Tony Hetherington was his Legal Secretary — the top official in the Law Officers' Department. Havers told me that he had known and liked Hetherington for 15 years: 'I've trusted him and respected his judgment, and so it makes co-operation between us very much easier,' he said. And in an interview Sir Michael Havers gave me in the summer of 1986, he summed up what he saw as the constitutional relationship between the Director of Public Prosecutions and the Attorney General:

It is in fact a unique situation, because he's independent but under my general superintendence. What that means is that if I wanted a particular administrative policy to be followed I'd discuss it with him and we might argue it out. But I've never had, and would not ever want, to give him a direct order. The truth is that over the seven years that I've been Attorney we've never had any difficulty at all. We keep very close contact, meet frequently, telephone frequently, and it's for him to identify the sort of case that comes into his office which he thinks I ought to know about quickly: spy cases, inevitably, but other ones which are sensitive politically, or sensitive in other ways which he has — after his years in my department — learned to recognise as involving something the Law Officers ought to know about.

When a particularly difficult case arises the Director will go to see the Attorney at his room in the Law Courts. 'There are certain cases where the public interest may outweigh the need for a prosecution,' Sir Michael Havers told me, 'and those will be very carefully discussed between us.' But how, I asked him, does that square with the Director's independence?

Because I'm also being non-political in these decisions. All these decisions whether to prosecute are entirely independent of the government. It's always said 'the government is prosecuting . . .' but it's not: the government has no say in it at all. I'm the only person the Prime Minister can't direct on matters like this; other ministers she can give orders to but our independence has been established for many many years.

This is an argument some people simply refuse to accept. The Attorney General is a member of the government. He is elected to Parliament by the government's supporters and he holds office for as long as he commands the Prime Minister's confidence. On the other hand, he is also a lawyer, and lawyers are used to giving independent advice. Lawyers must also be able to exclude irrelevant considerations from their thoughts: that, after all, is something they seem to expect juries to manage. But those who maintain that all the Attorney's decisions are invariably political will argue that no mere mortal, when weighing up the public interest and — for example — deciding whether a civil servant should be prosecuted for breaking the Official Secrets Act, can ever completely exclude from his thoughts the interests of the government he serves. As I say, it's something that the Attorney of the day vehemently denies.

The issue came to a head early in 1987 when Sir Michael Havers obtained an injunction against the journalist Duncan Campbell preventing him from telling anybody about a plan to build a British spy satellite, known as Project Zircon. As it was a civil matter, not a criminal prosecution, Havers was acting on behalf of the government and could only go ahead with the support of his Cabinet colleagues, support which was given so late that by the time the injunction was granted Campbell had already written about Zircon in the *New Statesman*. That article drew on a television programme Campbell had written for the BBC in Scotland; it was the BBC's decision to withdraw the programme on grounds of national security which prompted the *New*

Statesman article, as you may remember from Chapter 3.

When the article appeared there was some criticism of the government for not having applied for an injunction much earlier. But it was only at this stage that criminal proceedings under the Official Secrets Act became a possibility. Sir Michael Havers naturally wanted to know who Campbell's sources were and suggested to Sir Thomas Hetherington that he should invite the police to make enquiries. The Director of Public Prosecutions duly spoke to the police and, of course, they did as he asked: it is an offer they never refuse. Scant regard was paid to the police special branch raid on Duncan Campbell's home and his office at the *New Statesman*; but when the police obtained a warrant (at the third attempt) to search the BBC offices in Glasgow, and removed five untransmitted programmes in the same series as well as the Zircon programme, there was uproar in Parliament. In vain the government protested that the decisions taken by the Attorney and his Scottish equivalent, the Lord Advocate, to authorize police enquiries were taken independently of the government: people simply did not understand how he could put out of his mind the factors which, only a week earlier, had prompted him to advise his colleagues that an injunction would be in the government's interests.

The former Attorney General, Lord Shawcross, outlined the Attorney's role in his Commons speech of 29 January 1951. He stressed that in deciding whether to prosecute 'there is only one consideration which is altogether excluded and that is the repercussion of a given decision upon my personal or my party's or the government's political fortunes: that is a consideration which never enters into account.' But Shawcross also made it clear that the Attorney did not have to make up his mind in a vacuum:

> The true doctrine is that it is the duty of the Attorney General, in deciding whether or not to authorise a prosecution, to acquaint himself with all the relevant facts, including for instance the effect which the prosecution, successful or unsuccessful as the case may be, would have on public morale and order, and with any other consideration affecting public policy. In order so to inform himself he may, although I do not think he is obliged to, consult with any of his colleagues in the government, and indeed, as Lord Simon once said, he would be a fool if he did not. On the other hand, the assistance of his colleagues is confined to informing him of particular considerations which might affect his own decision, and does not consist, and must not consist, in telling him what that decision ought to be ... If political considerations which in the broad sense that I have indicated affect government in the abstract arise it is the Attorney General, applying his judicial mind, who has to be the sole judge of those considerations.

The Attorney's independence is said to be demonstrated by the fact that he is not, as such, a member of the Cabinet — although he sees Cabinet papers and can ask to attend meetings of the Cabinet and its committees. This distinction seems unimportant. The only way of demonstrating the Attorney General's complete independence from the government would be to make him an unelected public servant — like the DPP, I was going to say, but as you may have gathered by now I do not see how the DPP can be regarded as completely independent of the Attorney.

Lord Shawcross has spoken in favour of creating a more independent Attorney, such as exists in many Commonwealth countries. That view received some support from another former Attorney, Lord Rawlinson. But his successor, Lord Silkin, strongly disagreed. In his *Parliamentarian* article, Silkin said he regretted that the Attorney General did not sit at the Cabinet table, unless invited, because he was convinced that 'the more intimately the government's principle legal adviser is aware of the battles and the arguments and the stresses and strains that eventually result in policy, the better able he is to assist in ensuring that if there is a lawful and a proper way of achieving its objectives, that way will be found'.

Superintendence: Views from Below

Sir Theobald Mathew, Director of Public Prosecutions from 1944 to 1964, said (in the lectures I mentioned in Chapter 2) that as the Director never gave the reasons for his decision in any particular case he was therefore 'in a quasi-judicial position with regard to the exercise of his discretion'. But Mathew then went on confidently to assert that he was answerable to Parliament, through the Attorney General, for his decisions. 'The Director,' he said, 'remains the servant — the proud servant possibly — of the public, through parliament which represents them, and of the executive which, through parliament, is responsible to them, and he is in no sense the master of either.'

His successor, Sir Norman Skelhorn, emphasized in his memoirs that he was not subject to political direction. He quoted the example of a motor accident in 1964 involving a car driven by the Duke of Edinburgh. Skelhorn duly read statements made to the police by Prince Philip and the other driver, and then decided (with the advice of counsel) that there was no evidence to support a prosecution against the Duke of Edinburgh (although the other driver was prosecuted and convicted). 'However,' wrote Skelhorn, 'the important fact is that the case was considered and decided irrespective of the eminence of the person involved, and that no pressure whatever was brought to bear on me.' Skelhorn recalled that, although he was responsible between 1964 and 1977 to four different Attorneys, 'never once was any pressure put on me to exercise my discretion in a particular way, not even when the activities of the Home Secretary himself came under review'. The Home Secretary in question was the Conservative MP, Reginald Maudling, whose financial involvement with the corrupt Yorkshire businessman John Poulson led eventually to a decision by Skelhorn (with the advice of two Queen's Counsel) that there was 'insufficient evidence to justify criminal proceedings'.

Sir Norman Skelhorn drew an important distinction between being told what to do and asking for 'advice':

> Obviously, in sensitive cases where I had to consider where the public interest lay, it was my duty to keep the Attorney General informed — secrets

cases, for example, or those involving foreign nationals such as Leila Khaled [the Palestinian hijacker released by Britain in exchange for hostages] — and on such occasions I myself might seek his advice, but never his instructions, although under the Regulations he could have given me instructions.

There had been ample evidence that Leila Khaled had committed numerous serious offences; the question for the Director was whether it was in the public interest to prosecute her or to let her leave the country. Skelhorn said that 'in this particular instance, involving political issues, I was only too happy to lean on the Attorney General . . . I did not regard myself as the best person to decide what was in the public interest'. The Attorney General, Sir Peter Rawlinson, said later he had asked the Foreign Secretary what he thought would happen to the hostages if Khaled were to be charged with the hijacking. 'On each occasion,' said Rawlinson in remarks quoted by Professor Edwards, 'I was advised that a charge would increase the danger to their lives. Accordingly, I informed the government that I did not, in the circumstances then prevailing, intend to charge Leila Khaled. That was my decision and mine alone.' Of course, one must accept what Lord Rawlinson says. But I repeat: there still seems to be a fine dividing line between being told what to do and asking for advice. In practice what must happen is that a decision is reached after discussions between the Director of Public Prosecutions and the Attorney General, or between the Attorney and his colleagues in government. It is then announced as the Director's decision, or indeed as the Attorney's decision. But it is more likely to be a consensus view than the decision of one man who has simply been sounding out opinions.

Sir Thomas Hetherington, in his evidence to the Philips Royal Commission, was another Director who stressed that the decisions he made were his own and not those of the Attorney. He said the majority of cases his department dealt with were never seen or heard of by the Attorney General. Sir Thomas Hetherington believed that his independence from political influences was a factor of considerable importance in maintaining public confidence in the fair and impartial administration of the criminal law. But the Director then went on to explain that there was a 'close and regular relationship of consultation' between himself and the Attorney:

> It is my practice to consult the Attorney General in cases of special importance or difficulty even where there is no legal requirement for the Attorney to be involved. It is, for example, customary for me to consult the Attorney General in cases involving possible contraventions of Rhodesia sanctions. Cases in which the Attorney's fiat [approval] is required are considered by me, and the Attorney takes his decision only after my advice has been received. If the Attorney General gives his consent to criminal proceedings, I have conduct of the case.
>
> This position has two practical results. On the one hand, the Attorney's 'superintendence' does not require him to exercise control in detail over my work. On the other hand, I and my department have to be perceptive

enough to identify the type of case about which the Attorney General is
likely to be concerned in the public interest.

One such case was the prosecution of Jeremy Thorpe, which I described
in Chapter 3. But that had its own problems. Hetherington told me that
quite early on, before any decisions had been taken, he had discussed the
sensitivity of any decision to prosecute with the then Attorney, Sam Silkin.
'I offered and Sam agreed that I should take all my own decisions, not
consulting him but just keeping him informed,' Hetherington told me. 'Even
though Sam Silkin was absolutely straight, it could have appeared that he
was politically motivated, whatever the decision. It's on that sort of occasion
that the Director must take his own decision.' Some would say that the case
of Duncan Campbell and the Zircon project was equally sensitive, and that
the Director should have taken full responsibility — so far as he was able
to — for that case, too.

In his Upjohn lecture, Sir Thomas Hetherington stressed that

> the Attorney does not exercise control over the majority of the Director's
> decisions and the Attorney is not, and never has been, responsible for the
> Director to the extent that a minister is responsible for his officials. On
> the other hand, because of his general superintending role the Attorney
> is responsible to parliament for the way the Director carries out his duties.

I asked Sir Thomas Hetherington for examples of cases he discussed with
Sir Michael Havers.

> Some of the City fraud cases — involving Lloyds and Johnson Matthey
> Bankers — because there is so much legitimate public interest in what is
> going to happen. Cases involving public figures — such as Derek Hatton,
> the Deputy Leader of Liverpool Council, where we decided not to prosecute:
> that was one where we kept the Attorney informed, rather than asking
> him to take a decision.

More frequently though, the Director discusses questions of policy with
the Attorney. Hetherington told me he had recently discussed pornography:
what should be done if the Film Censors had approved a video recording
and the DPP's staff still thought it was obscene? The policy then adopted
was to keep the censors fully in touch with the DPP's views, so that they
could take account of recent prosecutions in deciding what video tapes to
license.

John Wood mentioned the example of homosexual law reform in the 1960s.
A committee chaired by Sir John Wolfenden had recommended a change
in the law to allow homosexual behaviour between consenting adults in
private. The government announced legislation, but a change in the law
was inevitably some months off. At that stage the then Director, Sir Norman
Skelhorn, asked the then Attorney, Sir Elwyn Jones, what to do about cases
coming to light while the Sexual Offences Bill was going through Parliament.
The Attorney said the Bill had support from all parties and was expected
to get through; he therefore thought it wrong for the Director to continue

to prosecute people whose conduct would no longer be an offence once the Bill had become law. He 'advised' the Director to bring no more prosecutions.

Superintendence: Revealed

The view taken by the Attorney General's advisers in 1987 was that the power to superintend had always included the power to direct. Nothing had changed when the 1985 Act failed to mention directions: if the Attorney ever wanted to insist on a prosecution, it was argued that the power to superintend the Director meant he could still do so.

When we discussed the Director's constitutional position, Sir Thomas Hetherington accepted that if the Attorney General were to insist on a prosecution he would ultimately feel bound to comply with the Attorney's wishes — even though the Attorney's formal power to direct a prosecution had now vanished. So in the last resort, Hetherington conceded that he was not fully independent of the Attorney. But in practice he said Attorneys had felt it right to leave decisions to the Director, and in answering Parliamentary questions they took care not to say whether they agreed or disagreed with a particular decision a Director had taken.

Let's sum up. What we have is a Director of Public Prosecutions who takes most of his decisions by himself, but who consults the Attorney in a small number of difficult cases. We have an Attorney General who makes up his mind on his own, but consults his Cabinet colleagues in a small number of difficult cases. The Attorney asserts his independence from the government, because other ministers must not tell him what to do (though they can offer him advice). But the Director is not able to assert his independence from the Attorney, because the Attorney can effectively exercise control over the Director's decisions.

As I said, the Director and the Attorney have a close and intimate relationship. They need it to make the system work. What has been demanded of past office holders has been almost impossible. Parliament has wanted a Director of Public Prosecutions with enough independence of the government to avoid being subservient to it; and enough supervision by the government to ensure that he is ultimately answerable, through the Attorney, to Parliament. What was wanted was a DPP who was not prepared to be pushed around by the government — unless the government had decided to push him around. It seems to be one of those peculiarly English compromises: the product of an unwritten constitution which relies on conventions rather than law. It is one of those relationships which depends on the individuals concerned; for the past sixty years it has been made to work. It will carry on working for as long as the Director and the Attorney continue to play the game.

APPENDIX

Code for Crown Prosecutors

Introduction

1.   This Code is issued pursuant to Section 10 of the Prosecution of Offences Act 1985, and as provided for in Section 10(3) of the Act will be included in the Director's annual report to the Attorney General. In accordance with Section 9 of the Act, the report will be laid before Parliament and published. The Code, therefore, is a public declaration of the principles upon which the Crown Prosecution Service will exercise its functions. Its purpose is to promote efficient and consistent decision-making so as to develop and thereafter maintain public confidence in the Service's performance of its duties. Amendments to the Code may be made from time to time.

2.   The principles endorsed by the Attorney General's criteria for prosecution, which had hitherto guided all who prosecute on behalf of the public, have been drawn upon to indicate the basis upon which decisions are to be made. Having regard, however, to the specific statutory duties with which the Service is charged, it is right that the Code should be, and be seen to be, an independent body of guidance designed for and aimed directly at those who prosecute in its name.

3.   Crown Prosecutors at every level in the Service will have great scope for the exercise of discretion at various stages of the prosecution process and in respect of many different functions. The responsible use of that discretion, based on clear principles, can better serve both justice, the interests of the public and the interests of the offender, than the rigid application of the letter of the law. The misuse of discretionary powers, on the other hand, can have severe consequences not only for those suspected of crime, but also for the public at large and the reputation of justice and the Service itself.

The evidential sufficiency criteria

4.   When considering the institution or continuation of criminal proceedings the first question to be determined is the sufficiency of the evidence. A prosecution should not be started or continued unless the Crown Prosecutor is satisfied that there is admissable, substantial and reliable evidence that a criminal offence known to the law has been

committed by an identifiable person. The Crown Prosecution Service does not support the proposition that a bare prima facie case is enough, but rather will apply the test of whether there is a realistic prospect of a conviction. When reaching this decision the Crown Prosecutor as a first step will wish to satisfy himself that there is no realistic expectation of an ordered acquittal or a successful submission in the Magistrates' Court of no case to answer. He should also have regard to any lines of defence which are plainly open to, or have been indicated by, the accused and any other factors which in his view would affect the likelihood or otherwise of a conviction.

5.   The Crown Prosecutor in evaluating the evidence should have regard to the following matters:—

(i)   In respect of any evidence, having regard to the requirements of the Police and Criminal Evidence Act 1984 and Codes of Practice, are there grounds for believing that breaches of the requirements may lead to the exclusion of the evidence under Part VIII of the Act? The Act and its Codes of Practice contain provisions for the detention, treatment and questioning of persons by the police which are designed to ensure the proper treatment of people in police custody and the reliability of evidence derived from confessions or other statements made to the police. Crown Prosecutors will wish to satisfy themselves that confession evidence has been properly obtained and is not exposed to the suggestion of oppressive behaviour. In considering other evidence, Crown Prosecutors will need to consider whether it has been obtained improperly and, if it may have been, whether a court might feel it right to exclude it on the grounds that its admission would have an adverse effect on the fairness of the proceedings. The possibility that certain evidence might be excluded should be taken into account when the sufficiency of evidence to justify the proceedings is initially reviewed and, if it is crucial to the case, may substantially affect the decision whether or not to proceed.

(ii) If the case depends in part on admissions by the accused, are there any grounds for believing that they are of doubtful reliability having regard to the age, intelligence and apparent understanding of the accused?

(iii) Does it appear that a witness is exaggerating, or that his memory is faulty, or that he is either hostile or friendly to the accused, or may be otherwise unreliable?

(iv) Has a witness a motive for telling less than the whole truth?

(v)   Are there matters which might properly be put to a witness by the defence to attack his credibility?

(vi) What sort of impression is the witness likely to make? How is he likely to stand up to cross-examination? Does he suffer from any physical or mental disability which is likely to affect his credibility?

(vii) If there is conflict between eye-witnesses, does it go beyond what one would expect and hence materially weaken the case?

(viii) If there is a lack of conflict between eye witnesses, is there anything which causes suspicion that a false story may have been concocted?

(ix) Are all the necessary witnesses available and competent to give evidence, including any who may be abroad?

(x) Where child witnesses are involved, are they likely to be able to give sworn evidence?

(xi) If identity is likely to be an issue, how cogent and reliable is the evidence of those who purport to identify the accused?

(xii) Are the facts of the case such that the public would consider it oppressive to proceed against the accused?

(xiii) Where two or more defendants are charged together, is there a realistic prospect of the proceedings being severed? If so, is the case suffiently proved against each defendant should separate trials be ordered?

6.   This list is not of course exhaustive, and the factors to be considered will depend upon the circumstances of each individual case, but it is introduced to indicate that, particularly in borderline cases, the Crown Prosecutor must be prepared to look beneath the surface of the statements. He must also draw, so far as is possible, on his own experience of how evidence of the type under consideration is likely to 'stand-up' in Court before reaching a conclusion as to the likelihood of a conviction.

The public interest criteria

7.   Having satisfied himself that the evidence itself can justify proceedings, the Crown Prosecutor must then consider whether the public interest requires a prosecution. The Crown Prosecution Service will be guided by the view expressed in a House of Commons debate by Lord Shawcross when he was Attorney General, and subsequently endorsed by his successors:—

> 'It has never been the rule in this Country—I hope it never will be—that suspected criminal offences must automatically be the subject of prosecution. Indeed the very first Regulations under which the Director of Public Prosecutions worked provided that he should . . . . . prosecute 'wherever it appears that the offence or the circumstances of its commission is or are of such a character that a prosecution in respect thereof is required in the public interest.' That is still the dominant consideration.' (H. C. Deb., Vol. 483, col. 681, January 29th 1951)

He continued by saying that regard must be had to 'the effect which the prosecution, successful or unsuccessful as the case may be, would have upon public morale and order, and with any other considerations affecting public policy.'

8.   The factors which can properly lead to a decision not to prosecute will vary from case to case, but broadly speaking, the graver the offence, the less likelihood there will be that the public interest will allow of a disposal less than prosecution, for example, a caution. Where, however, an offence is not so serious as plainly to require prosecution, the Crown Prosecutor should always apply his mind to the public interest and should strive to

ensure that the spirit of the Home Office Cautioning Guidelines is observed. If the case falls within any of the following categories this will be an indication that proceedings may not be required, subject of course to the particular circumstances of the case.

(i) *Likely Penalty*

When the circumstances of an offence are not particularly serious, and a Court would be likely to impose a purely nominal penalty, Crown Prosecutors should carefully consider whether the public interest would be better served by a prosecution or some other form of disposal such as, where appropriate, a caution. This applies particularly where the offence is triable on indictment when Crown Prosecutors should also weigh the likely penalty with the likely length and cost of the proceedings.

(ii) *Staleness*

Regard must be had not only to the date when the last known offence was committed, but also the length of time which is likely to elapse before the matter can be brought to trial. The Crown Prosecutor should be slow to prosecute if the last offence was committed three or more years before the probable date of trial, unless, despite its staleness, an immediate custodial sentence of some length is likely to be imposed. Less regard will be paid to staleness, however, if it has been contributed to by the accused himself, the complexity of the case has necessitated lengthy police investigation or the particular characteristics of the offence have themselves contributed to the delay in its coming to light. Generally, the graver the allegation the less significance will be attached to the element of staleness.

(iii) *Youth*

The stigma of a conviction can cause irreparable harm to the future prospects of a young adult, and careful consideration should be given to the possibility of dealing with him or her by means of a caution.

(iv) *Old age and infirmity*

(a) The older or more infirm the offender, the more reluctant the Crown Prosecutor should be to prosecute unless there is a real possibility of repetition or the offence is of such gravity that it is impossible to overlook. In general, proceedings should not be instituted where a Court is likely to pay such regard to the age or infirmity of the offender as to induce it to impose only a nominal penalty, although there may be exceptional circumstances, such as where the accused still holds a position of some importance, when proceedings are required in the public interest regardless of what penalty may be imposed.

(b) It will also be necessary to consider whether the accused is likely to be fit enough to stand his trial. The Crown Prosecutor should have regard to any medical reports which have been made available by the defence solicitor and may arrange through him for an independent medical examination where this is necessary.

(v) *Mental illness or stress*

    (a) Whenever the Crown Prosecutor is provided with a medical report to the effect that an accused or a person under investigation is suffering from some form of mental illness or psychiatric illness and that the strain of criminal proceedings may lead to a considerable worsening of his condition, such a report should receive anxious consideration. This is a difficult field because in some instances the accused may have become mentally disturbed or depressed by the mere fact that his misconduct has been discovered and the Crown Prosecutor may be dubious about a prognosis that criminal proceedings will adversely affect his condition to a significant extent. Where, however, the Crown Prosecutor is satisfied that the probable effect upon the defendant's mental health outweighs the interests of justice in that particular case, he should not hesitate to discontinue proceedings. An independent medical examination may be sought, but should generally be reserved for cases of such gravity as plainly to require prosecution but for clear evidence that such a course would be likely to result in a permanent worsening of the accused's condition.

    (b) The Crown Prosecutor should not pay as much regard to evidence of mental instability not coupled with a prognosis as to the adverse effect of proceedings, as such instability may increase the likelihood that the offence will be repeated. The accused's mental state will, of course, be relevant in considering any issue of mens rea or fitness to plead.

(vi) *Sexual offences*

    (a) Whenever two or more persons have participated in the offence in circumstances rendering both or all liable to prosecution the Crown Prosecutor should take into account each person's age, the relative ages of the participants and whether or not there was any element of seduction or corruption when deciding whether, and if so in respect of whom, proceedings should be instituted.

    (b) Sexual assaults upon children should always be regarded seriously, as should offences against adults, such as rape, which amount to gross personal violation. In such cases, where the Crown Prosecutor is satisfied as to the sufficiency of the evidence there will seldom be any doubt that prosecution will be in the public interest.

(vii) *Complainant's attitude*

In some cases it will be appropriate for the Crown Prosecutor to have regard to the attitude of a complainant who notified the police but later expresses a wish that no action be taken. It may be that in such circumstances proceedings need not be pursued unless either there is suspicion that the change of heart was actuated by fear or the offence was of some gravity.

(vii) *Peripheral defendants*

Where an allegation involves several accused, as a general rule the Crown Prosecutor should have regard to the need to ensure that proceedings are continued only against those whose involvement goes to the heart of the issue to be placed before the Court. The inclusion of defendants on the fringe of the action and whose guilt in comparison with the principal offenders is minimal can lead to additional delay and cost, as well as unnecessarily clouding the essential features of the case.

9.   Finally, if having weighed such of the above factors as may appertain to the case, the Crown Prosecutor is still in doubt as to whether proceedings are called for, he will throw into the scales the attitude of the local community and any information about the prevalence of the particular offence in the area or nationally. Should doubt still remain, the scales will normally be tipped in favour of prosecution as if the balance is so even, it could properly be said that the final arbiter must be the Court.

Discontinuance

10.   The use by the Crown Prosecutor of his power to terminate proceedings whether by using the procedure under Section 23 of the Prosecution of Offences Act 1985 or the continuing power to withdraw or offer no evidence, is in many ways the most visible demonstration of the Service's fundamental commitment towards ensuring that only fit and proper cases are taken to trial. Unless, of course, advice has been given at a preliminary stage, the police decision to institute proceedings should never be met with passive acquiescence but must always be the subject of review. Furthermore, the discretion to discontinue is a continuing one, and even when proceedings are under way Crown Prosecutors should continue to exercise their reviewing function. There may be occasions when time and other practical constraints limit the depth of the initial review of the case. It is important that cases should be kept under continuous review, not least because the emergence of new evidence or information may sometimes cast doubt on the propriety of the initial decision to proceed. Crown Prosecutors must be resolute when made aware of evidence or information of this nature and should not hesitate to bring proceedings to an end in appropriate cases. Public confidence in the Service can only be maintained if there is no doubting its commitment to taking effective action at whatever stage whenever it is right to do so. Prosecutions instituted in circumstances apparently falling outside the spirit of the Home Office Cautioning Guidelines should be queried with the police and may be discontinued where the Crown Prosecutor is satisfied that proceedings would not be in the public interest. It will be the normal practice to consult the police whenever it is proposed to discontinue proceedings instituted by them. The level of consultation will depend on the particular circumstances of the case or the accused, but the final decision will rest with the Crown Prosecutor.

11.   The broad heading of discontinuance also includes the question of the acceptance of pleas. To a large extent this area is bound up with charging practice—the selection of charges will sometimes affect the scope of the

discretion to accept pleas, but equally there will always be occasions calling for the judicious exercise of that discretion. This could include, for example, the situation where charges are preferred in the alternative or where the defendant is prepared to admit part only of the ingredients of a particular offence itself amounting to another offence; burglary reducing to theft by virtue of a denial of the element of trespass is a common example. The over-riding consideration will be to ensure that the Court is never left in the position of being unable to pass a proper sentence consistent with the gravity of the defendant's actions; having accepted a plea, the Crown Prosecutor must not then open the case on the basis that what the defendant actually did was something more serious than appears in the charge. Administrative convenience in the form of a rapid guilty plea should not take precedence over the interests of justice, but where the Court is able to deal adequately with an offender on the basis of a plea which represents a criminal involvement not inconsistent with the alleged facts, the resource advantages both to the Service and the Courts generally will be an important consideration.

Charging Practice

12.   It is axiomatic that there must be available admissible evidence which supports all the ingredients of the offence or offences charged. The Service will exercise its discretion on the choice of charge on the basis of the following principles:—

(i) Every effort should be made to keep the number of charges as low as possible. A multiplicity of charges imposes an unnecessary burden on the administration of the Courts as well as upon the prosecution, and often tends to obscure the essential features of the case. Where the evidence discloses a large number of offences of a similar nature, the use of specimen charges should always be consideed. Where numerous different types of offence are disclosed, the ability to present the case in a clear, simple manner should remain a key objective.

(ii) Multiplicity of charging should never be used in order to obtain leverage for the offering of a plea of guilty.

(iii) The charges laid should adequately reflect the gravity of the defendant's conduct and will normally be the most serious revealed by the evidence. Provided, however, that the offence charged is not inappropriate to the nature of the facts alleged and the Court's sentencing powers are adequate, the Crown Prosecutor should take into account matters such as speed of trial, mode of trial and sufficiency of proof which may properly lead to a decision not to prefer or continue with the gravest possible charge. The Crown Prosecutor should also take into account probable lines of defence when exercising his discretion.

Mode of Trial

13.   Where an offence is triable either on indictment or summarily, the Magistrates' Court must consider which mode of trial appears more

suitable, having regard to the matters mentioned in Section 19(3) of the Magistrates' Court Act 1980 and any representations made by the prosecutor or accused. The aim of the Crown Prosecutor when making representations as to venue should be to assist the Court in the exercise of its judicial discretion and in making such representations he should focus on those matters to which the Court is obliged to have regard, namely:

(i) The nature of the case;

(ii) Whether the circumstances make the offence one of serious character;

(iii) Whether the Magistrates' powers of punishment would be adequate; this must not, of course, extend to any expression of view by the Crown Prosecutor as to the nature or range within which the punishment should fall.

(iv) Any other circumstances which appear to make the offence more suitable for trial in one way than another.

While the attraction of an expeditious disposal should never be the sole reason for a request for summary trial, the Crown Prosecutor is entitled to have regard to the delay in the administration of justice likely to be occasioned by proceeding on indictment, together with the additional cost and possible adverse effect upon witnesses.

14. Where the case involves co-accused additional considerations may apply. As a general principle it will be in the interests of justice for all co-accused to be tried at the same Court. Accordingly, if the Court decides that one accused should be tried on indictment, the Crown Prosecutor should generally urge that mode of trial for his co-accused. Summary trial in these circumstances is only likely to be requested by the Crown Prosecutor rarely and will generally arise where the role of one defendant in the offence or offences is out of all proportion to that of his co-accused and where his absence seems unlikely to have any adverse effect on their trial or sentence.

Juveniles

15. It is a long standing statutory requirement that the Courts shall have regard to the welfare of the juvenile appearing before them, in criminal as in civil proceedings. It is accordingly necessary that in deciding whether or not the public interest requires a prosecution the welfare of the juvenile should be fully considered.

16. There may be positive advantages for the individual and for society, in using prosecution as a last resort and in general there is in the case of juvenile offenders a much stronger presumption in favour of methods 'of disposal which fall short of prosecution unless the seriousness of the offence or other exceptional circumstances dictate otherwise. The objective should be to divert juveniles from court wherever possible. Prosecution should always be regarded as a severe step.

17. The Home Office has issued guidelines to the police on cautioning juvenile offenders and on related decision making. Where the police are

unable to make an immediate decision to caution, the guidelines suggest that there may be advantages in their seeking the advice and views of other interested agencies, such as the Social Services Department, the Probation Service and the Education Welfare Service, on whether to caution or institute proceedings. Where the Crown Prosecutor decides that the public interest does not require the institution or continuation of proceedings against a juvenile and it appears that there has been no prior consultation, the Crown Prosecutor should consider whether to ask the police to bring the circumstances of the individual's involvement to the attention of the appropriate agency. Crown Prosecutors should be aware of the general arrangements and procedures for inter-agency consultation in their areas and are encouraged to contribute their experience to the development and improvement of such arrangements. Crown Prosecutors must satisfy themselves that the spirit of the Cautioning Guidelines has been applied before continuing a prosecution instituted by the police against a juvenile. The Crown Prosecutor should, taking account of the views of all the agencies concerned of which he is aware and having regard to the Cautioning Guidelines, refer back to the police any case where he considers that a lesser disposal eg a caution would be an adequate response and, in the final analysis, will not hesitate to exercise his power to discontinue proceedings where he is satisfied that a prosecution is not required in the public interest. When considering whether or not to continue proceedings, the Crown Prosecutor should have regard to the circumstances of any previous cautions the juvenile may have been given by the police. Where these are such as to indicate that a less formal disposal in respect of the present offence would prove inadequate, a prosecution will be appropriate.

18.   It will never be right to prosecute a juvenile solely to secure access to the welfare powers of the court. Where the Crown Prosecutor thinks that there may be grounds for care proceedings and that this might better serve the public interest and welfare of the individual he should invite the police to put this possibility to the local social services authority.

Mode and venue of trial considerations affecting juveniles

19.   (i)   Juveniles charged alone: Where the juvenile has attained the age of 14 and is charged with certain grave offences (as defined by Section 53(2) of the Children and Young Persons Act 1933) other than homicide, it is the Court's duty, having heard representations, to consider whether it ought to be possible to sentence the juvenile up to the maximum adult sentence. (Section 24(1)(a) Magistrates' Courts Act 1980). Accordingly, the Crown Prosecutor should put the relevant facts dispassionately before the Court and generally assist as required by the Court.

(ii)   Juveniles charged with adults: A charge against a juvenile may be heard in an adult Magistrates' Court if an adult is charged at the same time where either is charged with aiding, abetting, etc the other's offence, or where the juvenile is charged with an offence arising out of circumstances which are the same as, or connected with, those giving rise to an offence with which the adult is charged at the same time. There is also a discretion to commit for trial where the juvenile is charged with an indictable offence jointly with an adult and the Court considers it necessary in the interests of justice to commit them both for trial. In making representations as to venue in these circumstances, the prime task of the Crown Prosecutor will be to assist the Court in its judicial considerations. In reaching his decision as to the mode of trial to be requested, the Crown Prosecutor will wish to take several factors into account. These will include, for example, the respective ages of the adult and the juvenile, the seriousness of the offence, the likely plea, whether there are existing charges against the juvenile before the Juvenile Court and the need to deal with the juvenile as expeditiously as possible consistent with the interests of justice.

This Code is Crown copyright and is reproduced here with permission of the Controller of HMSO.

Bibliography

Only books quoted in the text are listed here. The books by Mansfield and Peay (1987) and Edwards (1984) both have very full bibliographies.

Arthur Andersen & Co, Management Consultants
Crown Prosecution Service, Home Office, 1985

Barker, D
Lord Darling's Famous Cases, Hutchinson, 1936

Edwards, J.L.J.
The Law Officers of the Crown, Sweet & Maxwell, 1964
The Attorney General, Politics, and the Public Interest, Sweet & Maxwell, 1984

Fisher, Sir H.
Report of an Inquiry by the Hon Sir Henry Fisher into the circumstances leading to the trial of three persons on charges arising out of the death of Maxwell Confait and the fire at 27 Doggett Road, London SE6, HMSO, 1977

Hall, R.
The Well of Loneliness, Cape, 1928; Virago, 1982

Home Office, Law Officers' Department
An Independent Prosecution Service for England and Wales, HMSO, Cmnd 9074, 1983

Hooper, D.
Official Secrets, Secker & Warburg, 1987

Jackson, R.
Case for the Prosecution, A Biography of Sir Archibald Bodkin, Arthur Barker, 1962

Jesse, F. Tenyson,
Trials of Timothy John Evans and John Reginald Halliday Christie, William Hodge, 1957

Kennedy, L.
10 Rillington Place, Gollancz, 1961; Panther, 1971

Law Officers' Department
Proposed Crown Prosecution Service: the distribution of functions between the Headquarters and Local Offices of the Service, HMSO, Cmnd 9411, 1984

Lawrence, D.H.
Lady Chatterley's Lover, Penguin, 1960

Leigh, L.H.
Police Powers in England and Wales (2nd edition), Butterworths, 1985

Mansfield, G. and Peay, J.
The Director of Public Prosecutions, Tavistock, 1987

Mortimer, J. (ed)
Famous Trials, Penguin/Viking, 1984

Philips, C. (Chairman)
Report of the Royal Commission on Criminal Procedure, HMSO, Cmnd 8092, 1981

Palmer, T.
The Trials of Oz, Blond & Briggs, 1971

Ponting, C.
The Right to Know: The Inside Story of the *Belgrano* Affair, Sphere, 1985

Price, C. and Caplan, J.
The Confait Confessions, Marion Boyars, 1977

Robertson, G. and Nicol, A.
Media Law, Oyez Longman, 1984

Roskill, Rt Hon Lord (Chairman)
Fraud Trials Committee Report, HMSO, 1986

Rozenberg, J. and Watkins, N.
Your Rights and the Law, Dent, 1986

Skelhorn, N.
Public Prosecutor, the Memoirs of Sir Norman Skelhorn, Harrap, 1981

Taylor, A.J.P.
English History 1914-1945, Oxford, 1965

Winfield, K.J. and Lee, A.
The Director of Public Prosecutions, a Short History to 1984, (unpublished: held in DPP's Library)

Index